THE HARLEM RENAISSANCE

CRITICAL STUDIES ON
BLACK LIFE AND CULTURE
(VOL. 2)

GARLAND REFERENCE LIBRARY
OF THE HUMANITIES
(VOL. 278)

Volume 2

Critical Studies on Black Life and Culture

Advisory Editor
Professor Charles T. Davis, Chairman
Afro-American Studies, Yale University

Assistant Advisory Editor
Professor Henry-Louis Gates
Afro-American Studies, Yale University

THE HARLEM RENAISSANCE
An Annotated Bibliography and Commentary

Margaret Perry

GARLAND PUBLISHING, INC. • NEW YORK & LONDON
1982

Library of Congress Cataloging in Publication Data

Perry, Margaret, 1933–
   The Harlem Renaissance.

   (Critical studies on Black life and culture ; v. 2)
   (Garland reference library of the humanities ; v. 278)
   Includes indexes.
   1. Afro-American arts—New York (N.Y.)—Bibliography.
   2. Harlem Renaissance—Bibliography.   I. Title.
   II. Series.   III. Series: Garland reference library of
   the humanities ; v. 278.
   Z5956.A47P47   1982   016.82'09'97471   80-9048
   [NX511.N4]
   ISBN 0-8240-9320-8

Printed on acid-free, 250-year-life paper
Manufactured in the United States of America

Dedicated to

My godchildren, David John and Sara Margaret Wivell
and to
Nancy Packard Anderson, who aided me greatly during
my last month of writing this work

CONTENTS

PREFACE

This bibliography attempts a comprehensive, though not exhaustive, listing of works by and about black writers of what has come to be known as the Harlem Renaissance—a period extending from the early 1920s through the early 1930s. The Introduction discusses the period in more detail. In addition to major and minor works of the period, peripheral items are included in order to provide a broad picture of the ambiance of the times. Therefore, news items, miscellaneous information about the social and cultural milieu, editorials, letters to the editor, and material on film and filmstrip have been included.

Articles concerning influences or influential people (e.g., spirituals, item 681, or Garvey, item 164) are included to provide a rounded sense, a fuller portrait of the period. Inclusiveness is the overall aim, in order to help students and others locate as much as possible that is directly about or related to the spirit of the Harlem Renaissance.

Archival material is listed in the section for materials by an author unless the bulk of the items is about rather than by the author. Masters and doctoral theses, both in English and in French, have been listed. For United States doctoral theses, persons may consult *Dissertation Abstracts* and *Dissertation Abstracts International* for ordering information. None of the theses have been annotated, since not all could be obtained and uniformity of treatment was desired for this section. With a few exceptions, no post–1980 material is cited herein.

Authors were chosen on the basis of two factors: authors who clearly indentified themselves with this movement, and authors who lived during this epoch and produced work that literary historians identify as Harlem Renaissance work. Countee Cullen is representative of the former and Sterling Brown is among the latter. Because writers like Brown and Langston Hughes, or

W.E.B. Du Bois span a longer period than the Harlem Renaissance, writings listed for all authors are for what I have always defined as flexibly as possible to be the Harlem Renaissance (ca. 1919–34, but not past 1937).

The arrangement is alphabetical, word by word, by author or title. An introductory explanation for each section is given. Generally, the notion has been to group the major books and articles about Afro-American literature in one section and to put books dealing specifically with the Harlem Renaissance in another section. Because information about the Harlem Renaissance occurs in small sections of many books or articles, this separation was made deliberately. Truthfully, very few books exist that focus on the Harlem Renaissance alone.

Book reviews are selectively included in Section III. Reviews of books published by artists during the Harlem Renaissance are listed after the annotation for each book.

Materials found in special collections are noted in descriptive detail in Section VII.

The annotations are descriptive for the most part. Some opinion is obvious, however; this is deliberate and probably does indicate a bias. But no overall viewpoint is expressed: as much information as could be found in the time allotted to complete this book has been included. Human error will make for omissions that may prove to be embarrassing, but the book must end somewhere. Material listed in this book covers books and articles from about 1919 to 1980. Annotations for material written in French are based on my own reading of the material. Cross-references are made for clarification of contents, either in terms of a specific argument in a text or for publication information.

ACKNOWLEDGMENTS

All annotations are my own, and all books and articles were read by me unless indicated as not seen. Nevertheless, many acknowledgments for help must be made—first and not least of all to my mother, who has had to live with me during the writing of this book. (There is a lot behind that modest statement!)

Others who have aided greatly are: Ann A. Shockley and Beth Howes, Fisk University; Donald Gallup and Ann Whelpley, Yale University; Ernest Kaiser and Susan Davis, Schomburg Center, New York Public Library; Janet Sims and Esme Bahn, Howard University; Lee Alexander, Gloria J. Mims, and Jewel A. Player, Atlanta University; Florence E. Borders, Dillard University; Edward Lyon, Syracuse University; and members of my library staff at Rush Rhees Library, University of Rochester—Carol Cavanaugh in Interlibrary Loans and Photoduplication, who helped me beyond the call of duty, Jo Ann Gamble, my secretary, who was always willing to give extra help, and my whole division, whose members were always patient with me when I went around with a slightly glazed look and who were also patient with my absences from the library. My manuscript typist, Dori Troicke-Green, deserves praise for her fine and speedy work. My sincere thanks to my editor and Production Manager Barbara A. Bergeron, for sensitive and skillful editing of the final manuscript. Last, but certainly not least, my sincere thanks to Robert R. France, Vice President for Planning and Director of Budgets, who aided me in my pursuit of a grant from the National Endowment for the Humanities. As in the past, he has been extremely supportive of my writing and research activities, and his aid this time was also invaluable.

SOURCES CONSULTED

Major sources used in gathering information in this book are listed below.

Travel for research and other expenses were partially underwritten by a grant (Summer Stipend) from the National Endowment for the Humanities.

Abstracts of English Studies, 1960–. Boulder, Colorado: National Council of Teachers of English.

Barksdale, Gaynelle W., comp. *Graduate Theses of Atlanta University*. Atlanta: Atlanta University, 1948, 1955, 1962.

Catalogue des Thèses de Doctorat. Paris: Cercle de la Librairie, 1960–.

Directory of Afro-American Resources. Edited by Walter Schatz. New York: Bowker, 1970.

Dissertation Abstracts, 1938–1969.

Dissertation Abstracts International, 1969–.

Fairbanks, Carol, and Eugene A. Engeldinger, comps. *Black American Fiction: A Bibliography*. Metuchen, N.J.: Scarecrow, 1978.

Hinding, Andrea, and Suzanna Moody, comps. *Women's History Sources*. New York: Bowker, 1979.

Index to Periodical Articles by and about Blacks. Compiled by the staff of the Hallie Q. Brown Memorial library. Boston: G.K. Hall, 1960–70, 1971–79.

Inge, M. Thomas, ed. *Black American Writers: Bibliographical Essays*, Vol. I. New York: St. Martin's Press, 1978.

MLA International Bibliography, 1921–80.

Patterson, Geoffrey M., and Joan E. Hardy, eds. *Index to Theses*. London: ASLIB, 1968–.

Rush, Theresa Gunnels; Carol Fairbanks Myers; and Esther Spring Arata, eds. *Black American Writers Past and Present: A Biographical and Bibliographical Dictionary*. 2 volumes. Metuchen, N.J.: Scarecrow Press, 1975.

Metuchen, N.J.: Scarecrow Press, 1975.
Turner, Darwin T., comp. *Afro-American Writers*. New York: Appleton-Century-Crofts, 1970.
Wagner, Jean. *Black Poets of the United States*. Urbana: University of Illinois Press, 1973.

Margaret Perry
Rochester, New York

INTRODUCTION

No art can exist without a reference to something outside of its actual production, whether this reference is inside the author's psyche or refers to the present or past world from which the creator draws inspiration, or identity, recognition, or repudiation, or some other conclusion; but a connection to external or internal forces lives in an artistic production. For the black artists (the writers, to be sure) of the early part of the twentieth century there was no art without acknowledgment of the past. Arthur A. Schomburg, the Puerto Rican-born Negro lawyer and businessman, summed this up in his 1925 essay, "The Negro Digs Up His Past": "The American Negro must remake his past in order to make his future."[1] And in invoking the appellation Harlem Renaissance, there is implied a referring back to a preceding age of cultural and artistic endeavors, such as the one during the fourteenth to sixteenth centuries in Europe. But renaissance, per se, means a rebirth. Many persons, including blacks, found it difficult to perceive of a black past outside one of slavery and barbarism. As Paul U. Kellogg, writing in 1925 about the portraits of blacks drawn by the Austrian artist Winold Reiss, observed: "There were Negroes who protested against his [Reiss's] series of racial types; they clung to the prevailing ideals of beauty and these heads were not beautiful to them. As others were quick to point out, from the picture supplements that reached their homes the Sunday before, they had been encompassed by Nordic conventions. Their imagery had been so long thwarted and warped that they could not grasp the rare service rendered by this Bavarian artist. . . ."[2] More importantly, these portraits accompanied a special section of *Survey Graphic*, featuring literature by the "New" Negroes. (This will be discussed briefly below.)

By the early 1920s there was something special emerging among the blacks, who—in the language of the day—were called colored or negro (small "n"), and the one thing that seemed to emerge was an interest in the black person's past. Perhaps the activity of this whole decade was no more than the following definition suggests; but the main notion is all-important nevertheless: "The Harlem Renaissance was a renaissance in one sense only, namely in the renewed interest in the African part of the black American consciousness, which resulted in the programmatic use of the true values kept alive in black folklore."[3] The past would be the touchstone, then—the black person's true ancestral past, which was rooted in Africa.

The definition of a period some claim did not exist[4] represents a challenge that cannot be ignored: the Negro Renaissance, the Harlem Renaissance, the decade of the New Negro—whatever one pleases to call it—did exist in fact as well as in spirit. The term Harlem Renaissance is the most widely known and used, for it seems to help focus on the informing spirit that served to inspire black artists to produce poetry and novels, short stories and essays, music, and art. During this expanded decade—spanning approximately 1919–1934—the black world came of age in an artistic sense. It does not seem too strained to compare this volatile period to fifteenth-century Italy, as Walter Pater described the cultural setting: "Here artists and philosophers and those whom the action of the world has elevated and made keen, do not live in isolation, but breathe a common air, and catch light and heat from each other's thoughts. There is a spirit of general elevation and enlightenment in which all alike communicate. It is the unity of this spirit which gives unity to all the various products of the Renaissance. . . ."[5] By the time World War I ended, black writers—just like the now more forceful, ordinary, non-artist blacks—felt freer and unshackled from the old images of the past. Emphasizing, in part, a commonality of the spirit that shaped their lives—that is, the African—the writers attempted to translate this newly found awareness into poems, plays, novels, short stories, and related literature.

The movement that gradually declared itself was self-consciously Afro-American: the African heritage was reclaimed and then proclaimed; slowly, and without a definite pattern, it was reshaped into an American idiom that supposedly stretched and spanned the years from capture, the "middle-passage," slavery, and the putative emancipation, up through freedom in a multitude of forms, to the variously defined period of the 1920s. If this decade, plus a few years, was ill-defined by its participants (and observers), it could be looked upon as a time of partial approaches towards self-realization, a time (in Harold Cruse's estimation) of "inspired aimlessness."[6]

Many forces operated to create the distinctive quality of this period, just as there were individual as well as collective manifestations that helped to define this period in one way or another. For instance, Langston Hughes wrote his famous essay, "The Negro Artist and the Racial Mountain,"[7] in the tone and shape of a manifesto; *Fire!!*, the abortive magazine, was an effort by many of the young artists to demonstrate the vitality and variety of black writing. Finally, it seems certain that the more one attempts to define this period, the more one pulls away from speculating about its existence; the Harlem Renaissance did, in fact, exist. The following discussion describes the reasons why and how the Harlem Renaissance evolved, the setting, the people, and their literature, in order to provide some prior reference for using the heart of the book: the bibliography.

The Harlem Renaissance was not a rare flower that grew suddenly upon a desert—rootless, unshaped, uninformed by any past. There are indicators that give one guideposts to the movement, to the atmosphere in and around it. There was, for instance, the migration of blacks to the city. This development of the urban Negro—New York City alone had an increase of black population of 66% between 1910 and 1920[8]—created a black population that was increasingly demanding about rights and freedom. The World War experiences of blacks increased this desire to participate more fully in American life. Even if the black soldier did not have complete equality, he was exposed to a wider range of opportunities and expected greater freedom when he returned from the war. Other factors that helped to create this artistic movement were the effects of the race riots of 1919. Blacks, instead of depicting docility, fought back during this wave of hatred and intolerance. The militancy displayed by blacks surprised not only whites but other blacks as well; the New Negro was being born. Claude McKay captured this spirit in his oft-quoted poem, "If We Must Die":

> Like men we'll face the murderous, cowardly pack,
> Pressed to the wall, dying, but fighting back!

There was generally greater interest in black life and culture by such artists as Eugene O'Neill, Ridgely Torrence, and Winold Reiss, who drew the portraits for the anthology *The New Negro*. The fragmented nature of culture both in the United States and Europe served to reduce the influence of the genteel tradition; thus, interest in black life was less sensational and, therefore, less stereotyped than formerly.[9]

The diversity of influences upon developing the Harlem Renaissance extend to such an occurrence as *Shuffle Along* as well as the emergence of that spectacular and controversial individual, Marcus Garvey.

Shuffle Along, an all-black musical—the book and the music, the director and the actors were all black—appeared on the scene in 1921. "*Shuffle Along* did anything but shuffle. It exploded onto the stage,"[10] said one critic. Langston Hughes also noted the importance of this show in shaping the period: "The 1920's were the years of Manhattan's black Renaissance. It began with *Shuffle Along, Running Wild,* and the Charleston. Perhaps some people would say even with *The Emperor Jones*, Charles Gilpin, and the tom-toms at the Provincetown. But certainly it was the musical revue, *Shuffle Along*, that gave a scintillating send-off to that Negro vogue in Manhattan."[11] It was a real boost to the self-image of blacks, it was an informing spirit of the time that "spread to books, African sculpture, music, and dancing." Moreover, the show created an ambiance of blackness—an example of the racial vitality and rhythmic swing and sway that whites would attempt to emulate and even steal.

Marcus Aurelius Garvey was unique and spectacular: his thesis was that the black person didn't have a chance in the United States, because it wasn't the racial homeland; therefore, blacks ought to return to Africa. He never got there—but this didn't hinder him from devoting his life to this effort, born out of a philosophy that was more appealing than a real journey back to Africa: this undergirding philosophy was that all black people needed to be reunited in order to have racial strength and self-assurance; in this way, the yoke of white oppression could be cast aside. As Garvey would shout, "Up you mighty race! You can accomplish what you will!" The masses, who were his major followers, could sense racial pride and self-confidence. This sentiment reflected the period that was changing into the "Jazz Age," the "Lost Generation," the "Negro Renaissance," and the intellectuals' disapprobation of Garvey does not lessen the philosophical influence he had or reflected during the 1920s. His appearance on the scene was certainly a factor in the development of the Harlem Renaissance.

In suggesting influences that may have had a direct relationship on the evolution of this period, it should be mentioned as well that the importance of the black press was not negligible; certainly, publications helped to spread information about personalities and happenings as well as to present literary works. Periodicals such as *The Crisis* (1910), published by the NAACP, *Opportunity* (1922), the organ of the National Urban League, or *The Messenger* (1912), the socialist journal published by A. Philip Randolph (National Sleeping Car Porters) and Chandler Owen provided black writers with the opportunity to see their short prose, poetry, and drama in print in periodicals that presumably reached the eyes of large numbers of black as well as white readers. There were other periodicals; indeed, this was a time of abundancy in the Negro press:

> In the number of newspapers and magazines on the newsstands, and in the percentage of blacks reading them, the Renaissance press outstripped any other in American history. The size of the press mushroomed as journalists capitalized on the dramatic story of the World War, on the mass migration of blacks from the rural South to northern cities, and on the rediscovery of black culture. Essays, poems, short stories and serialized novels were published, not only in black magazines but in black newspapers as well. Historical articles, literary criticism, and, to a lesser degree, theatre and art criticism were regular features in the Renaissance press. . . . The social and political power wielded today by television was in the Renaissance era largely in the domain of the press.[12]

The wide range of reasons behind the development of the Harlem Renaissance merge in a sense of defining the overall ambiance, the tone, of the decade: a release from the restraints and fears of the past, with an interest in the black racial past and a belief that the black race understood basic human values in a less corrupt, less compromised sense. If the movement was self-propelled by a lack of clear definition at the time it was developing, there was, nevertheless, a recognition that something new and different was occurring:

> The most outstanding phase of the development of the Negro in the United States during the past decade had been in the recent literary and artistic emergence of the individual creative artist. . . . The thing that has happened has been so marked that it does not have the appearance of a development; it seems rather like a sudden awakening, like an instantaneous change.[13]

Of course, it did not literally explode into being; there was a development. There is also, in retrospect, a glory to a period that not all can agree existed, or which cannot be defined with precision. The best way, finally, to comprehend this decade of artistic history is to be exposed to the works that were produced, and to explore the minds and interests of the persons who were a part of this volatile decade.

The major writers of the Harlem Renaissance were few; the number of writers were many. Jean Toomer stands out as the most creative, because he experimented with style and form and the uses of symbols. Langston Hughes, who was much closer idiomatically to black life and to art that depicted ordinary black life, was the most inventive and unrestricted of the literary artists. In addition to these two most lasting examples of Renaissance writing talent are the following, in alphabetical order:

> Countee Cullen
> W.E.B. Du Bois
> Jessie R. Fauset
> Rudolph Fisher
> Zora Neale Hurston
> James Weldon Johnson
> Nella Larsen
> Claude McKay
> Willis Richardson

Anne Spencer
Wallace Thurman
Walter White

The poets seemed to dominate the period, although some poets combined genres and produced fiction as well; Hughes, Cullen, and McKay, as well as Toomer, come to mind immediately. More short stories than are known were published; yet few Harlem Renaissance writers achieved mastery of this form. Rudolph Fisher was probably the best short story writer; McKay and Hurston also wrote some moving and well-told stories. Hughes represents the problem of attempting to define the Harlem Renaissance within the space of specific years: his best short stories appear in print from 1933 forward. The important consideration, however, is to discover what these writers wrote, to move from this knowledge to the works and then to commentaries about them and the authors in the bibliography.

One of the most consciously literary artists was Jean Toomer; he was deeply conscious of trying to shape his experiences and what he thought were the experiences of blacks into a form that became a work of art. His efforts to order experience into form, with meaning and emotion, were linked with his struggles to discover his personal spiritual and moral center. Toomer was also one of the few black writers who spent significant time with his white counterparts in Greenwich Village and in Europe. Thus, it is possible to connect him spiritually and thematically with some of the ideas that other writers of this period both in America and abroad were pondering—the lost generation writers, for instance: modern man's spiritual dearth, his lack of spiritual values; a rejection of bourgeois values; an obsession with death. Added to these areas of concern was Toomer's interest for a time in his genesis as an Afro-American—that strange anomaly that could make him black, although his own color was "white," as were his two wives. (Later, he was to repudiate his color, declaring he was of no race but solely of the human race.)

There are critics who may argue the aesthetics of Jean Toomer, writer—for he was enigmatic and contradictory.[14] But he produced a complex, rich book about Negro life—*Cane*—which was published in 1923, demonstrating (particularly in the last section, "Kabnis") an artistic search for the black person's roots. As

Robert Bone has stated, the figure of Father John in this section emphasizes ﹐Toomer's concern for this "link with the Negro's ancestral past."[15] Indeed, Toomer himself describes the following influence upon his life: "A visit to Georgia last fall [1921] was the starting point of almost everything of worth that I have done. I heard folk-songs come from the lips of Negro peasants. I saw the rich dusk beauty that I had heard many false accents about, and of which till then, I was somewhat skeptical. And a deep part of my nature, a part that I had repressed, sprang suddenly to life and responded to them."[16]

Cane is divided into three sections; the first and the last are set in the rural South and the middle section takes place primarily in Washington, D.C. One has portraits of black life interspersed with impressionistic poetry. As an insistence, for example, upon the connection with the black race's past, Toomer writes: "the Dixie Pike has grown from a goat path in Africa."[17] Toomer explores, often viscerally, the rural black life as it affects the poor men and women—especially the women. The circumscribed, restricted life of these individuals is the world of Toomer's imagination and craft. We see this in such stories as "Fern," or "Esther," or in "Karintha"—the woman who is full of the seed for future generations, desired only for her body and not for her self. There is no escape for these women who demonstrate the waste resulting from incomplete lives—lives stunted and twisted by the fate of being black and poor in the white man's South of the 1920s.

The importance of *Cane* can be demonstrated by the last story, "Kabnis," which tells of a young man, Ralph Kabnis, moving from fear and ignorance to a greater awareness of himself and his roots. Within a brief space Toomer erects an illuminating edifice with characters inside who live forever in the reader's mind—Halsey, Lewis, Carrie K., Layman, for instance—because they each help Kabnis to define and find himself. And there is Father John, the archetypal father of blacks; a former slave, he is a symbol of the true past of the American Negro. With his enigmatic aid, along with that of others, Kabnis begins to come to grips with the past, not only by claiming his ties with the American South (i.e., Africa transplanted) but also by admitting to the past indignities of slavery and oppression.

Finally, in his efforts to find self, Toomer has explored the varieties of blacks living in the South and in the city in this small but impressive collection of tales that pulse with a vibrancy and intensity. *Cane* scholars battle with Toomer's meanings, for it is a complex book—as complex, probably, as the man who wrote it and mused: "[*Cane* was] a swan song. It was a song of an end. . . . And why people have expected me to write a second and a third and fourth book like 'Cane' is one of the queer misunderstandings of my life."[18]

While Toomer brought the African past into the rural South for that self-journey into one's true origins, Countee Cullen approached the meaning of his race and his place in American society with all of the contradictory emotional and psychological ambivalence that characterized the black bourgeoisie's probe into Afro-American cultural history. On the one hand Cullen stated, "I want to be known as a poet and not as a Negro poet,"[19] and on the other hand, "Most things I write I do for the sheer love of the music in them. Somehow I find my poetry of itself treating of the Negro, of his joys and his sorrows—mostly the latter—and of the heights and depths of emotion I feel as a Negro."[20]

Countee Cullen was primarily a lyricist, influenced by romantic poets of the nineteenth and twentieth centuries; but he was also a man who was committed to pointing out the indignities heaped upon his people. Still, he was a true disciple of beauty, and he wanted his writing to reveal a sense of style and form and a consciousness of writing as art instead of polemic. Keats was perhaps the poet that Cullen most admired; also, his most characteristic lyrics show a penchant toward the style of A.E. Housman, Millay, and E.A. Robinson. Jay Saunders Redding called him the Ariel of Negro poets, one who "cannot beat the tom-tom above a faint whisper nor know the primitive delights of black rain and scarlet sun," a writer of "delightful love lyrics."[21] Therefore, it is not surprising to note that, besides the race problem, Cullen's two most constant themes were love and death. Although considered by many critics as the least race-conscious poet, nevertheless, Cullen will be remembered, Charles Glicksberg[22] has suggested, for his poems that deal with race or the race problem.

In defining the aspects of good poetry, Cullen stated: "Good poetry is a lofty thought beautifully expressed . . . poetry should not be too intellectual; it should deal more . . . with the emotion.

The highest type of poem is that which warmly stirs the emotions, which awakens a responsive chord in the human heart. Poetry, like music, depends upon feeling rather then intellect, although there should of course be enough to satisfy the mind, too."[23]

In trying to be raceless as well as to address the problems of the Afro-American in American civilization, Cullen represents the dichotomized black artist who would not repudiate his heritage but does not want to be judged solely in terms of it. Jessie Redmon Fauset, another Harlem Renaissance writer, was also of this persuasion, although her novels always dealt with the woes of the prejudice that the middle-class black faced. Langston Hughes, on the other hand, was of a vastly different cast of mind.

Hughes swaggered above the hurts and pressure of being black in America; he reveled in his blackness. A person—black or white—who did not know about or appreciate the ways of black folk was the deprived one in Hughes's canon of culture. And in his manifesto about art and culture Hughes declared: "We younger Negro artists who create now intend to express our individual dark-skinned selves without fear or shame. If white people are pleased we are glad. If they are not, it doesn't matter. We know we are beautiful. And ugly too. . . . If colored people are pleased we are glad. If they are not, their displeasure doesn't matter either."[24] And Hughes was true to his declaration, frequently being castigated for his love of common blacks and his preoccupation with writing jazz and blues poetry. Nevertheless, it was at the beginning of his career—in 1925, when he won the *Opportunity* magazine's first prize for poetry with "The Weary Blues," a poem that was songful, idiomatic in vocabulary, full of jazz and blues sounds, with a tone that was unmistakably negroid—that Hughes demonstrated he was a poet to acknowledge.

The most distinct feature of Hughes's poetry, then, the metaphor of music—jazz and the blues—was a vital mode for expressing what the poet saw as the unique quality of black life in America. As he wrote in "Lenox Avenue; Midnight":

> The rhythm of life
> is a jazz rhythm—

Hughes can also be characterized as a poet of the city; in particular, Harlem is *his* city, and the people there are *his* people. His love for both place and people permeates his poetry, utilizing the themes of protest and pride, love for freedom, hatred and despair deriving from prejudice, and belief that the world will get better for blacks. Undergirding these themes is Hughes's strong belief in American democracy. As he once said in an interview, his primary aim was "to interpret and comment upon Negro life, and its relation to the problems of Democracy."[25]

A writer who was much more critical of American life and American blacks was Claude McKay, who was born in Jamaica, West Indies, and who was a published author by the time he came to the United States in 1912. In his novel *Banjo* (a book berated by more conservative literary Negroes, such as W.E.B. Du Bois), McKay's character, Ray, who reflects his own thoughts, says: "We educated Negroes are talking a lot about a racial renaissance. And I wonder how we're going to get it. . . . If this renaissance we're talking about is going to be more than a sporadic and scabby thing, we'll have to get down to our racial roots to create it . . . [but] you're a lost crowd, you educated Negroes, and you will only find your self in the roots of your own people. You can't choose as your models the haughty-minded educated white youths of a society living on its imperial conquests."[26] And, of course, many of the Harlem Renaissance writers thought they were going back to their roots when they portrayed "authentic" views of black life. McKay wasn't sure his fellow black writers were being that honest; yet it was McKay who repudiated his first poems, written in Jamaican dialect, and he avoided experimental forms and militant themes in most of his poetry. Even his inspiring poem "If We Must Die," written in 1919—supposedly in protest against the race riots (he later disclaimed this)—was in sonnet form.

Indeed, McKay employed the most traditional forms of poetic expression, the sonnet and other rhymed verse in iambic pentameter. There are vigor and passion in his poetry; there is also tenderness of the most romantic sort. His themes were remarkably consistent and they were reasserted later in his novels and short stories. There was the theme stemming from his being a black man—a bitter denunciation of racial prejudice. Then, McKay's nostalgia for Jamaica was exhibited in those poems celebrating the freer life, one that is close to earth and sky and water. This reverence for nature reveals the poet's longing for religion (nature, at first, is his religion). His subsequent conversion to Catholicism was not as uncharacteristic as some would have it. Even the symbols he used in his nature poetry point toward a preoccupation not only with anti-metropolis sentiments but also with humanity's religious dependency. The theme of alienation is iterated in McKay's poetry; but this concern is most vividly expressed through Ray, a character in two of his novels—a spokesman, obviously for McKay. This strong sense of alienation is expressed on two levels: black in the white world (black against white, and vice versa), and black against black. The latter level is almost exclusively portrayed in his novels, whereas the former emotion sustains the theme of many McKay poems, such as "Outcast," "Baptism," "Courage," and "America." McKay was also a talented short story writer who evoked the vital spirit of the ordinary Negro as well as the spiritual duality of the black intellectual.

Reminiscences, memories about World War I, do not haunt the writings of most Harlem Renaissance writers, but Claude McKay's work is a notable exception to this. Still, his productions can hardly be said to be overly concerned with the psychological inheritance of this war. Indeed, there may be a mockery of it as the "white man's war," inasmuch as Banjo—McKay's character who has had war experiences—is a deserter who proves the black man's invisibility in America: Banjo's status is neither validated nor invalidated as a defender or deserter of his country. He is simply ignored by America; he finds his place among the rejects of society.

Some people—Du Bois in particular—felt McKay exploited the theme of Negro primitivism. McKay, like Cullen, did not seem to live up to his expectations; thematic limitations may have been a major cause of this for both of these writers. Still, if McKay failed to live up to his potential he was also companion to others besides Cullen in this category of talented black writers of the 1920s and early 1930s. Wallace Thurman, aspiring to the greatness of masters such as Tolstoy, Melville, or Proust, turned bitter about the period that brought these writers accolades and attention.

Wallace Thurman wanted to be great and talented. He was the latter, but he squandered his talent and died young—as if to prove he was right to be disillusioned about his times. Langston Hughes describes him vividly:

> Thurman . . . was a strangely brilliant black boy, who had read everything, and whose critical mind could find something wrong with everything he read. . . . He wanted to be a *very* great writer, like Gorki or Thomas Mann, and he felt that he was merely a journalistic writer. His critical mind, comparing his pages to the thousands of other pages he had read, by Proust, Melville, Tolstoy . . . found his own pages vastly wanting. So he contented himself by writing a great deal for money, laughing bitterly at his fabulously concocted "true, stories," creating two bad motion pictures for the "Adults Only" type for Hollywood, drinking more and more gin, and then threatening to jump out of windows at people's parties and kill himself.[27]

Thurman was extremely skillful in writing about Harlem; indeed, he excelled at nonfiction, whereas he was weak as a novelist. Still, he must be mentioned for his acerbic novel about the Harlem Renaissance that cynically explores the people and the tenor of this time. In *Infants of the Spring* there is bitterness and tension; it is a book full of caricatures, a *roman à clef* that spares no one, not even himself.

Wallace Thurman was a confused intellectual who remained frustrated in both his personal and professional life; yet if he could have written as he lived, what an outstandingly interesting book he would have produced! Sadly, he died destitute at an early age—died after months of agony in the incurable ward on Welfare Island one cold December day. He was, perhaps, as Dorothy West reminisced, "the most symbolic figure of the Literary Renaissance in Harlem."[28]

By contrast, Rudolph Fisher, B.A. and M.A. (Brown University, 1919 and 1920), M.D., Phi Beta Kappa, novelist and outstanding short story writer of the Harlem Renaissance, died in December 1934 as well—but in the Edgecombe Sanitorium in New York, in as much comfort as one can give a dying man. Fisher and Thurman, the first of the Harlem Renaissance writers to die, demonstrate the distinctions that existed among the black writers of this period.

Rudolph Fisher, who possessed a keen wit, a basically optimistic view of life, an observant mind, wrote short stories and novels (two) in a clear, direct, tidy style. He was a traditionalist in his manner of living and in his writing; yet he also had great humor and jollity. Once again, Langston Hughes captures a contemporary artist-friend:

> The wittiest of these New Negroes of Harlem, whose tongue was flavored with the sharpest and saltiest humor, was Rudolph Fisher, whose stories appeared in the *Atlantic Monthly*. His novel, *Walls of Jericho*, captures but slightly the raciness of his own conversation. He was a young medical doctor and X-ray specialist, who always frightened me a little, because he could think of the most incisively clever thing to say—and I could never think of anything to answer.[29]

Certainly *The Walls of Jericho* was Fisher's major work, but he made his greatest contribution as a short story writer. (He was also the author of the first mystery novel by an American black: *The Conjure-man Dies*.) Fisher wrote the well-made novel and short story: everything is intact—theme, character, setting, dialogue— so that the reader is never at a loss about what the author is trying to accomplish. Fisher also possessed a witty style in both narration and dialogue: his language and style evoke experiences genuinely and appealingly. He captured black idiomatic language perfectly, and used it with grace and humor as well as with salty vigor.

In the short story, Fisher demonstrates a classic grasp of this most American of literary forms: from his stories there emerges a single effect, growing out of careful characterization and close attention to establishing and maintaining the features of a beginning, a middle, and an end. Yet Fisher never loses sight of his desire to go beyond the mere artistry of the form; he also stresses values that are important to Negroes within their unique culture, such as racial solidarity.

One important goal stressed by the well-educated, black bourgeois—such as Fisher or W.E.B. Du Bois or James Weldon Johnson—was that the depiction of Negroes in imaginative literature should show the wide range of Negro life and culture. The diversity of the Negro had suffered, it was felt, under the polarized, one-dimensional portraits painted by white post-bellum writers (and, in some cases, by black writers, too, such as Charles Chesnutt). James Weldon Johnson, whose tastes were broad and varied, exemplified this diversity in both his life and in his writings. A poet, diplomat, novelist, musician, and lawyer, Johnson was a precursor of the Harlem Renaissance as well as a participant in the movement. In his autobiography, *Along This Way*, Johnson noted: "This was the era in which was achieved the Harlem of story and song; the era in which Harlem's fame for exotic flavor and colorful sensuousness was spread to all parts of the world; when Harlem was made known as the scene of laughter, singing, dancing, and primitive passions, and as the center of the new Negro literature and art. . . . But the sterner aspects of life in Harlem offer a unique and teeming field for the writer capable of working it. Under these aspects lie real comedy and real tragedy, real triumphs and real defeats. The field is waiting, probably for some Negro writer."[30] Johnson was wise enough to see both sides of life, the real and the fictional. He contributed one novel—first published in 1912 and then reissued in 1927, during a vital year of the period. *The Autobiography of an Ex-Coloured Man* uses the standard theme of the "tragic mulatto," inherited from the late nineteenth- and early twentieth-century stories dealing with light-skinned blacks. But Johnson's skillful characterization, vivid descriptions of life in all strata, and his effective use of irony lift the novel above the ordinary ones that deal with this romantic idea (i.e., that the Negro who forsakes his own race suffers deep psychological and cultural loss that the "freedom" of whiteness can never replace).

Johnson was one of the older persons to achieve and maintain a large measure of fame during the Harlem Renaissance. Another was W.E.B. Du Bois, writer, editor of *The Crisis* (organ of the National Association for the Advancement of Colored People), pan-Africanist, and a person who was never without a strong opinion. For Du Bois, the Afro-American artist was inescapably enmeshed in the cultural and sociological atmosphere that had declared the black a second-class citizen. Therefore, to this vigorous intellectual giant of the twentieth century, "All art is propaganda." It was the dictum by which he wrote; it is not surprising that his fiction was weak and discursive, just as his essays and journalistic writings were insightful and challenging to the reader. His opinionated cast of mind made him difficult; but he was also a great encourager of the young writers of the Harlem Renaissance. Certainly his publication, *The Crisis*, provided an outlet for the publication of many pieces of literature that were produced during this period.

Du Bois and James Weldon Johnson, however, were not alone in providing encouragement and sustenance for the black writers who were emerging at this time. Charles S. Johnson, for instance, continues to be underrated as an important influence on the literary and personal lives of Harlem Renaissance writers; yet Langston Hughes has declared he "did more to encourage and develop Negro writers during the 1920's than anyone else in America."[31] A specialist in race relations, and the first black president of the famous southern university Fisk (then for blacks only), Johnson's connection with the Harlem Renaissance was that of encourager, practical helper, and participant. He was the editor of *Opportunity*, and he found the money to support the prize contests of that magazine. He was also the editor of the collection of literature and the arts *Ebony and Topaz* (see item 770), where he stated: "It is a venture in expression, shared, with the slightest editorial suggestion, by a number of persons who are here much less interested in their audience than in what they are trying to say, and the life they are trying to portray."[32] And as the editor of this miscellanea, Johnson fits the description of an "entrepreneur of the Harlem Renaissance [with] . . . the third dimension as that of interpreter."[33]

Alain Locke and Carl Van Vechten were likewise favorable and understanding interpreters of the period; and both were instrumental in helping the developing writers, even when these young people struck out on their own to produce a short-lived literary journal, *Fire!!* Carl Van Vechten's role has been inflated sometimes as well as being exaggerated in the other extreme to the point of minimizing the aid he provided. He introduced writers to publishers, invited blacks and whites interested in the arts to his parties, generally promoted black arts of all genre, and was the author of the infamous *Nigger Heaven* (a novel that outraged many blacks because of its title). Even after the Harlem Renaissance was long over, Van Vechten continued his interest in the writers, and he motivated his black friends to donate materials to

Yale University to what has become a rich reservoir in black literature and culture: The James Weldon Johnson Memorial Collection of Negro Arts and Letters (dedicated on 7 January 1950).

As soon as the Harlem Renaissance was underway, a request was made to Alain Locke to edit a special edition of *Survey* magazine's "graphic" publication. The 1 March 1925 special issue was entitled "Harlem: Mecca of the New Negro"; the introductory essay was by Alain Locke. This same section was published, with some changes, during the same year (*The New Negro*) and has become famous as the first anthology of writings by many of the Renaissance writers. Locke's pronouncements captured part of the spirit and aims of the "New Negro," and expressed an assimilationist desire to contribute to American civilization the vestiges of Afro-American culture. In his introduction he states: "He [the new Negro] now becomes a conscious contributor and lays aside the status of a beneficiary and ward for that of a collaborator and participant in American civilization. The great social gain in this is the releasing of our talented group from the arid fields of controversy and debate to the productive fields of creative expression. The especially cultural recognition they win should in turn prove the key to that revaluation of the Negro which must precede or accompany any considerable further betterment of race relationships."[34] The enthusiasm and optimism of the 1920s turned a bit sour in the heart of Alain Locke: he had not become bitter but he did question the quality of production, the sincerity of the praise and assessments, the depth of knowledge blacks really had of their past, and wondered if the overall failure to reach the heights he had expected had come from not shaping a new tradition out of the old.

But the age died slowly, and there were others who contributed to the period that should be recognized, persons whose viewpoints were closely allied to Locke's.

Robert A. Bone has labeled Locke, along with Jessie Fauset and Nella Larsen, the "rear guard,"[35] a term which he used to characterize those persons of the Harlem Renaissance who exemplified the high bourgeoisie and eschewed the more exotic elements of black life. Walter White, who later became involved almost exclusively in civil rights issues, was also categorized this way. The respectable, prim world of Jessie Fauset, however, was far different from the more varied world of Nella Larsen; and the two novels of White and the fiction of Du Bois (which could also be classed as "rear guard") were the work of writers who were not primarily interested in imaginative writing. Still, all of these writers added to the ambiance of a specialness among Negro writers at this time. Anyone who studies this period must investigate the minor as well as the major writers; the tamer, less experimental, less exuberant writers were a part of the Harlem Renaissance as well.

One writer who emerged at this time, and who lived well into the next decade and produced singular works of fiction which related directly to folk literature, was Zora Neale Hurston, author of four novels, numerous short stories, and folklore material. She also makes a definite, inflexible time frame for the Harlem Renaissance impossible, or at least untenable; her major novel in the mode of the period was published in 1937 (*Their Eyes Were Watching God*). Born in 1903, in Eatonville, Florida—a rural, all-black town—Hurston arrived late on the Harlem Renaissance scene but became quickly enmeshed in the soul and spirit of the movement. She even managed to be used as a character, Sweetie Mae Carr, in Thurman's *Infants of the Spring*.

In addition to her novels, Hurston published a number of creditable short stories during the Harlem Renaissance. Her characters live, for the most part, in an all-black world; when the white impinges on the black, each race maintains its societal role with abiding conviction. Thus, Hurston's black characters do not suffer from the sort of alternative black self-hatred/prideful self-love/hate-envy of white and black that characterize some of the Harlem Renaissance fictional creations (e.g., McKay's Ray, Toomer's Kabnis, Thurman's Mary Lou, or some of the characters in the short stories of Dorothy West). Hurston's fictional style and characterizations were both deeply influenced by the colloquial, folk atmosphere of her native Florida where she collected folklore materials in connection with anthropological work she was doing with Franz Boas.

Hurston also successfully handled the important elements of the short story form—plot, diction, narration, and, especially, mood. Hence, we can overlook some of her more obvious faults, such as stilted conversation when she is not using dialect, her intrusion in narrative passages, and the relating of events as narration rather than as action. The authenticity of setting and situation in Hurston's stories as well as in her longer works is so sure and sound that she emerges as one of the truly innovative writers of the Harlem Renaissance.

Nella Larsen was rather the opposite in her style and interests, although she shared Hurston's trait of emotional honesty in the portrayal of female characters. Her craftsmanship was good and showed promise of greater complexity and durability, but she gave up publishing (as far as we know up to this time) after 1930 when she was accused of plagiarism.[36] Born in the Virgin Islands of a Danish mother and a Negro father, Nella Larsen (sometimes Imes, her married name, is used by writers) wrote two novels by 1929—*Quicksand* (1928) and *Passing* (1929). Larsen's women characters possess the same sort of pent-up energy the author must have had; these characters also demonstrate the frustrations of those possessing a mixed racial heritage. Larsen, using women in a different milieu from those of Hurston, was nevertheless like the other in being able to render a range of female psychology convincingly through her characters. Her women have both material and sexual desires, for instance, at a period when virtue and modesty were favored traits for Negro women—both in fiction and in life, among the bourgeoisie.

Jessie Redmon Fauset, whose age was never openly revealed, was among the older members of the Harlem Renaissance and was a strong and open encourager of young talent. She worked as literary editor for *The Crisis* for seven years (1919–1926), so she knew practically all of the writers of the period.[37] In her novels and stories she depicted the sensitive, middle-class Negro who was the victim of prejudice (the black bourgeois who shared so many traits with his or her white counterpart). Except for Hurston, she wrote more novels than any other Harlem Renaissance author, and additionally, her importance in a survey of this period can be supported for at least two reasons: "There was the cumulative effect of her concentration upon certain themes. . . . She managed to bring before the reading public a view of a genuine milieu of Negro society that whites rarely saw or knew existed."[38]

Fauset, who wrote simply *everything*, every genre, was also a playwright—although none of her plays was ever produced. The black playwright during the 1920s did exist, however. John Matheus, primarily a short story writer at that time, wrote plays. And Wallace Thurman's *Harlem* was produced on Broadway. But the writer who devoted himself the most to playwriting, who had productions and whose plays were reprinted, was Willis Richardson.

Richardson, born in 1889 in Wilmington, North Carolina, began writing in 1920. His play *The Chip Woman's Fortune* was the first serious drama by a black to be produced on Broadway (1923). Despite this, and despite winning some drama prizes (e.g., Edith Schwarb Cup, Yale University Theater, 1928), Richardson's achievements were modest. Like some other writers of the Harlem Renaissance, Richardson wrote without fully developing an early, raw, technically flawed talent.

The major essayists, for the most part, were the older persons—Du Bois and the two Johnsons (James Weldon and Charles S.—not related). The major poets were joined by a respectable band of others who produced a smaller body of verse—Arna Bontemps, whose style was tinged with nostalgia for the racial past, Waring Cuney, who reached heights in "No Images" and could not repeat its effectiveness, Frank Horne, whose most famous poem, "Letters Found Near a Suicide," was published in 1925, Helene Johnson, Gwendolyn Bennett, Georgia Douglas Johnson (who spanned the time before and after the Renaissance and who wrote trite, romantic verse), and Anne Spencer, who cultivated her talent slowly and as scrupulously as she did her gardens in Lynchburg, Virginia. Spencer never came to New York to mingle with her peers, but her good friend, James Weldon Johnson, brought New York and the Harlem Renaissance to her. She remains, despite a recent biography,[39] a much underrated poet of this period. Finally, because he too spanned the decades, there was Sterling Brown, who wrote an American poetry of vigor and rich blackness—a poetry that reflected the ideas espoused but not always practiced during the Harlem Renaissance. He has said of this period: "The New Negro is not to me a group of writers centered in Harlem during the second half of the twenties. Most of the writers were not Harlemites; much of the best writing was not about Harlem, which was the show-window, the cashier's till, but no more Negro American than New York is America."[40]

By the end of 1934 Fisher and Thurman were dead, and some

of the writers were questioning if the Negro Renaissance was not over and dead. By 1930 magazines like *The Crisis* and *Opportunity* reflected the changed spirit of the times—the Depression, a general lackluster attitude, a downbeat mood in contrast to the upbeat ambiance that ushered in the 1920s. In a letter to James Weldon Johnson, Dorothy West expresses the notion that Harlem Renaissance aspirations had fallen on fallow times as she attempted to start something new, a new challenge—as, indeed, her short-lived journal of the 1930s was called (*Challenge* and then *New Challenge*). Locke himself had questioned in print the decade of the twenties, and speculated about its demise: "Has the afflatus of Negro self-expression died down? Are we outliving the Negro fad? . . . By some signs and symptoms. Yes."[41]

The writers of this period, in a self-conscious manner, had attempted to connect philosophy to art—the New Negro was one who had discovered his past and, therefore, was engaged in a cultural renaissance. There was also a relation to the nineteenth-century black "literature" of engagement—the slave narrative, which depicted life as it was in the words of blacks rather than the sentimentalized yet basically racist (or at least unconsciously condescending) literature written by whites. The black writer had reclaimed his past and was to be interpreter of his own experiences. The buying audience, however, was mostly white.

> I was there. I had a swell time while it lasted. But I thought it wouldn't last long. . . . For how could a large and enthusiastic number of people be crazy about Negroes forever?
> The ordinary Negroes hadn't heard of the Negro Renaissance. And if they had, it hadn't raised their wages any.[42]

And despite the desire to set the record straight, to correct the image, to explore or expunge the double consciousness, many of the writers failed to use their blackness to fullness and with total honesty in order to create that unique genre of American literature one calls black or Afro-American. When Langston Hughes declared in 1926: "We younger Negro artists who create now intend to express our individual dark-skinned selves without fear or shame," he was speaking for only a few of the writers. Most of the writers were not bold, nor were they blind to the implications of white patronage—whether direct (as in the case of Hughes's and Hurston's "godmother") or indirect through publishers and the reading public. The Afro-American soul was under close and curious scrutiny; it was a soul still awaiting a definition through imaginative art.

Still, the artistic world would never be quite the same: the exposure to black life, no matter how uneven, eager, frenetically presented, made an impact, if minor, upon the American cultural scene. The Harlem Renaissance movement basically existed outside mainstream America—including the literary scene. The work of the major black writers was reviewed, but the notion that this literature was an equal if colorful counterpart of literature produced by white writers did not exist in any strong sense. The black writer may have worked hard to correct the unfair and unrealistic images white writers had focused upon, but this didn't seem to matter in a national sense. There simply were no black parallels to Pound or Eliot, Fitzgerald or Hemingway or Faulkner. And the collective spirit vs. the individual's need for self-expression remained a frequently unspoken obstacle to creating a consistent, focused artistic movement. The complaint Cruse made in *The Crisis of the Negro Intellectual*—that the Harlem Renaissance was a period of "inspired aimlessness—is true in this sense of failing to emerge as a definite segment or stage in American literature and civilization during the time it existed. (One might safely question whether or not this is important.)

There was, of course, the precise economic factor that affected the movement—the Great Depression. Much white patronage simply disappeared. The movement petered out to an indefinite end. But in its heyday of glory and enthusiasm it was like nothing that had existed before or—some may argue—since that time. In any case, it may be possible to agree with the critic who summed up the Harlem Renaissance, in part, this way: "If today we can sometimes jog, rather than puff, down the road toward the self-definition, it would seem that the Harlem Renaissance was a father who should not go without thanks, or reverence."[43]

Notes

[1]Arthur A. Schomburg, "The Negro Digs Up His Past," in *The New Negro: An Interpretation*, ed. Alain Locke (New York: Albert and Charles Boni, 1925), p. 231.

[2]Paul U. Kellogg, "The Negro Pioneeers," in *The New Negro*, p. 277.

[3]Josef Jarab, "The Birth of the New Negro (The Harlem Renaissance Reconsidered)," *Prague Studies in English*, 15 (1973), 44–45.

[4]Sterling A. Brown tends to deemphaasize this period as a definite, recognizable movement, while recognizing the new spirit and the individual writers.

[5]Walter Pater, *The Renaissance: Studies in Art and Poetry* (New York: Macmillan, 1902), pp. xv–xvi.

[6]Harold Cruse, *The Crisis of the Negro Intellectual* (New York: Oxford, 1971), p. 37.

[7]Langston Hughes, "The Negro Artist and the Racial Mountain," *The Nation*, 122 (23 June 1926), 692–94.

[8]Gilbert Osofsky, *Harlem: The Making of a Ghetto* (New York: Harper & Row, 1966), p. 128. There was also a serious housing shortage as well. See also "The Effects of the Negro Migration on the North," *The Journal of Negro History*, 6, No. 4 (October 1921), 434–44. This overcrowding resulted in a black phenomenon of this period—the rent party. This type of setting was used in Harlem Renaissance literature (by Claude McKay and Rudolph Fisher, for instance), and Langston Hughes describes this setting in his autobiography, *The Big Sea* (New York: Hill and Wang, 1963), pp. 228–33.

[9]This is not to say that other, new stereotypes may not have emerged: "The Harlemites that emerged from the pages of novels by both white and Negro authors in this period were exotic primitives, whose dances . . . were tribal rituals. . . . 'Negroes have cornered the joy' was the theme of a Negro novelist, who did know better." Sterling A. Brown, "A Century of Negro Portraiture in American Literature," *The Massachusetts Review* 7, No. 1 (Winter 1966), [pp. 73–96].

[10]Lofton Mitchell, *Black Drama* (New York: Hawthorn Books, 1967), p. 76.

[11]Langston Hughes, The Big Sea (New York: Hill and Wang, 1963, c1940), pp. 223, 224.

[12]Theodore Vincent, ed., *Voices of a Black Nation: Political Journalism in the Harlem Renaissance* (San Francisco: Ramparts Press, 1973), p. 22.

[13]James Weldon Johnson, *Black Manhattan* (New York: Atheneum, 1968, c1930, c1958), p. 260.

[14]See discussion of this in Darwin Turner, *In a Minor Chord: Three Afro-American Writers and Their Search for Identity* (Carbondale: Southern Illinois University Press, 1971), p. 39.

[15]Robert Bone, *The Negro Novel in America*, rev. ed. (New Haven: Yale University Press, 1965), p. 88.

[16]Jean Toomer, *Cane* (New York: Harper & Row, 1969, c1923), p. ix.

[17]Ibid., p. 18.

[18]Quoted in Turner, *In a Minor Chord*, p. 30.

[19]*Light*, 3 (24 September 1927), 12.

[20]Countee Cullen, *Copper Sun* (New York: Harper & Bros., 1927), inside back cover.

[21]Jay Saunders Redding, *To Make a Poet Black* (Chapel Hill: University of North Carolina Press, 1939), p. 111.

[22]Charles J. Glicksberg, "Negro Poets and the American Tradition," *Antioch Review*, 6 (Summer 1946), 246.

[23]Winifred Rothermel, "Countee Cullen Sees Future for the Race," *St. Louis Argus*, 3 February 1928.

[24]Hughes, "The Negro Artist," p. 694.

[25]*Phylon*, 7 (Fourth Quarter, 1950), 307.

[26]Claude McKay, *Banjo* (New York: Harper & Bros., 1929), pp. 200, 201.

[27]Hughes, *The Big Sea*, pp. 234, 235.

[28]Dorothy West, "Elephant's Dance," *Black World*, 20 (November 1970), 85.

[29]Hughes, *The Big Sea*, p. 240.

[30]James Weldon Johnson, *Along This Way* (New York: Viking Press, 1968, c1933, c1961), pp. 380, 381.

[31]Hughes, *The Big Sea*, p. 218.

[32]Charles S. Johnson, ed., *Ebony and Topaz: A Collectanea* (New York: Opportunity, 1927), p. [11].

[33]Patrick J. Gilpin, "Charles S. Johnson: Entrepreneur of the Harlem Renaissance," in *The Harlem Renaissance Remembered*, ed. Arna Bontemps (New York: Dodd, Mead & Co., 1972), p. 236.

[34]Locke, *The New Negro*, p. 15.

[35]Bone, *The Negro Novel*, p. 95.

[36]Nella Larsen, *Quicksand* (New York: Macmillan, 1971, c1928), p. 16 ["Introduction"].

[37]She even managed to get faint praise from the irascible radical of those times, Claude McKay: "She was prim, pretty and well dressed, and talked fluently and intelligently. All the radicals liked her, although in her social viewpoint she was away over on the other side of the fence." Claude McKay, *A Long Way from Home* (New York: Harcourt, Brace & World, 1970, c1937), p. 112.

[38]Margaret Perry, *Silence to the Drums: A Survey of the Literature of the Harlem Renaissance* (Westport, Conn.: Greenwood Press, 1976), p. 98.

[39]J. Lee Greene, *Time's Unfading Garden: Anne Spencer's Life and Poetry* (Baton Rouge: Louisiana State University Press, 1977).

[40]Sterling A. Brown, "The New Negro in Literature (1925–1955)," in *The New Negro Thirty Years Afterward*, ed. Rayford Logan (Washington, D.C.: Howard University Press, 1955), p. 57.

[41]Alain Locke, "This Year of Grace," *Opportunity*, 9, No. 2 (February 1931), 48.

[42]Hughes, *The Big Sea*, p. 228.

[43]George E. Kent, "Patterns of the Harlem Renaissance," in *The Harlem Renaissance Remembered*, p. 50.

I. BIBLIOGRAPHICAL AND REFERENCE MATERIAL

Includes bibliographies, guides to materials in collections, and first printing information.

*   Dickinson, Donald C. *A Bio-bibliography of Langston Hughes.* (See item 298.)

1.   Fleming, Robert E. *James Weldon Johnson and Arna Wendell Bontemps: A Reference Guide.* Boston: G.K. Hall, 1978.

Annotated bibliography of writings (articles, books, parts of books, and book reviews) about Johnson and Bontemps, arranged chronologically by publication dates of their works and, subsequently, by dates of writings about them up to 1976.

2.   F[uller], H[oyt] W. "Arna Bontemps: Dedication and Bibliography." *Black World,* 20 (September 1971), 78-79.

Individual and collaborated books written by Bontemps between 1931 and 1971 are listed. No articles, except contributions to encyclopedias, are included.

3.   Gross, Seymour L. "The Negro in Southern Literature," in *A Bibliographical Guide to the Study of Southern Literature,* ed. Louis D. Rubin, Jr. Baton Rouge: Louisiana State University Press, 1969. Pp. 58-66.

Does not adhere strictly to Southern literature in this checklist, proposing that much Afro-American literature touches on attitudes fostered in the South and, therefore, should be included in his list. Includes material by Negroes as well as works concerning them, primarily literary essays on literature.

4.   *Guide to the Microfilm Edition of the Countee Cullen
        Papers, 1921-1969.* Prepared by Florence E. Borders.
        New Orleans, La.: Amistad Research Center, 1975.

        A detailed, item-by-item description of manuscripts
        and correspondence in this collection.

5.   Hatch, James V., and Abdullah OMANii [sic]. *Black
        Playwrights, 1923-1977: An Annotated Bibliography of
        Plays.* New York: R.R. Bowker, 1977.

        The following information is supplied for playwrights:
        name, play title(s), date of composition or copyright,
        genre, brief description, casting, length, production,
        publication in book form, agent. Harlem Renaissance
        authors covered are: Grimké, Cullen, Bontemps, Hughes,
        Hurston, Matheus, and Richardson. Addresses of agents
        and agencies, as well as notation about awards given
        to black theatre and its artists. List of taped
        interviews (Hatch-Billops Archives, New York City)
        includes interviews with: Ida Cullen (re Countee
        Cullen), Langston Hughes, John Matheus, and Willis
        Richardson.

6.   Jackson, Blyden. "Langston Hughes," in *Black American
        Writers: Bibliographical Essays.* Volume I: *The
        Beginnings Through the Harlem Renaissance and Langston
        Hughes.* Edited by M. Thomas Inge, et al. New York:
        St. Martin's Press, 1978. Pp. 187-206.

        Description of bibliographies about Hughes, editions
        of his books, Hughes manuscripts and letters, biographies,
        and critical books about Hughes's writings. Many of
        the titles cited about Hughes are also assessed for
        their value to researchers.

7.   Kaiser, Ernest. "The Literature of Harlem." *Freedomways,*
        3, No. 3 (Summer 1963), 276-91.

        Pages 277-80 give a bibliographical overview of the
        publications issued during the Harlem Renaissance.

8.   —————. "Selected Bibliography of the Published
        Writings of Langston **Hughes**." *Freedomways,* 8 (1968),
        185-91.

        This item not seen.

9. "Langston Hughes, 1902-1967," in *First Printings of American Authors;* Vol. 3, eds. Matthew J. Bruccoli, C.E. Frazer Clark, Jr., Richard Layman, and Benjamin Franklin, V. Detroit: Gale Research Co., 1978. Pp. 157-81.

   Identification of the first American and the first English printing of books and broadsides by Hughes, as well as selected sheet music. Secondary publications, such as books edited or translated by Hughes, also appear.

10. Locke, Alain, comp. *A Decade of Negro Self-Expression.* Charlottesville, Va.: Trustees of the John F. Slater Fund, 1928. (Occasional Papers No. 26.)

    A classified, briefly annotated bibliography of books published by Negroes since World War I, representing the Negro's new efforts toward self-expression in conveying the unique black culture of America.

11. McDowell, Robert E., and George Fortenberry, eds. "A Checklist of Books and Essays about American Negro Novelists." *Studies in the Novel*, 3, No. 2 (Summer 1971), 219-36.

    General and individual author entries in this bibliography. Authors represented are: Cullen (Ferguson book only), Jessie Fauset, Fisher, Hughes, Hurston, J.W. Johnson, McKay, and Toomer.

12. Mandelik, Peter, and Stanley Schatt, comps. *A Concordance to the Poetry of Langston Hughes.* Detroit: Gale Research Co., 1975.

    An inclusive, key-word index to the most recent editions of Hughes's poetry (e.g., revised versions of some poems that appeared in *The Weary Blues* and *Fine Clothes to the Jew*), as well as for poetry published in various magazines and newspapers.

13. Miller, Elizabeth W., comp. *The Negro in America: A Bibliography.* 2nd ed. rev. Cambridge, Mass.: Harvard University Press, 1970.

    A full, wide-ranging listing of articles and books on nearly every subject one could wish or imagine. For the Harlem Renaissance, check the following areas: Biography and Letters; Folklore and Literature; The Negro in Literature and the Arts. Has a guide to materials to consult for further research.

14.   Miller, Ruth, and Peter J. Katopes. "The Harlem
        Renaissance: Arna Bontemps, Countee Cullen, James
        Weldon Johnson, Claude McKay, and Jean Toomer," in
        Black American Writers: Bibliographical Essays.
        Volume 1: *The Beginnings Through the Harlem Renaissance
        and Langston Hughes.* Edited by M. Thomas Inge,
        et al. New York: St. Martin's Press, 1978. Pp.
        161-206.

        Combines background history, bibliographic analysis
        (including mention of reprints), and criticism of
        books and articles about the Harlem Renaissance. A
        major introductory bibliographical essay because of
        its inclusiveness and, in particular, the explicit
        descriptions of specific manuscript collections (e.g.,
        James Weldon Johnson Memorial Collection at Yale; the
        Amistad Research Center in New Orleans). Includes
        brief explication of major thesis in each of the various
        articles written about the five authors. An extensive
        bibliographical essay.

15.   "The Negro in Literature." *The Crisis*, 36, No. 11
        (November 1929), 376-77, 392.

        Lists articles and books nationwide about the Negro
        in print from May through September 1929.

16.   ———. *The Crisis*, 37, No. 2 (February 1930) 51.

        Lists most important books by Negroes appearing in
        1929, followed by others of lesser importance, which
        were written by both blacks and whites. Also includes
        periodical articles.

17.   O'Daniel, Therman B. "Langston Hughes: A Selected
        Classified Bibliography." *CLA Journal*, 11, No. 4
        (June 1968), 349-66.

        Arranged by type of writing (e.g., poetry, autobio-
        graphies, short stories, etc.), covers only material
        written by Hughes, not anything about him.

18.   Olsson, Martin. *A Selected Bibliography of Black
        Literature: The Harlem Renaissance.* Exeter, England:
        University of Exeter, American Arts Documentation
        Centre, 1973.

        A succinct but penetrating introduction and analysis
        of what the Harlem Renaissance was and its cultural
        and literary significance. The bibliography is very

inclusive up to 1972, and there are brief, critical annotations. A highly useful bibliography for the scholar who needs a comprehensive introduction to the literature of this period.

19.   Partington, Paul G. "A Checklist of the Creative Writings of W.E.B. Du Bois." *Black American Literature Forum*, 13, No. 3 (Fall 1979), 110-11.

Brief narration of Du Bois's publications career, indicating that most of his creative writings appeared before the Harlem Renaissance. Du Bois rarely used *The Crisis* for publishing his creative work; poems that did appear, however, are not listed in this bibliography. Books containing short stories, poems, short fiction, and dramas are listed for the years 1907-1963.

*   Perry, Margaret. *A Bio-Bibliography of Countee P. Cullen*. (See item 238.)

20.   Reilly, John M. "Jean Toomer: An Annotated Checklist of Criticism." *Resources for American Literary Study*, 4, No. 1 (Spring 1974), 27-56.

An annotated bibliography of articles, book reviews, parts of books, and dissertations concerning Toomer, organized by year, with an alphabetical index by author at the end. Covers the years 1923-1973. Because of the cutoff date, the numerous articles (annotated in this bibliography) that appeared in *CLA Journal* during June 1974 are not listed in this well-conceived, insightful bibliography.

21.   Tucker, Veronica E., ed. *An Annotated Bibliography of the Fisk University Library's Black Oral History Collection*. Nashville: Fisk University, 1974. (Internships in Ethnic Studies Librarianship.)

Report of the contents, date of interview, and length of interviews of prominent Negroes who are connected with the history and culture of Afro-Americans.

22.   Turner, Darwin T. "Jean Toomer," in *A Bibliographical Guide to the Study of Southern Literature*, ed. Louis D. Rubin, Jr. Baton Rouge: Louisiana State University Press, 1969. Pp. 311-12.

A brief introduction to major articles and parts of books devoted to Toomer up to 1967. Bibliography contains twelve entries.

23.   "Wallace Thurman, 1902-1934," in *First Printings of
        American Authors*, Vol. 4, eds. Matthew J. Bruccoli,
        C.E. Frazer Clark, Jr., Richard Layman, and Benjamin
        Franklin, V. Detroit: Gale Research Co., 1979. P. 373.

        Identification of first American printings of Thurman's
        books, including the Haldeman-Julius Little Blue Book
        (n.d.). Facsimile of the title pages.

24.   Whiteman, Maxwell. *A Century of Fiction by American
        Negroes, 1853-1952: A Descriptive Bibliography*.
        Philadelphia: Albert Saifer, 1968.

        An alphabetical listing, by author, of books that are
        then annotated descriptively. A year-by-year
        chronology is attached, as is a brief supplement and
        a one-page list of "excluded titles" (with explanations).

25.   Whitlow, Roger. "The Harlem Renaissance and After:
        A Checklist of Black Literature of the Twenties and
        Thirties." *Negro American Literature Forum*, 7
        (December 1973), 143-46.

        An unannotated bibliography of novels, poetry collec-
        tions, individual collections of verse (e.g., Cullen's
        books), plays, and folk literature. No introduction, so
        criteria for inclusion of items is not clear.
        Includes most entries that appear in his critical
        history of Negro literature (see item 50).

26.   Williams, Ora. *American Black Women in the Arts and
        Social Sciences: A Bibliographic Survey*. Metuchen,
        N.J.: Scarecrow Press, 1978.

        Bibliographic information about Harlem Renaissance
        writers such as Zora N. Hurston, Jessie Fauset,
        Alice Dunbar-Nelson, and Anne Spencer--but not a
        first source to check. Although there is an index,
        the arrangement of entries tends to hamper easy
        access to information one might find elsewhere.
        Photographs.

II. LITERARY HISTORIES

Primarily general histories of Afro-American literature which feature significant discussion concerning the Harlem Renaissance.

27. Abramson, Doris E. *Negro Playwrights in the American Theatre, 1925-1959*. New York: Columbia University Press, 1969.

 Although there is a brief chapter entitled "Beginnings," which goes back prior to 1925 theatrical history, there is no mention of Angelina Grimké or the most prolific Harlem Renaissance playwright, Willis Richardson. The chapter on the 1920s concentrates on two plays: *Appearances*, by Garland Anderson, and *Harlem*, by Wallace Thurman. The chapter concerning the 1930s focuses attention on the dramatization of Rudolph Fisher's detective novel, *Conjure-Man Dies*.

28. Arata, Esther Spring, and Nicholas John Rotoli. *Black American Playwrights, 1800 to the Present: A Bibliography*. Metuchen, N.J.: Scarecrow Press, 1976.

 Lists works and criticism both of individuals and of their plays; Grimké, Richardson, Matheus, and Hughes are represented.

29. Bell, Bernard W. *The Folk Roots of Contemporary Afro-American Poetry*. Detroit: Broadsides Press, 1974.

 Book not seen. Source states the use of folk preaching by James Weldon Johnson is discussed.

30. Berzon, Judith R. *Neither White Nor Black: The Mulatto Character in American Fiction*. New York: New York University Press, 1978.

Provides an historical review of belief and practices
concerning blacks in America: belief in black in-
feriority led to fear of mixing races; when this did
happen, the offspring represented not only a contra-
diction in philosophy but also created confusion about
the social status of this type of person. Thus, the
mulatto became a popular character in fiction; in
Harlem Renaissance novels, when many espoused the
"black is beautiful" notion, the mulatto was used to
promote the viewpoint that passing, or being white,
was a less desirable state of existence. To pass
was to deny the true self. The major attack against
the obsessive concern for color is found in Schuyler's
Black No More. In exploring the interest in the
mulatto, the stereotypes, the mythology, much of the
Harlem Renaissance literature is discussed, e.g.,
work by Du Bois, Hughes, Hurston, J.W. Johnson,
Larsen, Toomer, and Schuyler.

31.   Bone, Robert. *Down Home: A History of Afro-American*
        Short Fiction from Its Beginnings to the End of the
        Harlem Renaissance. New York: G.P. Putnam's Sons,
        1975.

        Taking Frank O'Connor's thesis that the short story
        has grown from "submerged population groups," Bone
        applies his own theory of the "pastoral and anti-
        pastoral" influences on the black short story writer.
        Writers discussed in detail are Hurston, Fisher,
        McKay, Walrond, Toomer, Hughes, and Bontemps.

32.   ———. *The Negro Novel in America*, rev. ed. New
        Haven: Yale University Press, 1965.

        Views Harlem Renaissance writers as representing eithe
        "assimilationism [or] Negro nationalism," which limits
        his categorization of novels that may not fit into
        these two definitions. Has included *Cane*, presumably
        because he considers it the major work of fiction to
        emerge from the Harlem Renaissance. Sees Toomer
        emphasizing modern society's dehumanization of
        individuals. Also discusses the work of J.W. Johnson,
        Du Bois, McKay, Hughes, Cullen, Larsen, Fauset,
        Fisher, and Walter White in Part II: "This Discovery
        of the Folk, 1920–1930."

33.   Brawley, Benjamin. *The Negro Genius: A New Appraisal of the Achievement of the American Negro in Literature and the Fine Arts*. New York: Dodd, Mead & Co., 1937.

Chapters 8-10 review the work of Renaissance writers. A conventional narration of biographical and publication information about such writers as James Weldon Johnson, Georgia Douglas Johnson, Countee Cullen, Alain Locke, Claude McKay, Rudolph Fisher, Jessie Fauset, Sterling Brown, Arna Bontemps, Zora Neale Hurston, and Willis Richardson. The scope alone is useful to anyone wishing to have an overview of writers and their primary interests. Tends to be tolerant of technical weaknesses and to favor the subject of a book at the expense of style. Does assess some of the minor writers with clarity and fairness. In general, a genteel literary history.

34.   Brown, Sterling A. *The Negro in American Fiction*. Port Washington, N.Y.: Kennikat Press, 1967. Reprinted, New York: Arno Press, 1969 (with *Negro Poetry and Drama*).

First published in 1937, Chapter 9, entitled "The Urban Scene" (pp. 131-50), covers what Brown calls "The Harlem School," writers attempting to present "new characters in a new milieu," concerned with the middle class as well as the more exotic elements of the city, but generally failing to select significant issues or to have a vision that transcended apeing white values. Summarizes plots of major Harlem Renaissance authors (e.g., McKay, Cullen, Fisher, Fauset), and ends chapter with discussion questions. Excellent, trenchant criticism stated in a modicum of words.

35.   ———. *Negro Poetry and Drama*. Washington, D.C.: The Associates in Negro Folk Education, 1937. Reprinted, New York: Arno Press, 1969 (with *Negro in American Fiction*).

Chapter 5, "Contemporary Negro Poetry (1914-1936); the New Negro" states that the major new spirits of the times were self-respect and self-reliance, which produced poetic reactions against "sentimentality, didacticism, optimism, and romantic escape." Interest in African past, producing poems of race pride, as well as propaganda and protest poems, emerged during the Harlem Renaissance. Poets discussed briefly are

J.W. Johnson, McKay, Spencer, Fauset, Toomer, Cullen,
Hughes, Cuney, Helene Johnson, Bontemps, and himself.

36.   Davis, Arthur P. *From the Dark Tower: Afro-American
         Writers 1900 to 1960*. Washington, D.C.: Howard
         University Press, 1974.

         The first 135 pages are devoted to "The New Negro
         Renaissance," discussing the work of Du Bois, J.W.
         Johnson, McKay, Toomer, Locke, Hughes, Cullen,
         Bontemps, J. Fauset, Larsen, Fisher, Schuyler,
         Thurman, Hurston, and Sterling Brown. Presents
         background and social history from 1900 because
         "Like all similar movements, the Renaissance had
         its roots in the past." Generally sees this movement
         as one expressing a new viewpoint, a freshness, with
         an acknowledgment of the problem of a dual heritage.
         Still, it was not a movement to be rigidly defined:
         "There was no one type of black writer." What drew
         writers together was the new spirit, the ambiance of
         newness, high aspirations for revealing what true
         blackness was. Does not see the Renaissance as a
         total failure, despite shortcomings he points out in
         discussions of individual authors. Bibliography.

37.   Ford, Nick Aaron. *The Contemporary Negro Novel: A
         Study in Race Relations*. Boston: Meador Publishing
         Co., 1936. Reprinted, College Park, Md.: McGrath
         Publishing Co., 1968.

         A pioneer review and assessment of Harlem Renaissance
         novels, which Ford gently but firmly calls not up to
         standard because of weak technique and the tendency
         to write sociology instead of works of art. Suggests,
         therefore, that perhaps black writers should give up
         "the pretensions of pure artistry and boldly [take]
         up the cudgel of propaganda."

38.   Gayle, Addison, Jr. *The Way of the New World: The
         Black Novel in America*. Garden City, N.Y.: Anchor
         Press/Doubleday, 1975.

         A sociological interpretation of literature, suggesting
         that "it is necessary that one live the black experience
         in a world where substance is more important than
         form, where the social takes precedence over the
         aesthetic...." Many of the Harlem Renaissance writers
         are seen as conforming to white standards, or at
         least not fully shaking the influence of Van Vechten's

sensational novel, *Nigger Heaven*. Van Vechten is
the villain of this period, to the point of making
the sociological thesis tiresomely self-serving.
Finally states, without strong proof, that works by
Renaissance writers at least helped to start the
shift from concern for the black middle class to
greater emphasis on the proletariat. (See Perkins,
item 152, for a brief but opposite point of view.)

39.   Gloster, Hugh. *Negro Voices in American Fiction*.
       Chapel Hill: University of North Carolina Press, 1948.

       Sees the Renaissance as the period that broke with
       the past literary stereotypes and advanced black
       American literature greatly: a more self-revelatory
       literature emerged. Describes major works of fiction
       in summary format. Useful notes and bibliography.
       Chapters 3 and 4 cover the Renaissance period.

40.   Green, Elizabeth Lay. *The Negro in Contemporary
       American Literature: An Outline for Individual and
       Group Study*. Chapel Hill: University of North
       Carolina Press, 1928. Reprinted, College Park, Md.:
       McGrath Publishing Co., 1968.

       Describes writings of many Harlem Renaissance writers--
       Cullen, Hughes, J.W. Johnson, Eric Walrond, Toomer,
       Arthur Huff Fauset, and Rudolph Fisher--followed by
       study questions and bibliography.

41.   Harrison, Paul Carter. *The Drama of Nommo*. New
       York: Grove Press, 1972.

       An interpretation of drama from the non-Western point
       of view, stating observations in terms of African
       concepts, e.g., knowing a person's feelings through
       his body movements. Sees Toomer's *Cane* as an example
       of a work that expressed an authentic black vision,
       a book that "epitomizes a world-view peculiar to the
       African sensibility." Believes Thurman, in his play
       Harlem, catered to the exploitation that was a part
       of the Harlem Renaissance. It was Hughes, McKay,
       and Toomer who attempted to portray the uniqueness
       of the black personality in a renaissance, the author
       contends, that never ceased.

42.   Jackson, Blyden, and Louis D. Rubin, Jr. *Black
       Poetry in America: Two Essays in Historical
       Interpretation*. Baton Rouge: Louisiana State
       University Press, 1974.

       Production by poets of the Renaissance did not match
       their press or the attention focused on them. McKay,
       Cullen, and Hughes are examined in some detail as
       examples of both the weak and strong elements in
       Renaissance poetry. Of the three, Hughes is judged
       to be the best: where he lacked depth or the ability
       to synthesize ideas and emotions he had the ability
       to create impressionistic verse that possessed the
       authentic voice of the ordinary Negro. Also discusses
       the poetry of Sterling Brown, who "accepted the
       major·premise of the Renaissance--its championship
       of Negro materials presented with Negro means."

43.   Kerlin, Robert T. *Negro Poets and Their Poems*.
       Washington, D.C.: Associated Publishers, 1923.

       A history and interpretation of Negro poets, laudatory
       (even when criticizing), diffusely written. An early
       introduction, however, to some poets who would blossom
       during the Harlem Renaissance: Claude McKay, Langston
       Hughes, Anne Spencer, Georgia Douglas Johnson,
       Angelina Grimké, and Jessie Fauset. A period piece
       in literary history, but essential in examining the
       Harlem Renaissance in a total manner. Photos of the
       authors. See also article concerning Kerlin (item 665).

44.   Littlejohn, David. *Black on White: A Critical Survey
       of Writing by American Negroes*. New York: Grossman
       Publishers, 1966.

       Has little positive to say about Afro-American
       literature; finds it bleak, unrelenting in detailing
       injustices to blacks, and poorly written. Seems to
       dislike most of the literature he has read: calls
       The Walls of Jericho "trash" (pp. 49-50); sees
       Langston Hughes in a positive light, however, but has
       grudging praise for Cullen. Expresses great admiration
       for Du Bois. His bias against black literature is
       curiously strong, despite his avowed interest in
       it (but his overall attitude makes it difficult
       for the reader to have much faith in what is
       expressed).

45.   Margolies, Edward. *Native Sons: A Critical Study
        of Twentieth-Century Negro American Authors*.
        Philadelphia: J.B. Lippincott, 1968.

        "The First Forty Years: 1900-1940," the opening
        chapter, characterizes the Harlem Renaissance as a
        romantic, self-congratulatory movement. Describes
        the work of Hughes, whom he calls "primarily a folk
        artist who writes *for* the people he is writing *about*"
        (p. 37), and Toomer, whose *Cane* is assessed as having
        thematic unity. Also briefly discusses Claude McKay,
        Cullen, Schuyler, Wallace Thurman, and Nella Larsen.
        Sees the Harlem Renaissance as opening up wider
        possibilities for writers because new and broader
        interests and points of view were being espoused.

46.   Redding, J. Saunders. *To Make a Poet Black*. Chapel
        Hill: University of North Carolina Press, 1939.
        Reprinted, College Park, Md.: McGrath Publishing
        Co., 1968.

        Chapter 4 deals with the Harlem Renaissance, highlightin,
        the work of McKay, Toomer, Fauset, Hughes, Cullen,
        Rudolph Fisher, and James Weldon Johnson. Contends
        that there was a new sociological interest in the
        Negro from 1910 onwards, due to migration and the
        urban problems. The literature gradually reflected
        changes in Negro attitude, from apologetic to
        declamatory about the strengths and strivings of
        the race. By 1921 the interest in the Negro matched
        his interest in himself; thus, the Negro renaissance
        began to emerge. Sees the movement in literature as
        starting with Claude McKay; by 1924 the movement was
        identifiable and definitely in place. Suggests there
        was pessimism and cynicism in the work of many--a
        "black despair," for instance, as he writes about
        Nella Larsen. Notes the experiments in form of
        Langston Hughes, one of the few to try new forms and
        experiments with language. Ultimately sees the period
        as one where the urban setting became an obsession
        and the literature was that of escape. Seduced by
        the new interest in them and the urban hold upon
        them, the writers of the Harlem Renaissance were
        a confused, unevenly talented lot who had strayed
        perhaps too far from their earth-bound roots.

47.   Rosenblatt, Roger. *Black Fiction*. Cambridge,
        Mass.: Harvard University Press, 1974.

        Sees a dominant theme in black literature as a search
        for a base for the race's cultural history. Also
        believes that black fiction has examined the same
        problem as found in most American fiction, i.e.,
        self-definition. Approaches his study of black
        fiction by concepts rather than by chronology, in
        order to examine what he sees as the cyclical pattern
        inherent in it--a cyclical pattern that emerges from
        the history of blacks in America. Discusses the
        following books: *Cane, Their Eyes Were Watching God,
        Not Without Laughter, Autobiography of an Ex-Coloured
        Man*, and *Home to Harlem*.

48.   Schraufnagel, Noel. *From Apology to Protest: The
        Black American Novel*. Deland, Fla.: Everett/Edwards,
        1973.

        Presents a brief overview of the Renaissance, not so
        much as a movement as a summary of writings by
        participants, in Chapter 1. A superficial and
        sometimes inaccurate treatment of the literature
        (e.g., literary historians now avoid crediting
        Van Vechten with inspiring McKay, but Schraufnagel
        persists in promulgating this notion).

49.   Starke, Catherine Juanita. *Black Portraiture in
        American Fiction: Stock Characters, Archetypes, and
        Individuals*. New York: Basic Books, Inc., 1971.

        Harlem Renaissance writers--Cullen, Hughes, McKay,
        J.W. Johnson, and Toomer--are discussed as either
        individuals or as among the following major arche-
        types in black literature: tragic mulatto, sacrificial
        symbol, beloved mammy, natural primitive, or alter-
        ego symbol. Sees black individuals as persons
        moving "from subservience to self-assertion."
        With theoretical framework, examines briefly such
        literature as *Cane, Not Without Laughter, One Way
        to Heaven*, and *The Autobiography of an Ex-Coloured
        Man*.

50.   Whitlow, Roger. *Black American Literature: A Critical
        History*. Chicago: Nelson-Hall, Co., 1973.

        Straightforward historical overview of the 1920s,
        with excerpts from the literature scattered in the
        text. Provides a separate section on the following

Harlem Renaissance writers, detailing publications
and major thematic interests, in Chapter V: Claude
McKay, Jean Toomer, Langston Hughes, Nella Larsen,
George Schuyler, Arna Bontemps, and Zora Neale Hurston.

51.   Young, James O. *Black Writers of the Thirties*. Baton
        Rouge: Louisiana State University Press, 1973.

        Stresses shift of ideas from those of race men, who
        upheld blackness in genteel terms (e.g., James Weldon
        Johnson), to newer blacks who viewed black life from
        an economic frame of reference. Therefore, many
        Harlem Renaissance writers represented a past ideal
        that did not exist and wrote inconsequential literature
        that was "disappointingly shallow." Examines in some
        detail the following writers and their work: Cullen's
        The Black Christ and his novel, *One Way to Heaven*;
        Hughes's 1930s poetry and his first novel, *Not
        Without Laughter*; the novels of Thurman, Hurston,
        Schuyler, McKay, and Fauset; and the poetry of Sterling
        Brown. Also writes about literary critics of the
        1920s and 1930s. Useful as a contrast between two
        decades that served as influences upon Harlem
        Renaissance writers.

III. GENERAL STUDIES AND
STUDIES OF SEVERAL AUTHORS

This section is divided into two parts: A. Books,
Articles, and Parts of Books; B. Selected Book and Drama
Reviews.

A. Books, Articles, and Parts of Books
(About Literature and the Period in General)

52.   Arden, Eugene. "The Early Harlem Novel." *Phylon*,
        20 (1959), 25-31.

        Descriptive narration of novels about black life
        from Dunbar to Cullen, giving an inordinate amount
        of space to Carl Van Vechten's *Nigger Heaven*.
        Believes a stereotype of Harlem was created by
        writers who wrote in the Van Vechten mode. Finally,
        considers that the important feature to remember
        about the Harlem Renaissance novel is the creation
        of a new character: the urban Negro.

53.   Barnes, Albert C. "Negro Art, Past and Present."
        Opportunity, 4, No. 41 (May 1926), 148-49, 168-69.

        Saw the Negro artist as one who has natural gifts
        that had not been lost; but Barnes also thought
        greater appreciation by both whites and blacks needed
        to be given to African art in order to allow the
        then-current black artists to express this "natural"
        gift.

54.   Barret, Eseoghene. "The Harlem Renaissance."
        Nigeria Magazine, 122-23 (1977), 125-28.

        Argues, not too convincingly, that the writers of
        this period were united in trying to express a common
        racial sentiment. Overstates the influence of the
        writers on ordinary members of their own race. The

notion of a new assertiveness among black writers
is accurate, although the overall description of the
period tends to be too general, too speculative,
lacking in convincing examples to undergird arguments.

55.   Bearden, Romare. "The Negro Artist and Modern Art."
        Opportunity, 12, No. 12 (December 1934), 371-72.

        Accuses the Negro artist of being mediocre and
        derivative, of failing to appreciate his own black
        heritage, and of not having an ideology or social
        philosophy. Also states that foundations like the
        Harmon Foundation foster this mediocre art in a
        patronizing manner.

56.   Berghahn, Marion. *Images of Africa in Black American
        Literature*. Totowa, N.J.: Rowman and Littlefield,
        1977. Pp. 118-51.

        A special section on the Harlem Renaissance and the
        influence of Africa and primitivism on Afro-American
        writers.

57.   Berry, Faith. "Did Van Vechten Make or Take Hughes'
        'Blues'?" *Black World*, 25, No. 4 (February 1976),
        22-28.

        Argues that Van Vechten's influence on the writing
        of Hughes has been exaggerated; that his major
        contribution to Hughes was as a useful contact in
        the business end of the literary world.

58.   ————. "Voice for the Jazz Age, Great Migration,
        or Black Bourgeoisie." *Black World*, 20, No. 1
        (November 1970), 10-16.

        Stresses that the Renaissance movement was a middle-
        class phenomenon that depicted a Harlem that did not
        really exist. The literature devoted little space
        to the masses; however, attention to black life and
        artistic work was a distinct contribution of these
        well-educated bourgeois writers.

59.   *Black World*, 20, No. 1 (November 1970).

        Issue devoted to the Harlem Renaissance. See
        individual articles, items 58, 74, 76, 132, 133,
        142, 170, 212, 476, 694.

60.   Bland, Edward. "Racial Bias and Negro Poetry."
        Poetry, 63 (March 1944), 328-33.

        Using examples from verse by Cullen, McKay, and other
        Harlem Renaissance writers, argues that poetry by
        Negroes is limited by "pre-individualistic values"
        which stress group rather than individual experiences.

61.   Bontemps, Arna. "The New Black Renaissance." *Negro
        Digest* (November 1961), 52-58.

        In suggesting the black writers of the early 1960s
        have more in common with Harlem Renaissance writers
        than those of the immediately preceding decades,
        makes comparison between Toomer and Ellison,
        discusses Wallace Thurman (seeing him as perhaps a
        failed Baldwin), and sees the same informing spirit
        in Julian Mayfield's work as was in that of Rudolph
        Fisher.

62.   Braithwaite, William Stanley. "Alain Locke's
        Relationship to the Negro in American Literature."
        Phylon, 18 (1957), 166-73.

        Views Locke as trying to help black writers of the
        1920s understand their spiritual link with Africa
        (e.g., group consciousness) and its culture. Uses a
        scene from Wallace Thurman's *roman à clef*, *Infants
        of the Spring* (where Locke is Dr. Parkes), to prove
        that Locke believed "that the roots of the American
        Negro imagination were fertilized in the primitive
        arts of Africa."

63.   ————. "The Negro in Literature." *The Crisis*,
        28, No. 5 (September 1924), 204-10.

        States that James Weldon Johnson was the first black
        poet since Dunbar to rise above mediocrity. Goes on
        to discuss Claude McKay's poetry, which he feels is
        weakened by his propagandistic verses. Praises Du
        Bois excessively when he cites the novel *The Quest
        for the Silver Fleece* as notable. Comments favorably
        on Jessie Fauset's novel *There is Confusion*, and
        ends with a paean to Jean Toomer, whom he describes
        as "a bright morning star of a new day of the Race in
        literature!" Braithwaite makes literary judgments
        in terms more often of race than of objective literary
        criteria. A shorter, revised version of this article,
        entitled "The Negro in American Literature," appears
        in *The New Negro*, edited by Alain Locke (see item 772).

64.   ———. "Some Contemporary Poets of the Negro Race."
           The Crisis, 17, No. 6 (April 1919), 275-80.

           Proposes that Paul Laurence Dunbar represents the end
           of an era, not the beginning of a tradition in Negro
           literature. Rather, it was Du Bois's *The Souls of
           Black Folk* (1903) that established a poetic spirit
           that poets of the 1920s would carry forward--a spirit
           that reflects the idealism and aspirations of the New
           Negroes. Poets discussed in the light of this thesis
           are: Claude McKay, Roscoe C. Jamison (dead by the time
           this article was published), Georgia Douglas Johnson,
           and James Weldon Johnson.

65.   Brawley, Benjamin. "The Negro Literary Renaissance."
           The Southern Workman, 56 (April 1927), 177-84.

           A genteel, fusty assessment of writers: Walrond and
           McKay are praised, Cullen is found lacking mastery of
           poetry so greatly that "we can find in it not one
           quotable passage," and Hughes is chastised for his
           blues and jazz poetry, which are characterized as
           "imitative and coarse." Brawley is puzzled but
           impressed by Toomer's work; but the critical attitude
           is basically narrow and rigid. A period-piece essay
           that expresses an unsympathetic, contemporary view
           of the Harlem Renaissance.

66.   ———. "The Promise of Negro Literature." *Journal
           of Negro History*, 19, No. 1 (January 1934), 53-59.

           Not so much about the Renaissance as about the author's
           relief that the decade of self-expression (which he
           saw as one lacking in self-control) was being replaced
           by a literature that was on the threshold of telling
           about black "struggles, of our aspiration and
           yearning, of our most earnest striving," which he
           felt was not always found in the more exotic literature
           of the Renaissance.

67.   Brown, Sterling A. "The Blues as Folk Poetry," in
           Folk-Say: A Regional Miscellany, 1930, ed. B.A.
           Botkin. Norman: University of Oklahoma Press,
           1930. Pp. 324-39.

           Blues songs need closer study to reveal the real
           poetry as well as the genuine folk experience of
           Negroes. The blues show "two great loves, the love
           of words and the love of life, poetry results."

68.   ————. "The Negro in Literature (1929-1955)," in
           The New Negro Thirty Years Afterward, ed. Rayford
           Logan, Eugene C. Holmes, and G. Franklin Edwards.
           Washington, D.C.: Howard University Press, 1955.
           Pp. 57-72.

           The increased interest in Negro life and culture during
           the 1920s is acknowledged, but skepticism is expressed
           about the emphasis on the exotic qualities of Negro
           life at the expense of the idealism expressed by an
           individualist such as Langston Hughes. The early days
           of the Depression forced the writers to do some
           soul-searching (among them, Alain Locke, the "Dean"
           of the Renaissance), and new directions emerged as
           the Renaissance drew to a close.

69.   Butcher, Margaret Just. *The Negro in American Culture*.
           New York: Alfred A. Knopf, 1957.

           Based on notes and articles left by Alain Locke,
           references to the Harlem Renaissance period appear
           throughout the book, primarily in the chapters "Formal
           Negro Poetry" and "The Negro in Modern American
           Fiction." Argues in overall terms that features of
           black American culture derive from folk life of the
           past. Slavery held back the development of black
           culture, but it did not kill the spirit of the
           people or the heritage from which the black race
           sprang.

70.   Calverton, V.F. "The Negro's New Belligerent
           Attitude." *Current History*, 30, No. 6 (September
           1929), 1081-88.

           Recounts the past history of blacks in Africa, and
           claims that this proves that Afro-Americans have a
           heritage of which to be proud—a history that stands
           behind the new Negro writers of the Harlem Renaissance.
           Does not see this period as a transitory phenomenon
           in American cultural history, even though many of
           the writers are overly praised by persons who think
           in terms of race rather than art. Concludes that
           "if this new literature of the negro [sic] in America
           does not constitute a renaissance, it does signify
           rapid growth in racial art and culture." This same
           article appeared in his *Anthology of American Negro
           Literature* under the title of "The Growth of Negro
           Literature," and in Cunard's *Negro* (see item 763).

71.   Carter, Elmer A. "Crossing Over." *Opportunity*, 4,
        No. 48 (December 1926), 376-78.

        A study of "passing," a theme of many novels written
        during the Harlem Renaissance.

72.   Chamberlain, John. "The Negro as Writer." *The
        Bookman*, 70, No. 6 (February 1930), 603-11.

        An overview of Afro-American poetry and prose that is
        both perceptive and representative of a narrow racial
        bias against black literature: assessments of Cullen
        and McKay seem just, but complete dismissal of some
        minor writers (e.g., Fauset, Larsen, Bontemps) seems
        arbitrary and haughty. A useful article, however,
        for capturing the tone of criticism written during
        this period concerning writing by black authors.

73.   Chapman, Abraham. "The Harlem Renaissance in Literary
        History." *CLA Journal*, 11 (September 1967), 38-58.

        As the Renaissance is a neglected phase in American
        literary history in 1967, argues that American critical
        history needs to be desegregated in order to place
        the Harlem Renaissance in its various contexts, such
        as a movement to erase the false image of Negroes
        that had developed from the time of slavery. One
        problem Chapman points out is the primary conflict
        this movement had with the Protestant culture which
        had ignored the black contribution to American culture.
        After exploring the various contexts one might consider,
        concludes with a reminder that the Harlem Renaissance
        movement is fertile ground for more extensive
        scholarship by literary historians.

74.   Clarke, John Henrik. "The Neglected Dimensions of
        the Harlem Renaissance." *Black World*, 20, No. 1
        (November 1970), 118-29.

        Suggests that Marcus Garvey's contribution to the
        Renaissance movement was important because of his
        support from the black masses, which established a
        basis for the movement that emphasized the humanity
        of black and the importance of their African heritage.

75.   Coleman, Floyd, and John Adkins Richardson. "Black
        Continuities in the Art of the Harlem Renaissance."
        Papers on Language & Literature, 12, No. 4 (Fall
        1976), 402-21.

        The persistence of the African heritage in Renaissance
        literature and art is explored: the main premise is
        that blacks did not forget the culture they had known
        in Africa. Just as black language was not deviant
        but special, the whole of African culture was an
        influence also upon the black artists of the 1920s.
        For instance, the African heritage, blended into
        the aesthetics of Western art, resulted in a tendency
        towards modernism in painting and sculpture. Writers,
        painters, and sculptors are discussed.

76.   Collier, Eugenia [W.]. "Heritage from Harlem."
        Black World, 20, No. 1 (November 1970), 52-59.

        Believes that the roots of the arts movement in the
        1960s derive from the Harlem Renaissance writers who
        reshaped Afro-American literature through their use
        of black folklore, realistic portrayals of black
        life, and their expression of pride in their blackness
        and in their heritage.

77.   ————. "I Do Not Marvel, Countee Cullen." *CLA
        Journal*, 11, No. 1 (September 1967), 73-87.

        Seeking to find poetry that expresses the spirit of
        the Harlem Renaissance, examines poems that (1)
        demonstrate an interest in Africa; (2) utilize the
        blues, spirituals, and ballads; (3) use black speech
        idioms without resorting to dialect; and (4) portray
        black life realistically. Examples are drawn from
        Cullen, Sterling Brown, McKay, Waring Cuney, and
        Helene Johnson.

78.   Cruse, Harold. *The Crisis of the Negro Intellectual*.
        New York: William Morrow & Co., 1967.

        There are some overall theses that Cruse applies to
        the Negro in America which help one to understand his
        interpretation of the Harlem Renaissance movement.
        Sees a distinct mode of social opinion among Negroes,
        no matter the class, and considers Harlem pivotal in
        the "black world's quest for identity and salvation."
        He also believes that Afro-Americans are no less immune
        to the mythological American Dream than their white
        compatriots. Finally, the Negro intellectual is

socially separated from the major population of his
race. Therefore, it is not surprising that he finds
freneticism, ill-defined goals, a lack of an identifiable
cultural philosophy, and an "inspired aimlessness"
about the Harlem Renaissance. Shapeless, unable to
apply action and works to theory or expressed beliefs,
the Harlem Renaissance failed to establish and shape
a cultural presence that was clearly Afro-American.

79.   Cunard, Nancy. "Harlem Reviewed," in her *Negro: An
         Anthology*. London: Wishart, 1934. Reprinted, New
         York: Frederick Ungar Publishing Co., 1970. Pp. 47-55.

         Describes the people who live in Harlem, the buildings
         that house or entertain them, discusses the conflicts
         between West Indians and native-born blacks, describes
         the religious leaders, and provides some statistical
         information as well. Has an eye for the exotic, but
         also seriously attacks the Negro press, which she
         considers vulgar and uneven in coverage of important
         topics and events. Dismisses Van Vechten and blacks
         like him who are characterized as producing romantic
         as well as vulgar work. Ends with a hope that
         Harlemites will seek to become Communists.

80.   Davis, Arthur P. "Growing Up in the New Negro
         Renaissance: 1920-1935." *Negro American Literature
         Forum*, 2 (Fall 1968), 53-59.

         Sees the Harlem Renaissance period as one of a flourish
         of artistic outpourings and a time when Harlem was
         "delightful." The slums of today had not yet appeared.
         A genuine reminiscence of views, habits, activities,
         and entertainment enjoyed by the author as well as
         portraits of personalities like Wallace Thurman and
         Bruce Nugent.

81.   De Armond, Fred. "A Note on the Sociology of Negro
         Literature." *Opportunity*, 3, No. 36 (December
         1925), 369-71.

         Espouses the belief that poor race relations and
         inability to appreciate influences on black writers
         are the causes that inhibit understanding of Afro-
         American literature.

82.   Dorsey, Emmett E. "Political Ideologies of the New
        Negro," in *The New Negro Thirty Years Afterward*, ed.
        Rayford Logan, Eugene C. Holmes, and G. Franklin
        Edwards. Washington, D.C.: Howard University Press,
        1955. Pp. 33-40.

        Notes that it was interesting that political matters
        were not discussed in *The New Negro*, even though there
        was emerging a new type of political ideology during
        the Renaissance period: more concerned with urban
        problems, unionism, and a shift in loyalty from the
        Republican Party to the Democratic.

83.   Edmonds, Randolph. "Some Reflections on the Negro in
        American Drama." *Opportunity*, 8, No. 10 (October
        1930), 303-05.

        States failure to produce black drama derives from
        lack of apprenticeship experience among blacks, and
        the objections of the audience to watching "serious"
        Negro drama. The drama written by blacks, nonetheless,
        is considered poor, imitative, unable to "reveal the
        soul of the black man," and possessing "almost no
        theatric values." Urges black colleges to provide
        theatrical experience for blacks, both young authors
        and future audiences.

84.   Emanuel, James A. "America Before 1950: Black Writers
        Views." *Negro Digest*, 18, No. 10 (August 1969),
        26-34, 67-69.

        Sees the decade itself (pp. 29-30) as more important
        than the literature produced. Considers three novelists
        worth mentioning: Du Bois, McKay, and Nella Larsen,
        and then adds Rudolph Fisher's *The Walls of Jericho*
        to this exclusive list because of its satire.

85.   ————. "Renaissance Sonneteers." *Black World*,
        24, No. 11 (September 1975), 32-45, 92-97.

        Attempts to show the relevance of subjects used by
        Harlem Renaissance poets who wrote sonnets (and some
        poets mentioned are obscure and not specifically
        connected to "the movement") by emphasizing the
        racial elements in the poetry. Stresses the most
        pervasive overall theme of creating a positive image
        of blacks. Strains a bit to connect love with black
        interest in the seventies in "the maintenance of
        ecosystems, law and order, and revolution." Sees
        that it is perhaps impossible for today's writers to

use the sonnet but believes the Renaissance writers
used it effectively to express their own racial
beliefs and needs.

86.   Fauset, Arthur Huff. "American Negro Folk Literature,"
         in *The New Negro: An Interpretation*, ed. Alain Locke.
         New York: Albert and Charles Boni, 1925. Pp. 238-44.

         States that authentic folk tales of Negroes have been
         misinterpreted by white authors like Joel C. Harris,
         that there is a need to collect black folk tales in
         a scientific manner, or "some of the precious secrets
         of folk history are in danger of fading out in its
         gradual disappearance." Indicates that the folk
         literature possesses less self-consciousness, is nearer
         to nature, and has universal appeal. Therefore, hopes
         that investigation into aspects of folklore will bring
         forth authentic folk literature.

87.   Foreman, Ronald C., Jr. "The 20's and the Blues/Jazz
         of Black Fiction," in *Proceedings of the Fifth National
         Popular Culture Association*. Bowling Green, Ohio:
         Center for Archival Collections, University Library,
         1975, [Microfilm] PCA 1559-73.

         Traces the types of influence that authentic black
         music--jazz, blues, spirituals--had on the work of
         Jessie Fauset, J.W. Johnson, Jean Toomer, Langston
         Hughes, Claude McKay, Nella Larsen, and Countee
         Cullen. Some ignored the "existence of jazz and blues,'
         but this, too, is seen as significant in examining
         the fiction and poetry of the black authors of the
         1920s.

88.   Fox, R.M. "The Negro Renaissance." *Labour Magazine*
         (London), (November 1928), 306-08.

         Introduces this new movement to English readers by
         mentioning such influences as a reevaluation of racial
         heritage, a new self-confidence developed during World
         War I when more blacks entered the industrial life
         of the United States, and the importance of jazz as
         an example of the "riotous energy of the negro."
         Sees the movement starting with Dunbar, which remains
         an argument among critics (see items 64 and 132).

89.   Franklin, John Hope. "A Harlem Renaissance," in his
        From Slavery to Freedom: A History of Negro Americans,
        3rd ed. New York: Random House, 1947. Pp. 498-514.

        A panoramic sweep of the period, emphasizing social
        and economic changes as important factors upon the
        literary life. Notes that most of the Harlem Renaissance
        writers, however, ignored Socialism and Communism even
        though many wrote about the problems of the black
        race (with a certain artistic detachment, however).
        Mentions the work of the major writers by title and
        presents an overall description (but not synopses)
        of the works.

90.   Frazier, E. Franklin. *Black Bourgeoisie*. New York:
        The Free Press, c1957.

        Describes the Harlem Renaissance (pp. 119-29) as a
        nationalistic movement, because of the political and
        social aspects of this time.

91.   ————. "The New Negro Middle Class," in *The New
        Negro Thirty Years Afterward*, ed. Rayford Logan, Eugene
        C. Holmes, and G. Franklin Edwards. Washington, D.C.:
        Howard University Press, 1955. Pp. 26-32.

        Despite the efforts of writers to reevaluate culture
        in Afro-American terms, the new black middle class
        rejected the new literature and sought to escape into
        the make-believe world of possessions and white values.

92.   Fullinwider, S.P. *The Mind and Mood of Black America:
        20th Century Thought*. Homewood, Ill.: The Dorsey
        Press, 1969.

        After tracing sociological thought of E. Franklin
        Frazier, Du Bois, and Robert Park, shifts to Alain
        Locke, the philosopher "who picked up the various
        strands of thought and interpreted them in terms of
        art and literature." Locke helped to secure recognition
        and exposure for the emerging black artists, even
        when he was sometimes ridiculed for representing what
        some writers wanted to get away from (middle-class
        respectability). Others are cited, also--Charles S.
        Johnson, for example. The major writers are analyzed,
        with an attempt to probe the psychology behind the
        writer. Although different in other respects, each
        writer is seen as wanting to detail aspects of living
        as a black in America. Considers *Cane* the most
        beautiful book to come from this period. Spends a

great amount of time on Toomer's work, but also
delves into the life and work of Cullen (and mistakenly
indicates that his first wife never did join him in
Europe). Sees a weakness of many Renaissance writers
as a tendency towards too much introspection; added
to that was their dual heritage, which caused self-
hatred and then despair in some writers.

93.   Gayle, Addison, Jr. "The Harlem Renaissance: Toward
        a Black Aesthetic." *Midcontinent American Studies
        Journal*, 11 (Fall 1970), 78-87.

        Writers and critics during the Harlem Renaissance
        failed to establish a black aesthetic because they
        could not free themselves from white values. This is
        true, despite the achievements of Toomer, McKay,
        Hughes, and James Weldon Johnson (who is credited with
        breaking down traditional modes when he discouraged
        use of dialect and introduced idiomatic language).
        Still, the Renaissance writers "mapped out the
        contours of such a road [to a black aesthetic]."

94.   Gibson, Donald B., ed. *Modern Black Poets: A
        Collection of Critical Essays*. Englewood Cliffs,
        N.J.: Prentice-Hall, 1973.

        Reprints "The New Negro Poet in the Twenties," by J.
        Saunders Redding (see item 46)--a title used for this
        collection only, and also reprinting from page 101
        instead of from page 93 of Redding's *To Make a Poet
        Black*. Also reprints "The Good Black Poet and the
        Good Gray Poet: The Poetry of Hughes and Whitman,"
        by Donald Gibson (see item 304), and "I Do Not
        Marvel, Countee Cullen." by Eugenia Collier (see
        item 77).

95.   Gilpin, Patrick J. "Charles S. Johnson: Entrepreneur
        of the Harlem Renaissance," in *The Harlem Renaissance
        Remembered*, ed. Arna Bontemps. New York: Dodd,
        Mead & Co., 1972. Pp. 215-46.

        Describes Johnson's activities as editor of *Opportunity*
        and friend of many of the Harlem Renaissance writers.
        Encourages writers not to exploit their race but to
        explore and explain it by using the same standards of
        writing as those used by whites. Agrees with Langston
        Hughes (in *The Big Sea*, p. 218, item 286) about
        Johnson's importance as a major supporter of the
        movement--a supporter, unlike Du Bois, who did not
        try to dictate the direction of the Renaissance to
        conform with his own views.

96.   ————. "A Footnote on the Harlem Renaissance,"
         in *The Harlem Renaissance Generation*, ed. L.M.
         Collins. Nashville: Fisk University, 1972. Pp. 386-88.

         Discusses the importance of the Negro magazines
         Opportunity and *The Crisis* in aiding the Harlem
         Renaissance writers to become published.

97.   Glicksberg, Charles I.. "Negro Americans and the
         African Dream." *Phylon*, 8, No. 4 (Fourth Quarter,
         1947), 323-30.

         In his overall argument, which does not concern the
         Harlem Renaissance primarily, iterates his belief
         (see item 98) that the identity with Africa, with the
         black heritage stemming from that land, encouraged
         during the Harlem Renaissance was "an act of psychic
         suicide" (p. 326).

98.   ————. "The Negro Cult of the Primitive." *The
         Antioch Review*, 4 (Spring 1944), 47-55.

         Considers it parochial for Negro writers to be bound
         by race alone; believes the Renaissance writers,
         spurred by a repudiation of America, participated in
         a myth when they wrote their rhetoric of blackness.
         Considers the assimilationist views of Locke more
         tenable. Not primarily about the Harlem Renaissance,
         but significant for the argument against reveling in
         the primitive aspects of any race's past.

99.   ————. "Negro Poets and the American Tradition."
         The Antioch Review, 6 (Summer 1946), 243-53.

         Demonstrates the warring elements in the poetry of
         such writers as Hughes and Brown, where there is
         hatred as well as love for America in the poetry,
         where race pride is celebrated, and belief in the
         triumph of right on the side of blacks is seen in a
         poem like "America," by McKay. Sees eventually the
         writing focusing on wider interests and problems so
         that "Negro writers will become *American* writers."

100.   Gloster, Hugh M. "The Van Vechten Vogue." *Phylon*,
         6, No. 4 (Fourth Quarter, 1945), 310-14.

         Although Van Vechten exaggerated the exotic qualities
         of life in Harlem and black life in general during
         the 1920s, his influence on other writers and on the
         period itself helped to make it possible for black

writers to break away from taboos that had made it
difficult in the past to be more self-revelatory
about the black race, its culture, and its habits.

101.   Gross, Theodore. "The Negro Awakening: Langston
          Hughes, Jean Toomer, Rudolph Fisher, and Others."
          The Heroic Ideal in American Literature. New York:
          The Free Press, 1971, pp. 137-47.

          Described primarily as a movement of local colorists,
          the Harlem Renaissance is characterized as an awakening
          rather than a rebirth. The commentary concentrates
          on Toomer's *Cane*, which he sees escaping the local
          color formulae and "is the only volume written during
          the Negro Awakening that one can consider a significant
          contribution to our literature."

102.   Gruening, Martha. "The Negro Renaissance." *Hound &
          Horn*, 5, No. 4 (July-September 1932), 504-14.

          Believes the Harlem Renaissance failed because its
          lofty aims--e.g., group spirit, "spiritual emancipa-
          tion"--were not realistic or possible to fulfill
          completely. The movement succeeded on individual
          bases, such as in the work of Toomer. One problem
          was the acceptance of white values, which resulted
          in sterile, meritless writing (e.g., novels of
          Fauset). The best novels were written by poets--
          Hughes and McKay--who do not simply chronicle black
          life to prove a point but who imbue their writing
          with a story and characters that interest the reader.

103.   Hart, Robert C. "Black-White Literary Relations in
          the Harlem Renaissance." *American Literature*, 44,
          No. 4 (January 1973), 612-28.

          An overview of individual and group relationships
          between black and white writers: Van Vechten played a
          key role, both as promoter of writers and as a close
          friend and literary executor of James Weldon Johnson.
          Concludes, however, that there was little serious
          contact between the major white writers (such as
          Hemingway or Eliot) and the Harlem Renaissance
          authors. The relationships were, rather, of "white
          patron to black artist," which aided writers who had
          little or nothing from the past to build on and who
          served as strong precursors to the black writers of
          the 1930s and 1940s.

104.   Hay, Samuel. "Alain Locke and Black Drama." *Black
        World*, 21, No. 6 (April 1972), 8-14.

        Contends that Locke presaged revolutionary, social
        drama when he advised, in 1927, that black dramatists
        must write plays that serve Negro life, plays that
        grow from what is inherent in Negro life. The con-
        tradiction in his philosophy was his advising the
        writer to be detached from the elements that serve
        to inspire the drama.

105.   Helbling, Mark. "Carl Van Vechten and the Harlem
        Renaissance." *Negro American Literature Forum*, 10,
        No. 2 (Summer 1976), 39-47.

        Van Vechten, as the author points out, was important
        not only because of his controversial book, *Nigger
        Heaven*, but also because of the publishing help he
        gave to young Negro writers and the interracial
        gatherings he backed. Emphasis on *Nigger Heaven*
        and how it reflects his personal philosophy and
        connects with his earlier novel, *Peter Whiffle*.

106.   Hemenway, Robert, ed. *The Black Novelist*. Columbus,
        Ohio: Charles E. Merrill, 1970.

        A collection of essays reprinted from other publications:
        "Zora Neale Hurston," by Robert Bone (see item 32),
        "The Novels of Jessie Fauset," by William S.
        Braithwaite (see item 252), and "The Negro Renaissance:
        Jean Toomer and the Harlem Writers of the 1920's,"
        by Arna Bontemps (see item 441).

107.   Hercules, Frank. "An Aspect of the Negro Renaissance."
        Opportunity, 20, No. 10 (October 1942), 305-06,
        317-19.

        Depicts the Harlem Renaissance as a period of cross-
        fertilization between whites and blacks; indeed,
        expresses the notion that the period could not have
        existed without enlightened whites (not false, but
        poorly supported here). Sees the Renaissance as more
        of a rediscovery than a renaissance--a rediscovery
        "by an historically larger proportion of the white
        group than ever before of the artistic genius of the
        American Negro" (p. 318). Nevertheless, this is a
        disorganized, curiously-written article because it
        doesn't uphold its own thesis in a convincing manner.

108.   Holmes, Eugene C. "Alain Locke--Philosopher," in
        The New Negro Thirty Years Afterward, ed. Rayford
        Logan, Eugene C. Holmes, and G. Franklin Edwards.
        Washington, D.C.: Howard University Press, 1955.
        Pp. 3-7.

        Sees Locke as a cultural pluralist who was interested
        in trying to solve the conflicts he found in
        American society.

109.   ———. "The Legacy of Alain Locke." *Freedomways*,
        3, No. 3 (Summer 1963), 293-306.

        Sees Locke as the main force behind the New Negro
        movement. Biographical information about Locke is
        related, indicating how his background and education
        made it natural for him to encourage and call
        attention to new Negro artistic expressions.

110.   Hudlin, Warrington. "The Renaissance Re-examined,"
        in *The Harlem Renaissance Remembered*, ed. Arna
        Bontemps. New York: Dodd, Mead & Co., 1972. Pp.
        268-77.

        After a weak, poorly focused introduction, points out
        some of the major features of the period--racial
        pride, interest in African heritage and black folklore,
        and a sense of "cultural dualism." Divides the
        Renaissance into two parts: "Primary Black Propaganda
        (1921-24) to the eventual additional impetus of white
        society (1924-31)." Not so much a reassessment as a
        description of what has been written about the
        period, by both contemporaries and later critics.
        An inchoate article because of its poor organization.

111.   Huggins, Nathan Irvin. *Harlem Renaissance*. New York:
        Oxford University Press, 1971.

        Sees the 1920s through the eyes of those who lived
        then and finds that "their search for ethnic identity
        and heritage ... resonate what we hear about us now."
        Believes this search to be involved in the whole of
        American culture. Therefore, the white-black
        necessary, if difficult, relationship is emphasized
        in this coverage of the Renaissance. Discusses art,
        the theatre, as well as literature. Some literary
        comments are questionable (e.g., "The only contemporary
        poet to influence his [Cullen's] work was Amy
        Lowell"). An essential book for the study of
        this period, and the first full-length book about it.

112.   Hull, Gloria T.   "Black Women Poets from Wheatley to
         Walker." *Negro American Literature Forum*, 9, No. 3
         (Fall 1975), 91-97.

         Traces history of women poets and discusses, among the
         Harlem Renaissance poets, Anne Spencer, Georgia
         Douglas Johnson, Angelina Grimké, Jessie Fauset,
         Helene Johnson, and Gwendolyn Bennett. Says that
         the influence of these women poets was negligible
         because only G.D. Johnson published in book form,
         and most of them did not produce much nor was their
         work distinguished in quality. Also, most of them
         did not fraternize with the leading male poets: "Thus,
         they were out of the mainstream in more ways than one."

113.   ————.   "Rewriting Afro-American Literature: A Case
         for Black Women Writers." *The Radical Teacher*, Special
         Issue 6 (December 1977), 10-14.

         Sees black women writers as excluded from criticism
         and study in the academic world. In particular,
         considers this exclusion widespread in studies about
         the Harlem Renaissance. Includes a cleverly con-
         structed satire, "Rewriting the Renaissance," to
         point out how much rethinking needs to be done in
         order to give proper attention to poets like Angelina
         Grimké, Anne Spencer, and Gwendolyn Bennett.

114.   Isaacs, Edith J.R.   "The Negro and the Theatre: A
         Glance at the Past and a Prophecy." *Opportunity*, 13,
         No. 6 (June 1935), 174-77.

         Traces reasons why black theatre is weak, but sees a
         good future. Lack of experience within the theatre,
         writing for "a theatre in which the Negro himself.
         was a stranger," prohibited the black playwright from
         developing fully in the United States. Notes growing
         theatre movement in black communities and colleges,
         and sees this as forerunner to the production of
         first-rate drama written by Negroes.

115.   ————.   "The Negro in the American Theatre: A
         Record of Achievement." *Theatre Arts*, 26, No. 8
         (August 1942), 494-526.

         Narrative about on-stage dramas, comedies, and
         musicals, up to motion pictures. Discusses individual
         pieces, such as *Shuffle Along* and *Harlem*, and also
         mentions books that have also included commentary on
         the black theatre (e.g., *Black Manhattan*). Reminds

the reader that black theatre is not just what has
been produced for blacks or by them; many dramas have
been written by whites as well (e.g., Ridgely
Torrence's *Three Plays for a Negro Theatre*). The
first part of this theatre history covers the period
1917-1942. Illustrated with photographs of such
persons as Charles Gilpin, Josephine Baker, and a
scene from *Harlem*.

116.   Ivy, James W. "Écrits Nègres aux États-Unis."
       Présence Africaine, N.S. 26 (Juin-Juillet 1959),
       67-76.

A sketch covering the history of Afro-American
literature--emphasizing in the Harlem Renaissance
section the economic and social influences upon this
period. Sees it as a time when there was greater
unity among Negroes, and a time when there was a
search for a racial memory as exemplified by Toomer's
Cane. Briefly discusses Walrond, the objectivity of
his stories about poverty; calls Fauset more idealistic
than realistic, the creator of new stereotypes. Also
describes the poetry of Cullen, Hughes, and James
Weldon Johnson. Mentions Fisher's second book, but
ignores his *The Walls of Jericho*. A spotty, uneven
article.

117.   Jackson, Blyden. "Harlem Renaissance in the Twenties,"
       in his *The Waiting Years: Essays on American Negro
       Literature*. Baton Rouge: Louisiana State University
       Press, 1976. Pp. 165-78.

Expresses the mood as well as the mores of this period
descriptively--e.g., the places, the types of people,
the institutions that created a collective black
consciousness. Then discusses, at length, Langston
Hughes's *Not Without Laughter*--a novel often dismissed,
but one that creates the real, inner world of Negro
life. Because of this the novel can stand as a symbol
of the Harlem Renaissance as well as an example of
the cumulative process that extends the Renaissance
beyond its own time. *Additional note:* "The original
occasion for this essay was a session of a conference
at Southern Illinois University in the 1920s in
America."

118.   ————. "The Negro's Negro in Negro Literature."
        The Michigan Quarterly Review, 4 (1965), 290-95.

        Contends that Afro-American literature has blindly
        pursued black self-identity by being unable to escape
        the circumscribed world of oppressed blacks (and,
        therefore, produced "only one character"), although
        some Harlem Renaissance writers made efforts to
        promote the more positive aspects of the Negro
        character.

119.   ————. *The Waiting Years: Essays on American
        Negro Literature*. Baton Rouge: Louisiana State
        University Press, 1976.

        Reprinted essays, three directly concerning the
        writers of the 1920s: "Harlem Renaissance in the
        Twenties," "Largo for Adonis," and "Jean Toomer's
        Cane" (see items 117, 233, and 462).

120.   Jarab, Josef. "The Birth of the New Negro (The
        Harlem Renaissance Reconsidered)." *Prague Studies
        in English*, 15 (1973), 37-65.

        A summary of the major books published during the
        Harlem Renaissance, and an analysis of these works
        as well as an overall history of the period itself.
        The intentions and tone of the movement are interpreted
        to be self-conscious in nature; still, maintains the
        status of black writers was strengthened during this
        period, and that racial pride in general was stimulated
        through their creations. There was altogether an
        openness engendered that permitted black writers to
        feel free to come together in an attempt to forge a
        common, yet distinct, form of American literature.
        Thus, this was a period of self-revelation and self-
        assertion in a social as well as an artistic sense.

121.   Johnson, Abby Arthur, and Ronald Maberry Johnson.
        "Black Renaissance: Little Magazines and Special
        Issues, 1916-1930," in their *Propaganda and Aesthetics:
        The Literary Politics of Afro-American Magazines in the
        Twentieth Century*. Amherst: University of Massachu-
        setts Press, 1979. Pp. 66-96.

        Describes the art and literature in special issues of
        such "little magazines" as *The Carolina Magazine*
        (1928), which were devoted to featuring work by Negro
        artists. Also details history and philosophy of
        "little magazines that specialized in Afro-American

literature (e.g., *Stylus*), which were published by
Negroes themselves.

122.   ————. *Propaganda and Aesthetics: The Literary
Politics of Afro-American Magazines in the Twentieth
Century.* Amherst: University of Massachusetts
Press, 1979.

An inclusive but not complete (e.g., *Black Scholar*
not discussed) history of most magazines published
by and for blacks during the twentieth century.
Comments about editors, editorial policies, and
specific articles are clear and soundly discussed.
Strong bibliographic references. Chapters dealing
specifically with the Harlem Renaissance appear
separately in this bibliography (see items 121,
123, and 124).

123.   ————. "Renaissance to Reformation: House Organs,
Annual Reviews, and Little Magazines, 1930-40," in
their *Propaganda and Aesthetics: The Literary
Politics of Afro-American Magazines in the Twentieth
Century.* Amherst: University of Massachusetts
Press, 1979. Pp. 97-124.

Describing the 1930s publications as more diversified,
narrates the publishing history of *The Crisis*,
Opportunity, *Challenge*, and *New Challenge* during
this period, using archival material to give a full,
accurate picture of the economic and philosophical
problems (e.g., McKay felt that Dorothy West, *New
Challenge*, was too radical—an interesting shift in
the thinking of a person considered radical in the
1920s).

124.   ————. "Toward the Renaissance: *Crisis*, *Opportunity*,
and *Messenger*, 1910-1928," in their *Propaganda and
Aesthetics: The Literary Politics of Afro-Amèrican
Magazines in the Twentieth Century.* Amherst:
University of Massachusetts Press, 1979. Pp. 31-63.

Relates history of the magazines in the title above,
their editors and editorial policies. Describes, for
instance, specific articles published in the magazines.
Also goes into detail about the publishing philosophy
of W.E.B. Du Bois (editor of *The Crisis*), which
contrasted quite markedly with that of Charles S.
Johnson (editor of *Opportunity*).

125.   Johnson, Charles S. "Jazz Poetry and Blues." *The Carolina Magazine*, 58, No. 7 (May 1928), 16-20.

        The importance of black music to poetry is examined (e.g., in Langston Hughes).

126.   ————. "The Negro Enters Literature." *The Carolina Magazine*, 57, No. 7 (May 1927), 3-9, 44-48.

        Traces history of Negro literature; then discusses the overall new self-confidence and true literary (as opposed to historic or social) qualities of the 1920s. Sees James Weldon Johnson's "Creation" as a symbol of a break with the old style of black writers. Also indicates influences, such as the changed atmosphere after World War I, and other factors in the development of the Harlem Renaissance. Discusses other· well-known writers—Cullen, McKay, and Langston Hughes, for instance—but characterizes features of the youngest writers of this time, too—e.g., Frank Horne, Helene Johnson, and Gwendolyn Bennett.

127.   ————. "The Negro Renaissance and Its Significance," in *The New Negro Thirty Years Afterward*, ed. Rayford Logan, Eugene C. Holmes, and G. Franklin Edwards. Washington, D.C.: Howard University Press, 1955. Pp. 80-88.

        The significance of this period was the development of cultural freedom and personal freedom to express the true racial self. In this period of race consciousness, Alain Locke was noted for his giving of encouragement and guidance to the writers.

128.   ————. "The Rise of the Negro Magazine." *Journal of Negro History*, 13, No. 1 (January 1928), 7-21.

        Sees the newer magazines as helping to destroy the old image of the Negro, and cites prominent Harlem Renaissance periodicals *The Crisis*, *Opportunity*, and *The Messenger*. Mentions the editorials of *The Crisis*, credits *The Messenger* with bringing attention to social problems, and stresses *Opportunity*'s goal of helping Negroes to have a better self-image and encouraging those who were interested in creative writing.

129.   Johnson, James Weldon. "The Dilemma of the Negro
        Author." *American Mercury*, 15, No. 60 (December
        1928), 477-81.

        Focuses on the special problems Negro writers face,
        such as a dual audience or convincing readership of
        the authenticity of characters and situations in an
        imaginative work. Johnson thinks the best work comes
        from writers who can create literature that appeals
        both to blacks and to whites.

130.   ————. "Harlem: The Cultural Capital," in *The New
        Negro: An Interpretation*, ed. Alain Locke. New York:
        Albert and Charles Boni, 1925. Pp. 301-11.

        Relates the ongoing evolution of Harlem, which was a
        white neighborhood at the beginning of the century,
        but has become the cultural capital of the Negro race.
        Describes the setting--the black businesses, for the
        most part--and optimistically suggests that harmony
        and prosperity will reign in Harlem in the future.

131.   Keller, Frances Richardson. "The Harlem Literary
        Renaissance." *The North American Review*, 5, No. 3
        (Old Series: Vol. 253), (May-June 1968), 29-34.

        Sees the Harlem Renaissance movement as a search for
        an image other than one of protest: black American
        intellectuals and cultural leaders wanted to define a
        new image, a "sustaining model of the kind of American
        the Negro might become." The writers sought to
        express this quest in imaginative literature. Not
        able to look back to the immediate past because of
        slavery, Africa became the attraction for attention
        to the black person's past--even though the writers
        did not support Garvey's Back-to-Africa movement.
        Never able to fully settle upon an image, the writers
        nevertheless helped to destroy the old image of the
        Negro.

132.   Kent, George E. "Patterns of the Harlem Renaissance,"
        in his *Blackness and the Adventure of Western Culture*.
        Chicago: Third World Press, 1972. Pp. 17-35. Reprinted
        in *The Harlem Renaissance Remembered* (see item 212a).

        Provides a sweeping, overall picture of the setting
        of the Harlem Renaissance and of the various elements
        that helped to produce this cultural period: e.g.,
        the presence of Garvey, the race riots of 1919.
        Suggests that Dunbar "is thus both a precursor ...

and a sensibility against which to revolt." (See
Braithwaite, item 64, who took the opposite view.)
Also suggests the importance of Du Bois's *The Souls
of Black Folk* (1903) as an influence upon the
development of this artistic movement. Ends with
a summary of personalities and their literary productions, and assesses the overall movement as a step
forward for the black literary artist, making it
possible for later artists to be accepted more readily
by the arbiters of culture and literature. Inclusive
in its coverage of causes for the movement, the people,
the art produced, a major article for one who seeks
an abbreviated, intelligent introductory narration
about the whole period.

133.   Killens, John O. "Another Time When Black Was
        Beautiful." *Black World*, 20, No. 1 (November 1970),
        20-36.

        Stresses the notion that to be ignorant of one's
        black history is to be doomed to repeat it. Sees
        the 1920s as a fertile, creative, joyful time--not
        an authentic revolution but a time when there was
        liberation from white norms as writers wrote with
        love and feeling for their own race, for their
        African heritage. Summarizes the work of many writers
        --Toomer, Cullen, Brown, Hughes, Schuyler, Bontemps,
        Hurston, and Jessie Fauset.

134.   Kornweibel, Theodore, Jr. "Theophilus Lewis and the
        Theater of the Harlem Renaissance," in *The Harlem
        Renaissance Remembered*, ed. Arna Bontemps. New
        York: Dodd, Mead & Co., 1972. Pp. 171-89.

        Explains the nearly-forgotten career of theatre
        critic Theophilus Lewis, who wrote for *The Messenger*
        and continually stressed the need for black theatre.
        In his writings he suggested the prohibitions standing
        in the way of the development of such a theatre--lack
        of black actors of serious drama, and control of the
        theatres in Harlem by whites.

134a.   Lewis, David Levering. "Dr. Johnson's Friends: Civil
        Rights by Copyright." *Massachusetts Review*, 20,
        No. 3 (Autumn 1979), 501-19.

        Description of the social climate of the early 1920s
        and the attitudes of Negro intellectuals who saw
        themselves as ushering in a new literary age. There

is a slightly mocking tone that suggests these
intellectuals--Charles S. Johnson, Alain Locke, James
Weldon Johnson, for example--took their mission and
talents too seriously. Uses the Civic Club dinner
in honor of Jessie Fauset (21 March 1924) as a focus
for characterizing the euphoria that existed among
many black intellectuals at the beginning of the
Harlem Renaissance.

This article forms a part of a later book, *When
Harlem Was in Vogue* (see item 134c).

134b.   ————. "The Politics of Art: The New Negro, 1920-1935."
*Prospects: An Annual Journal of American Cultural
Studies*, 3. New York: Burt Franklin & Co., 1977.
Pp. 237-61.

An overview of the Harlem Renaissance that addresses
the double audience the artists faced (i.e., black/
white), the artistic and social ideas of the major
writers (e.g., Hughes, McKay), and the unproved notion
that artistic expression by blacks would positively
affect the social ills of the U.S. The role of
"helpers" is stressed; in particular, Charles S.
Johnson's contribution as a money raiser and general
supporter of the artists is reaffirmed (see item
95). Photographs.

This article forms a part of a later book, *When
Harlem Was in Vogue* (see item 134c).

134c.   ————. *When Harlem Was in Vogue*. New York:
Alfred A. Knopf, 1981.

A substantial, readable, sometimes chatty, sometimes
irreverent narrative about every aspect of the Harlem
Renaissance--the people and numerous stories of their
entangled relationships, the publications, the music,
the whites who associated with the movement (and
those, like Allen Tate, who refused to associate
with Hughes and J.W. Johnson in the South), the
racial problems, and discussions of individual books
or poems. There is vast research of primary and
secondary sources, personal interviews, oral histories,
which comprise the extensive notes. A generous number
of photographs, including some that have not appeared
in other books about this period (e.g., Hughes and
Thurman sitting on steps, supposedly sipping gin).
Exhuastive in details but never exhausting to read--
a major contribution to the examination of the
Harlem Renaissance.

135. Locke, Alain. "American Literary Tradition and the
      Negro." *Modern Quarterly*, 3, No. 3 (May–July 1926),
      215-22.

      While focusing on earlier literature to demonstrate
      American social attitudes towards Negroes, Locke ends
      his essay optimistically, predicting "a true
      literature of the Negro" because of writings by
      such authors as Rudolph Fisher, Jean Toomer, and
      Walter White.

136. —————. "Art or Propaganda?" *Harlem: A Forum of
      Negro Life*, 1, No. 1 (November 1928), 12.

      Article not seen by the author.

137. —————. "The Message of the Negro Poets."
      Carolina Magazine, 58, No. 7 (May 1928), 5-15.

      Declares that "There is poetry by Negro poets,--and
      then there is Negro poetry." His concern is with
      the latter, for he argues that there are identifiable
      racial traits in poetry being produced--for instance,
      the use of Negro idioms, use of forms inspired by
      black music (jazz, spirituals), and the demonstration
      of a link with the African past. Race, then, he
      advocates, "is stronger than nationality."

138. —————. "The Negro's Contribution to American Art
      and Literature." *The Annals of the American Academy
      of Political and Social Science*, 140 (November 1928),
      234-47.

      Explains the dual elements in the creative world of
      black artists--the African heritage and the American
      experience. Sees the "New Negro movement" growing
      from 1917 as the most outstanding artistic and
      cultural contribution made by Negroes up to that
      time. Traces background of Negro arts and ends
      with describing the "New Negro" literary movement.
      Bibliography.

139. —————. "The New Negro," in his *The New Negro: An
      Interpretation*. New York: Albert and Charles Boni,
      1925. Pp. 3-16.

      Theorizes that the Negro, once a problem not only to
      others but to himself as well, has finally made some
      progress towards breaking the barriers of prejudice.
      Allied to this is a new spirit among Negroes, one of

"group expression and self-determination," a spirit
of race and energy that will enrich American civilization as the new Negro becomes a fuller part of this
civilization.

140.   Logan, Rayford W.   "The Historical Setting of *The New
         Negro*," in his *The New Negro Thirty Years Afterward*,
         ed. with Eugene C. Holmes and G. Franklin Edwards.
         Washington, D.C.: Howard University Press, 1955.
         Pp. 18-25.

         Traces the social and political history of the world
         from Negro eyes from "his nadir" (the beginning of
         the century) to 1925. He sees this as a period of
         disenfranchisement of the Negro through a lack of
         leadership on the part of national leaders--from the
         President to newspaper editors; and black as well as
         white, noting Booker T. Washington in particular.
         Therefore, *The New Negro*, edited by Alain Locke, was
         a contribution in affirming the progress the Negro
         had made despite obstacles.

141.   Lomax, Michael L.   "Fantasies of Affirmation: The
         1920's Novel of Negro Life." *Phylon*, 16, No. 2
         (December 1972), 232-46.

         Addresses the idea that the literature of the 1920s
         was more uncompromising concerning race problems than
         assimilationist interpreters suggest. Indeed, "because
         the object of their artistic attack was white America,
         the literature of the period can be labelled 'protest.'"
         This theory is undergirded by selected excerpts from
         writings by such authors as W.E.B. Du Bois and
         Wallace Thurman.

142.   Long, Richard A.   "Alain Locke: Cultural and Social
         Mentor." *Black World*, 20, No. 1 (November 1970),
         87-90.

         Contends that Locke's influence was the key to racial
         spirit that was so important to the Harlem Renaissance.
         Defines this as Locke's *ancestralism*, which was his
         encouragement for artists to have "respect for the
         African past and for the folk spirit developed in
         the American South."

143.   McPherson, James M., et al., eds. *Blacks in America:
        Bibliographical Essays*. New York: Doubleday, 1971.

        Part VIII has a chapter on the Harlem Renaissance
        (pp. 241-53), but the coverage is brief, although
        evaluative in some cases.

144.   Makalani, Jabulani K. (Clovis E. Semmes). "Toward
        a Sociological Analysis of the Renaissance: Why
        Harlem?" *Black World*, 25, No. 4 (February 1976),
        4-13, 93-97.

        An introductory overview of factors that led to the
        Harlem Renaissance--e.g., intellectual development,
        migration of blacks--characterizing the period as
        full of "radicalism and cultural diversity." The
        analysis of this time stops short of examining why the
        period died, except to mention the Depression factor.

145.   Mays, Benjamin E. *The Negro's God As Reflected in
        His Literature*. Boston: Chapman & Grimes, 1938.
        Reprinted, New York: Atheneum, 1969.

        Sees a different attitude about God reflected in the
        literature after 1914--more disillusionment, a less
        traditional approach to the divine. Mentions (but
        not in equal or great depth) work by Cullen, Fauset,
        Hughes, Larsen, McKay, J.W. Johnson, Schuyler, and
        Walter White.

146.   Mitchell, Lofton. *Black Drama*. New York: Hawthorn
        Books, 1967.

        A small section of Part Two is devoted to 1917-1929,
        the Renaissance movement. Written in memoir style,
        there is immediacy but lacks full, precise information
        a scholar would need. Willis Richardson, for instance,
        is mentioned only twice--and fleetingly.

147.   Moore, Gerald. "Poetry of the Harlem Renaissance,"
        in *The Black American Writer*. Volume II: *Poetry and
        Drama*. Edited by C.W.E. Bigsby. Deland, Florida:
        Everett Edwards, 1969. Reprinted, Baltimore:
        Penguin Books, 1971. Pp. 67-76.

        Sees an "insularity" in the assessment of Harlem
        Renaissance critics such as Harold Cruse or David
        Littlejohn, who viewed the movement as "pampered"
        and aimless (Cruse) or more cultural than artistic
        (Littlejohn). Rather, argues that the poetry of the

Harlem Renaissance frequently exhibited an authentic
Afro-American voice that, in turn, greatly influenced
later black poets from other countries--such as the
Négritude poets, Senghor and Césaire, and served as
"a contributory cause of excellent poetry made by
other men in other continents."

148.   Moore, Richard B. "Africa Conscious Harlem."
        Freedomways, 3, No. 3 (Summer 1963), 315-34.

        The section devoted to the "Harlem literary renaissance"
        (pp. 323-27) briefly stresses the African influence
        and inspiration upon Harlem Renaissance writers,
        such as McKay, Toomer, and Cullen. Descriptive;
        not an assessment of writings.

149.   Mudimbe-Boyi, Mbulamuanza. "Sur quelques thèmes dans
        la poésie de la 'Harlem Renaissance.'" *Afrique
        Littéraire et Artistique*, 44 (1977), 2-13.

        Sees the Harlem Renaissance as an attempt by black
        poets to search the past for a reaffirmation of the
        self; a search, then, for one's roots, one's cultural
        heritage. Suggests the period evolved through a
        convergence of economic, social, and ideological
        conditions and concepts: poverty, racism, and Marxism.
        Confuses some 1930s tendencies with the 1920s, and
        unconvincingly includes P.L. Dunbar in his discussion.
        (One glaring error: attributes "Heritage" to Claude
        McKay instead of to Countee Cullen.) A conventional
        view of the period, even though some Harlem Renaissance
        themes are correctly cited (e.g., criticism of a
        mechanistic socity, or the search for one's
        racial identity).

150.   Muraskin, William. "An Alienated Elite: Short Stories
        in *The Crisis*, 1910-1950." *Journal of Black Studies*,
        1, No. 3 (March 1971), 282-305.

        In the section dealing with the period during the
        Harlem Renaissance (pp. 285-90), stories are
        characterized as dealing with the themes of alienation
        and the search for an identity. Sees the heroes
        as possessing bourgeois "white" values.

151.   Osofsky, Gilbert. *Harlem: The Making of a Ghetto. Negro
        New York, 1890-1930*. New York: Harper & Row, 1963.

        Presents the hard economic and social facts of Harlem
        during the Harlem Renaissance, which was evolving into

a slum while a "myth-world" was being created by
many of the Renaissance writers. Pages 179-87 deal
specifically with the movement, but information
about the whole period is dispersed throughout.

152.   Perkins, Eugene. "The Changing Status of Black
       Writers." *Black World*, 19, No. 8 (June 1970),
       18-23, 95.

       Sees the failure of the Harlem Renaissance stemming
       from the writers' failing to reach the black masses.

153.   Perry, Margaret. *Silence to the Drums: A Survey of
       the Literature of the Harlem Renaissance*. Westport,
       Conn.: Greenwood Press, 1976.

       Brief overview of the period, followed by description
       of the novels, poetry, and short stories produced
       during this time. Focus on both major and minor
       (e.g., Arthur Huff Fauset, John Matheus) writers,
       with some emphasis on the short story. Bibliography,
       and a chronology of events 1917-1934.

154.   Primeau, Ronald. "Frank Horne and the Second Echelon
       Poets of the Harlem Renaissance," in *The Harlem
       Renaissance Remembered*, ed. Arna Bontemps. New
       York: Dodd, Mead & Co., 1972. Pp. 247-67.

       Believing that the full meaning of the Renaissance
       cannot be understood without examining the minor
       poets of the period, describes the themes and style
       of Horne's poetry as well as that of Georgia Douglas
       Johnson, Waring Cuney, Arna Bontemps, Helene Johnson,
       Gwendolyn Bennett, Angelina Grimké, and Anne Spencer.
       Concentrates on Horne, who exemplifies the questing
       spirit of the 1920s cultural movement. Is generous
       and non-critical about some of the poetry discussed
       (e.g., calls Georgia Douglas Johnson's writing "some
       of the best poetry" of the Harlem Renaissance).

155.   Record, Wilson. *The Negro and the Communist Party*.
       Chapel Hill: University of North Carolina Press,
       1951. Reprinted, New York: Atheneum, 1971.

       One chapter covers the 1919-1928 period, which was
       characterized by the Party's inability to capture
       the interest of artists, intellectuals, and social
       leaders. Even Garvey's U.N.I.A. could not be
       transformed to suit Communist purposes. An
       interesting insight into an organization that

strove to influence blacks during a period when
they were susceptible to outsiders who courted them.

156.   Redding, J. Saunders. "American Negro Literature."
        The American Scholar, 18, No. 2 (Spring 1949),
        137-48.

        An overview of literature by black Americans from
        Dunbar to Wright and Margaret Walker. Brief, critical
        comments concerning the Harlem Renaissance, which is
        viewed as a time when writing was "arty, self-
        conscious and experimental," a period marked by
        naïveté and a certain air of hysteria.

157.   Schomburg, Arthur A. "The Negro Digs Up His Past,"
        in *The New Negro: An Interpretation*, ed. Alain Locke.
        New York: Albert and Charles Boni, 1925. Pp. 231-37.

        Notes growing trend toward group expression among
        Negroes. Stresses the need for the present generation
        to know about black history and culture of the past,
        to understand that the present artistic explosion and
        desire for self-expression is based on genuine values
        from a verifiable black history rooted in Africa.

158.   Scruggs, Charles W. "'All Dressed Up But No Place to
        Go': The Black Writer and His Audience During the
        Harlem Renaissance." *American Literature*, 48,
        No. 4 (January 1977), 543-63.

        The psychological and emotional duality of the black
        writers is explored in terms of who read the literature
        of this period and the audience the writers thought
        they wished to reach. The writers really wanted, in
        black terms, the Whitmanesque ideal audience, Scruggs
        argues, and this never existed; therefore, the Harlem
        Renaissance writers were supported by whites because
        the black writers had not found their place or role
        in the black community.

159.   Singh, Amritjit. "Black-White Symbiosis: Another Look
        at the Literary History of the 1920's," in *Studies in
        American Literature: Essays in Honor of William Mulder*,
        ed. Jagdish Chander and Narindar S. Pradhan. Delhi,
        India: Oxford University Press, 1976. Pp. 154-68.

        Explores reason why the relationships between blacks
        and whites interested in black life failed to produce
        more literature that did not reflect the fad of black

primitivism. Places much of the blame on Van Vechten and the influence of his novel *Nigger Heaven*.

160.   ————. *The Novels of the Harlem Renaissance: Twelve Black Writers 1923-1933*. University Park: Pennsylvania State University Press, 1976.

The twelve novelists are studied in relation to themes, aesthetics, and values. Provides background history of the movement, including discussion concerning using the appellation Harlem Renaissance. Considers the novelists fall into the Western literary tradition, and states that most of the novels did not concentrate on the problems important to the black masses. It was a bourgeois movement that drew support from a small black middle class and whites, a movement where novels were concerned with problems no longer a part of black literature (e.g., tragic mulatto, miscegenation). Sees this narrowness of vision as American, not simply Afro-American. The novelists who are examined are: Arna Bontemps, Countee Cullen, W.E.B. Du Bois, Jessie Redmon Fauset, Rudolph Fisher, Langston Hughes, Nella Larsen, Claude McKay, George S. Schuyler, Wallace Thurman, Jean Toomer, and Walter White. Ends with a review of previous research, giving value judgments on some of it (e.g., Bone's *Negro Novel* ... and Gloster's *Negro Voices*, see items 32 and 39).

161.   Singh, Raman K. "The Black Novel and Its Tradition." *Colorado Quarterly*, 20, No. 1 (Summer 1971), 23-29.

Cites Toomer as portraying soul in *Cane* because anti-materialism is stressed and there is a recognition of a positive element in the black style of living.

162.   Spence, Eulalie. "A Criticism of the Negro Drama As It Relates to the Negro Dramatist and Artist." *Opportunity*, 6, No. 6 (June 1928), 180.

Deplores the weak quality--in subject as well as in writing--of plays written by Negroes. Encourages the black writer to produce dramas that "portray the life of his people, their foibles ... and their sorrows and ambitions and defeats."

163.   Taussig, Charlotte E. "The New Negro as Revealed in
        His Poetry." *Opportunity*, 5, No. 4 (April 1927),
        108-11.

        Introduces readers to the then new literary movement
        by concentrating on the poets. States that in Harlem
        "group expression and self-determination have ...
        become possible," resulting in the publication of
        work by James W. Johnson, Georgia D. Johnson, and
        "the three Negro poets who represent the high-water
        mark of the new Negro poetry--Claude McKay, Langston
        Hughes, and Countee Cullen." Presents a standard
        description of each poet's writing.

164.   Taylor, Clyde. "Garvey's Ghost: Revamping the Twenties."
        Black World, 25, No. 4 (February 1976), 54-67.

        By reviewing several books about the Renaissance in
        relation to Garvey, the author urges literary and
        social historians to examine this period more
        critically and to probe again the reasons given
        for the development of this movement.

165.   Trimmer, Joseph F. *Black American Literature: Notes
        on the Problem of Definition*. Muncie, Ind.: Ball
        State University, 1971. (Publications in English,
        No. 16.)

        In examining how the black artist participates in his
        art as well as attends to the responsibilities of his
        race, suggests that Harlem Renaissance writers saw
        their preoccupation with race as positive, although
        later black writers have felt Renaissance writers sold
        out to "the paternalism of White intellectuals."

166.   Turner, Darwin T. *In a Minor Chord: Three Afro-
        American Writers and Their Search for Identity*.
        Carbondale: Southern Illinois University Press, 1971.

        The three writers are Jean Toomer, Countee Cullen,
        and Zora Neale Hurston--respectively described as
        "Exile," "The Lost Ariel," and "The Wandering
        Minstrel" (see items 242, 342, and 495).

167.   Vincent, Theodore G., ed. *Voices of a Black Nation:
        Political Journalism in the Harlem Renaissance*. San
        Francisco: Ramparts Press, 1973.

        Political and social ideologies of writers whose
        commentaries appeared in the black press in the 1920s

and 1930s are reprinted here under six general
headings: The Emerging New Negro; Questions of
Ideology; Economic Issues; The Black American and
The Third World; The Harlem Renaissance; Toward
the Future.

168.   Wagner, Jean.   "The Negro Renaissance," in his *Black
        Poets of the United States from Paul Laurence Dunbar
        to Langston Hughes*.   Urbana: University of Illinois
        Press, 1973.   Pp. 149-93.

        Characterizes the Renaissance as exhibiting a new
        spirit--one that demonstrates new assertiveness
        among blacks, a resistance to oppression, and imbued
        with a "new vision of the race's common past."
        Considers the poets the most noteworthy writers:
        Claude McKay, Jean Toomer, Countee Cullen, James
        Weldon Johnson, Langston Hughes, and Sterling Brown
        (see items 218, 243, 317, 368, 404, and 499).
        Mistakenly attributes much mass support to the
        Renaissance, but does accurately assess the importance
        of Du Bois and Marcus Garvey as influences upon the
        period.   Also indicates themes that were stressed:
        revolt, rediscovery of the past, and exaltation
        of blackness.

169.   Williams, Henry.   *Black Response to the American
        Left: 1917-1929*.   Princeton, N.J.: Princeton
        University Press, 1973.   (Princeton Undergraduate
        Studies in History: 1.)

        Chapter 5 is devoted specifically to the 1920s.
        Examines the thought of three groups of black in-
        tellectuals, the "conservative, middle and extremist."
        The ideas of Du Bois, Charles S. Johnson, and A.
        Philip Randolph, for instance, are explained.   Of
        the creative writers, only Claude McKay is mentioned.
        A book that interfaces well with Wilson Record's
        book on blacks and Communism (see item 155).

170.   Williams, John A.   "The Harlem Renaissance: Its
        Artists, Its Impact, Its Meaning."   *Black World*,
        20, No. 1 (November 1970), 17-18.

        Sees the Harlem Renaissance as an example of what
        black writers of today should avoid--i.e., a closed
        circle of writers who basically write and think alike.
        Believes the Harlem Renaissance writers were seen as
        exotic, whereas the writers of today are considered
        political.

B. Selected Book and Drama Reviews

171.   Atkinson, Brooks. "Up 'Harlem' Way." *New York
         Times*, sect. 8 [p. 1], 3 March 1929.

         A review of the play *Harlem*, which he calls
         "animalism ... crude, dark and coarse."

172.   Benchley, Robert. "'Hearts in Dixie." (*The First
         Real Talking Picture*)." *Opportunity*, 7, No. 4
         (April 1929), 122-23.

         An enthusiastic review of the film with Stepin
         Fetchit, whom Benchley calls "the best actor that
         the talking movies have produced."

173.   Bennett, Gwendolyn. "The Emperors Jones." *Opportunity*,
         8, No. 9 (September 1930), 270-71.

         Compares the interpretations of Charles Gilpin,
         Paul Robeson, and Weyland Rudd of this famous
         O'Neill character.

174.   Bontemps, Arna. "The Harlem Renaissance." *Saturday
         Review of Literature*, 30 (22 March 1947), 12-13, 44.

         Compares, in a review of Cullen's *On These I Stand*,
         the styles and points of views of Cullen and Hughes,
         which are characterized basically as traditionalist
         (Cullen) vs. non-traditionalist (Hughes). A few
         general comments, also, about the tenor of the
         twenties for the Negro writer.

175.   Bradstreet, Howard. "A Negro Miracle Play."
         Opportunity, 8, No. 5 (May 1930), 150-51.

         A review of *The Green Pastures*, which is characterized
         as capturing the mind of the Negro and yet transcending
         the strictures of color in a dramatic sense.

176.   Brown, Sterling [A.]. "Chronicle and Comment."
         Opportunity, 8, No. 12 (December 1930), 375.

         A review of books about black life that were published
         in 1930: a descriptive rather than evaluative overview
         of titles.

177.   ————. "The Literary Scene: Chronicle and Comment."
          Opportunity, 9, No. 2 (February 1931), 53-54.

          Observing that Negroes read little and, therefore,
          buy few books the author points out books and
          articles--such as George Schuyler's *Black No More*--
          that deal directly with the concerns of black people
          in America.

178.   ————. "More Odds." *Opportunity*, 10, No. 6
          (June 1932), 188-89.

          Uses a brief review of Edwin R. Embree's *Brown
          America* to expand on a major Sterling Brown thesis:
          namely, that the Negro must delve into the self, the
          black soul, to be able to present a true picture of
          the Negro. The Negro "intellectual" is castigated
          for being too far removed from the ordinary Negro,
          even though the writer protests he is not writing
          "a brief for folk-literature, or proletarian
          literature."

179.   ————. "The Negro in Fiction and Drama." *The
          Christian Register*, 114, No. 7 (14 February 1935),
          111-12.

          A variety of books by both black and white writers
          are reviewed, but the comments on Zora Neale Hurston's
          Jonah's Gourd Vine and Langston Hughes's *The Ways of
          White Folks* emphasize Harlem Renaissance features,
          e.g., the use of folk idioms by Hurston, and the
          effective characterizations of Harlemites by Hughes.

180.   ————. "Six Plays for a Negro Theatre." *Opportunity*,
          12, No. 9 (September 1934), 280-81.

          A review of a book of this same title, edited by
          Randolph Edmonds.

181.   Bruce, Richard. "The Dark Tower." *Opportunity*, 5,
          No. 10 (October 1927), 305-06.

          Cullen's guest editor discussed two books by the
          poet--*Copper Sun* and the anthology Cullen edited,
          Caroling Dusk--in addition to presenting news about
          Langston Hughes.

182.   Calverton, V.F.   "The Advance of the Negro."
         Opportunity, 4, No. 38 (February 1926), 54-55.

         A review of *The New Negro*, but the review is
         preceded by comments concerning the Negro's need
         to prove his intellectual and cultural capabilities
         to the race (white) that once was the ruling class.
         The New Negro should go a distance in correcting the
         old image of the black race.   Praises Toomer and Cullen,
         believes Hughes needs to pay more attention to form;
         generally assesses the book favorably, including the
         editorship of Alain Locke.

183.   Cullen, Countee.   "Poet on Poet."   *Opportunity*, 4,
         No. 38 (February 1926), 73-74.

         Cullen's review of *The Weary Blues* by Langston Hughes,
         which is generally favorable and ends by stating
         that Hughes is not just promising but has arrived.
         Cullen is impressed by Hughes's spontaneity and the
         verve and color of his poetry.   Does not like the
         jazz poems, however, which are characterized as
         "interlopers" among the poems Cullen admires.

184.   Dismond, Geraldyn.   "Mrs. Dismond Goes to the Play:
         'Box Seats' for the Family."   *Opportunity*, 6, No. 6
         (June 1928), 181-82.

         A retelling of the plot of this play, to demonstrate
         its weaknesses, is the mode of drama criticism used
         by this reviewer.

185.   Du Bois, W.E.B., and Alain Locke.   "The Younger
         Literary Movement."   *The Crisis*, 27, No. 4 (February
         1924), 161-63.

         High praise for Toomer's *Cane*, which Du Bois states
         has broken through conventional sex modes in black
         literature.   Indicates Toomer has great insight into
         humans as well as the artistry to write with the
         impressionist's touch.   Locke follows with a review
         of *There is Confusion*, by Jessie Fauset, which he
         calls a problem novel, praising it for its perspective
         and seeing it as "a social document of sterling and
         intimate character."

186.   Ely, Effie Smith. "American Negro Poetry." *Christian Century*, 40 (22 March 1923), 366-67.

In reviewing J.W. Johnson's *Book of American Negro Poetry*, finds much of the work imitative "as might be expected of beginners." Because she feels the poets should give the feelings of the race, the dialect poems by earlier writers are praised while a poem by Anne Spencer is called "obscure and pretentious." Also gives favorable attention to poems that possess a Christian spirit, which is a reminder to the reader of the source of the review journal and its bias.

187.   Fauset, Arthur Huff. "The Negro's Cycle of Song--A Review." *Opportunity*, 3, No. 35 (November 1925), 333-35, 348.

A review of Howard W. Odum's *The Negro and His Songs*.

188.   Gordon, Eugene. [Review of Gordon, Taylor. *Born to Be*, see item 641.] *Opportunity*, 8, No. 1 (January 1930), 22-23.

Praises Gordon's sense of narrative and the power of his language in this recounting of the musician's life and observations.

189.   Horne, Frank. "Black Verse." *Opportunity*, 2, No. 23 (November 1924), 330-32.

Review of *Anthology of Verse by American Negroes*, edited by Newman Ivey White and Walter C. Jackson. Sees much diligence involved in compiling the anthology, such as inclusion of brief biographies and bibliographic notes; but finds weaknesses in their critical remarks. Finds little that is new in the poetry selections, although praises editors for including poems by Countee Cullen and believes this alone justifies the book.

190.   [Johnson, Charles S.] "Some Books of 1924." *Opportunity*, 3, No. 26 (February 1925), 58-59.

A superficial overview of fiction and nonfiction by both black and white writers. In particular, mention is made of Jessie Fauset's book *There is Confusion*, "probably the first full fledged novel by a Negro woman."

191.   Johnson, Hall. "Porgy and Bess--A Folk Opera: A
         Review." *Opportunity*, 14, No. 1 (January 1936),
         24-28.

         Examines in detail the musical properties of this
         folk opera and presents some specific criticism.
         Questions if a white man can really capture the
         Negro folk qualities, and suggests that--even though
         Gershwin does write in the Negro vein sometimes--
         Negro writers and musicians must create a theatre
         where experiment and learning lead to a true recreation
         of Afro-American culture.

192.   Johnson, James Weldon. "Romance and Tragedy in
         Harlem--A Review." *Opportunity*, 4, No. 46 (October
         1926), 316-17, 330.

         Because of Carl Van Vechten's closeness to many
         persons during the Harlem Renaissance, Johnson's
         favorable review here of *Nigger Heaven* is useful for
         seeing how one half of the Negro intelligentsia viewed
         this controversial book. A review that is more
         descriptive than critical. (It must be remembered
         that Van Vechten submitted the book to Johnson
         before its final publication.)

193.   Kerlin, Robert T. "Singers of New Songs." *Opportunity*,
         4, No. 41 (May 1926), 162-64.

         Review of *Cane* by Toomer, *The Weary Blues* by Langston
         Hughes, and *Color* by Countee Cullen. Kerlin ends by
         stating: "It's in the lap of the gods whether Toomer,
         Hughes, and Cullen will be poets of unfulfilled re-
         nown or the creators of an epoch when it will no
         more seem a marvel 'To make a poet black, and bid
         him sing' [Cullen]."

194.   Larkin, Margaret. "A Poet for the People--A Review."
         Opportunity, 5, No. 3 (March 1927), 84-85.

         A favorable review of Langston Hughes's *Fine Clothes
         to the Jew*, wherein Hughes is described as the
         Robert Burns of the Negro race.

195.   Lewis, Theophilus. "If This Be Puritanism."
         Opportunity, 7, No. 4 (April 1929), 132.

         A review of Wallace Thurman's play *Harlem*, which is
         assessed favorably for being "a wholesome swing toward
         dramatic normalcy" in terms of the characterizations.
         See item 171 for a far different view.

196.   Locke, Alain.   "Black Truth and Black Beauty."
       Opportunity, 11, No. 1 (January 1933), 14-18.

       Review of books that appeared in 1932, praising
       Sterling Brown's *Southern Road* in particular.
       Worries about Negroes not living up to their promise
       in their writing.   Notes the abundance of prose in
       contrast to the poetry.   Finds Cullen's novel and
       Thurman's second one disappointing, but enjoys the
       detective novel of Rudolph Fisher.

197.   ————.   "Deep River: Deeper Sea: *Retrospective
       Review of the Literature of the Negro for 1935*."
       Opportunity, 14, No. 1 (January 1936), 6-10; 14,
       No. 2 (February 1936), 42-43, 61.

       Discusses the encroaching proletarian viewpoint among
       writers and sees this as a delimiting philosophy.
       Zora N. Hurston's *Mules and Men* is favorably noted,
       but drama is described as weak and limited; the fault
       with drama, suggests Locke, is with the playwrights
       and critics.   Notes new books of poetry by Cullen
       and J.W. Johnson, but decided their works "do not
       advance their poetic reputations."

198.   ————.   "The Eleventh Hour of Nordicism: *Retrospective
       Review of the Literature of the Negro for 1934*."
       Opportunity, 13, No. 1 (January 1935), 8-12; 13,
       No. 2 (February 1935), 46-48, 59.

       Notes a freeing of the black artists from the influence
       of whites—that is, demonstrating a more anti-bourgeois
       spirit and acquiring one with more skepticism and a
       more fatalistic air.   "Fatalism and futility brood
       over the scene like the heat and the fever," although
       the author points out that a move towards more
       proletarian thoughts has not yet taken hold.
       Mentions the small amount of poetry written by
       black authors during 1934.

199.   ————.   "1928: A Retrospective Review."   *Opportunity*,
       7, No. 1 (January 1929), 8-11.

       Notes the high production of fiction and points
       out the interest that black writers have in their
       African origins.

200.   ————. "This Year of Grace." *Opportunity*, 9,
           No. 2 (February 1931), 48-51.

           Subtitled "Outstanding Books of the Year in Negro
           Literature," we have a major statement of disappoint-
           ment, of real disaffection with the "much exploited
           Negro renaissance." Locke points out the faults,
           as he sees it, of the movement--in particular, a
           superficiality of vision and literary execution.
           He does praise Hughes's first novel, *Not Without
           Laughter*, and James Weldon Johnson's chronicle of
           Harlem, *Black Manhattan*; generally, however, this
           critic, who heralded the Renaissance, expresses
           concern that the writing of 1930 was "in the
           literature of criticism and interpretation rather
           than in the literature of creative expression."

201.   ————. "We Turn to Prose." *Opportunity*, 10,
           No. 2 (February 1932), 40-44.

           Review of literature appearing in 1931, which is
           characterized as a serious and sober year. Calls
           Black No More a success, and praises Fauset's *The
           Chinaberry Tree*.

202.   "Our Book Shelf." *Opportunity*, 1, No. 12 (December
           1923), 374-75.

           A significant first effort to probe the most startling
           early book of the Renaissance: *Cane*. Toomer's
           artistry and uniqueness are recognized early.

203.   ————. *Opportunity*, 10, No. 3 (March 1932), 88-89.

           Reviews of Jessie Fauset's *The Chinaberry Tree* and
           of Wallace Thurman's *Infants of the Spring*: a
           favorable assessment of the Fauset book by Edwin
           B. Burgum, who applauds the author's concentration
           on highly respectable, bourgeois Negroes, earning
           for Miss Fauset the reputation of a writer who
           "takes Negro life seriously." In contrast, Lois
           Taylor finds Thurman's book in the vein of the
           sensational and sordid--a flaw, it has been suggested,
           of many of the Harlem Renaissance novels.

204.   ————. *Opportunity*, 10, No. 10 (October 1932),
           320.

           A review of Rudolph Fisher's novel *The Conjure-Man
           Dies*, significant as the first detective novel
           written by a Negro.

205.   Rosenberg, Harold. "Truth and the Academic Style."
           Poetry, 49, No. 1 (October 1936), 49-51.

           Review of *St. Peter Relates an Incident, Selected
           Poems* sees Johnson as a polemicist and academician
           who misuses poetry for his cause (social justice).

206.   Skinner, R. Dana. "The Play." *Commonweal*, 9,
           No. 18 (6 March 1929), 514.

           Review of *Harlem* by Wallace Thurman. Considers it
           a drama that exploits the Negro and therefore does
           not present an honest portrayal of black life.

207.   Spence, Eulalie. "Negro Art Players in Harlem."
           Opportunity, 6, No. 12 (December 1928), 381.

           A negative review of this drama company's production
           of Ridgeley Torrence's *The Rider of Dreams*.

208.   Van Vechten, Carl. "Religious Folk Songs of the
           American Negro--A Review." *Opportunity*, 3, No.
           35 (November 1925), 330-31.

           Review by a white who absorbed much of Negro life.

IV. STUDIES OF INDIVIDUAL AUTHORS

Selected writings by major and minor literary artists and criticism that focuses on the literary work of these writers.

A. Bontemps, Arna (1902-1973)
1. His Writings (Selected)
a. Novel

209.   *God Sends Sunday*. New York: Harcourt, Brace
        & Co., 1931.

        Tale of Little Augie, a racetrack jockey whose
        fortunes rise and then fall and who, in late middle
        age, is seen as "a tiny withered man in a frayed and
        ancient Prince Albert and a badly battered silk
        hat"--his days of good fortune gone but his essential
        goodness intact.

        Reviews: *Boston Transcript*, 8 April 1931, p. 2;
        N.Y.H.T. Books, 22 March 1931, p. 16: G.B. Bennett;
        N.Y.T. Book Review, 15 March 1931, p. 7; *Opportunity*,
        9, June 1931, p. 188: Sterling A. Brown; *Saturday
        Review of Literature*, 7, 2 May 1931, p. 801;
        Springfield (Mass.) *Republican*, 12 April 1931, p. 7e.

                b. Other Writings

210.   *Arna Bontemps--Langston Hughes Letters, 1925-1967*.
        Selected and edited by Charles H. Nichols. New York:
        Dodd, Mead & Co., 1980.

        Approximately 500 letters selected to give literary
        and personal insights into these two personable
        authors. The number of letters that fall within the
        Harlem Renaissance period is small; but the interest
        in this period is always there, cropping up in later
        letters from time to time (e.g., 8 July 1954, p. 325,

or 23 April 1963, p. 460, where Hughes discovers
letters from the Renaissance days: "I came across
an enormous big dusty box full of 1920-30 letters
... and unopened until now: everybody in it--you
[Bontemps], Zora, Wallie [Thurman], Du Bois, Aaron
[Douglas], Bruce [Nugent], even Jean Toomer ... and
a real treasure trove of Jessie Fauset letters....").

*   "Arna Bontemps Talks About the Renaissance." (See
             item 514.)

211.   "The Awakening: A Memoir," in his *The Harlem Renaissance
             Remembered*. New York: Dodd, Mead & Co., 1972.
             Pp. 1-26.

             Recall of events and people of the early 1920's--
             Shuffle Along, Marcus Garvey--that helped to impel
             the beginning of the Harlem Renaissance. Not just a
             reminiscence about friends--Hughes, Cullen, Van
             Vechten--but also a factual review of publications
             and events like the *Opportunity* awards.

212.   "The Black Renaissance of the Twenties." *Black
             World*, 20, No. 1 (November 1970), 5-9.

             Chronicles the setting of pre-Renaissance days to
             demonstrate how difficult it was for black artists
             to thrive, because of America's racial history.
             Mentions the factors that helped the Renaissance to
             develop--the appearance of Garvey, the publication
             of poetry by McKay, the production of *Shuffle Along*--
             creating an air of excitement and gradual interest
             in Negroes.

*   "The Harlem Renaissance." (See item 174.)

212a.   *The Harlem Renaissance Remembered*, ed. Bontemps.
             New York: Dodd, Mead & Co., 1972.

             Essays written by participants in a study of this
             period when Bontemps was Curator of the James Weldon
             Johnson Collection at Yale. Each essay, including a
             memoir by Bontemps (see item 211), appears under
             individual authors in this book (see items 96, 110,
             132, 134, 154, 227, 256, 315, 332, 402, 429, and
             491).

*   "A Memoir: Harlem, the 'Beautiful' Years." (See
             item 538.)

*   "The Negro Renaissance: Jean Toomer." (See item 441.)

*   "The New Black Renaissance." (See item 61.)

*   *100 Years of Negro Freedom.* (See item 539.)

2. Writings About Him

*   Alexander, Sandra Carlton. "The Achievement of Arna
       Bontemps." (See item 802.)

213.   Arvey, Verna. "Arna Bontemps, Who Recreates
       Significant Moments in History." *Opportunity*, 22,
       No. 3 (July-September 1944), 126, 139.

       Biographical sketch of Bontemps and a brief description
       of his writings. A brief article that praises rather
       than assesses the work and achievements of the author.

*   Ashe, Betty Taylor. "Arna W. Bontemps, Man of Letters."
       (See item 805.)

*   Baker, Houston A., Jr. "Arna Bontemps: A Memoir."
       (See item 519.)

*   Brown, Sterling A. "Arna Bontemps: Co-Worker,
       Comrade." (See item 543.)

*   Conroy, Jack. "Memories of Arna Bontemps." (See
       item 550.)

*   Fleming, Robert E. *James Weldon Johnson and Arna
       Bontemps.* (See item 1.)

*   F[uller], H[oyt] W. "Arna Bontemps." (See item 2.)

*   Grissom, Ruby M. "Contribution of the Negro to
       American Literature." (See item 845.)

*   Miller, Ruth, and Peter J. Katopes. "The Harlem
       Renaissance." (See item 14.)

214.   Page, Denise. "Arna Bontemps: Opposing Routes in the
       Renaissance," in *The Harlem Renaissance Generation*,
       ed. L.M. Collins. Nashville: Fisk University, 1972.
       Pp. 220-28.

       Places Bontemps early in the Renaissance as a poet
       rather than as a prose writer. Believes his poetry

exemplifies Du Bois's "twoness," in that the twin
forces of African primitivism and conventional
religion merge to produce personal poetry that
reflects the Afro-American's dual religious and
cultural experiences. Also, states that Bontemps
always pays his debt to the past of the Afro-
American (i.e., the African).

*   Singh, Amritjit. *The Novels of the Harlem Renaissance.*
           (See item 160.)

*   Syracuse University. (See item 797.)

                B. Brown, Sterling A. (1901-   )
                   1. His Writings (Selected)
                      a. Book

215.   *Southern Road.* New York: Harcourt, Brace & Co., 1932.

           The poet's first collection; poems influenced by
           folk idioms, work songs, and the strong, racy bad
           men of myth as well as of reality. Does not eschew
           dialect.

           Reviews: *Boston Transcript*, 10 August 1932, p. 7;
           Commonweal, 16, 1 June 1932, p. 140; *The Nation*, 135,
           13 July 1932, p. 43; *New Republic*, 71, 27 July 1932,
           p. 297; *N.Y. Evening Post*, 14 May 1932, p. 7; *N.Y.H.T.
           Books*, 21 August 1932, p. 7: Eda Lou Walton; *N.Y.T.
           Book Review*, 15 May 1932, p. 13; *Opportunity*, 10,
           August 1932, pp. 250-51: Louis Untermeyer; *Pittsburgh*
           (Mo.) *Bulletin*, 37, October 1932, p. 62; *Saturday
           Review of Literature*, 8, 14 May 1932, p. 732: William
           Rose Benet; *Springfield* (Mass.) *Republican*, 5 June
           1932, p. 7e.

                      b. Other Writings

*   "The Blues as Folk Poetry." (See item 67.)

*   "Chronicle and Comment." (See item 176.)

*   "Concerning Negro Drama." (See item 544.)

*   "A Literary Parallel." (See item 545.)

*   "The Literary Scene." (See item 177.)

*   "More Odds." (See item 178.)

*   *The Negro in American Fiction*. (See item 34.)

*   "The Negro in Fiction and Drama." (See item 179.)

*   "The Negro in Literature." (See item 68.)

*   *Negro Poetry and Drama*. (See item 35.)

*   "Our Literary Audience." (See item 546.)

*   "Six Plays for a Negro Theatre." (See item 180.)

2. Writings About Him

*   Armstead, T.J. "The Social Realism of Langston Hughes and Sterling Brown." (See item 804.)

*   Brown, Sterling A. *Negro Poetry and Drama*. (See item 35.)

*   Davis, Arthur P. *From the Dark Tower*. (See item 36.)

216.   Henderson, Stephen A. "A Strong Man Called Sterling Brown." *Black World*, 19, No. 11 (September 1970), 5-12.

Stresses Brown's identification with black folklore, sermons, spirituals, the blues, and tales--the whole panoply of the roots of black culture. Sees him as remaining true to the black spirit, with humor, humanity, and a sense of racial history.

*   Jackson, Blyden. *Black Poetry in America*. (See item 42.)

217.   Locke, Alain. "Sterling Brown: The New Negro Folk-Poet," in *Negro: An Anthology*, ed. Nancy Cunard. London: Wishart, 1934. Reprinted, New York: Frederick Ungar Publishing Co., 1970. Pp. 88-92.

Praises the ability of the poet to celebrate black folk life not in dialect but in black idioms that characterize a particular area. Captures the truth of black life--of life within the "veil" and when the mask to fool the outside world is dropped.

*   Perry, Margaret. *Silence to the Drums*. (See item
       153.)

*   Redding, J. Saunders. *To Make a Poet Black*. (See
       item 46.)

*   Skinner, Beverly Lanier. "The Poems and Nature Prose
       of Sterling Brown." (See item 892.)

218.   Wagner, Jean. "Sterling Brown," in his *Black Poets
       of the United States from Paul Laurence Dunbar to
       Langston Hughes*. Urbana: University of Illinois
       Press, 1973. Pp. 475-503.

       One of the most complete discussions of Brown's
       poetry--a poet described here as a "poet *par
       excellence* of the soil." States that Brown respects
       his heritage but does not write about Africa or its
       meaning to blacks. Says some of the features of
       Brown's poetry are humor, cynicism, stoicism, and a
       profound, underlying faith in his people and their
       ability to rise above the humiliations and cruelties
       of life.

                 C. Cullen, Countee (1903-46)
                    1. His Writings (Selected)
                       a. Books

219.   *The Ballad of the Brown Girl: An Old Ballad Retold*.
       New York: Harper & Brothers, 1927.

       In traditional quatrains, the old story (English
       folklore) of the "Brown Girl's" love for Lord Thomas
       and the unhappy ending caused by racial difficulties
       and the rival love, "Fair London." An attempt to
       use a past tale to highlight the racism of the
       twentieth century.

       Reviews: *Boston Transcript*, 5 May 1928, p. 5; *Chicago
       Tribune*, 21 April 1928; *New Haven Times Union*, 28
       March 1928; *N.Y. American Hebrew*, 4 May 1928: Anne
       Kulique Kramer; *N.Y. Evening Post*, 7 July 1928, p. 8:
       A.K. Laing; *N.Y.H.T. Books*, 6 May 1928, p. 21; *N.Y.T.
       Book Review*, 29 April 1928, p. 12: Percy Hutchison;
       St. Louis Post-Dispatch, 28 March 1928; *Salt Lake
       City Tribune*, 27 May 1928; *San Francisco Chronicle*,
       29 April 1928; *Springfield* (Mass.) *Republican*, 17
       October 1928, p. 8; *Utica Press*, 19 May 1928.

220.   *The Black Christ, and Other Poems.* New York:
         Harper & Brothers, 1929.

         A twentieth century tale about the lynching of a
         Negro boy for a crime of violation he did not commit.
         The symbolism draws on the death and resurrection of
         Christ. The other poems are lyrics that dwell on
         love and death.

         Reviews: *Baltimore Afro-American*, 1 June 1928;
         Booklist, 26 February 1930, p. 195; *Boston Transcript*,
         31 December 1929, p. 2; *Carolina Magazine*, 1, 4 May
         1930, p. 1: Emile Trevelle Holley; *Chicago Defender*,
         9 November 1929: Dewey R. Jones; *Christian Century*,
         47, 11 June 1930, p. 757: Raymond Kresensky; *The Nation*,
         130, 12 March 1930, pp. 303-04: Granville Hicks; *Nation
         and Athenaeum* (London), 46, 7 December 1929, p. 380
         supplement: W. Palmer; *N.Y. Age*, 14 December 1929;
         N.Y. Evening Post, 14 December 1929, p. 13m: Vincent
         McHugh; *N.Y.H.T. Books*, 2 February 1930; *N.Y. Telegram*,
         30 November 1929; *N.Y.T. Book Review*, 1 December 1929,
         p. 7: Percy Hutchison; *N.Y. World*, 25 November 1929,
         p. 10m: Granville Hicks; *Opportunity*, 7 March 1930,
         p. 93: Clement Wood; *Outlook*, 153, 27 November 1929,
         p. 509: Louise T. Nicholl; *Poetry*, 24 February 1930,
         pp. 286-89: Bertha Ten Eyck James; *Salt Lake City
         Tribune*, 27 May 1928; *Southern Workman*, 59, February
         1930, p. 92: Edward Shillito; *Times* (London)*Literary
         Supplement*, 21 November 1929, p. 948; *Virginia
         Quarterly Review*, 6, January 1930, p. 158: James
         Southall Wilson.

*   *Caroling Dusk.* (See item 762.)

221.   *Color.* New York: Harper & Brothers, 1925.

         The poet's first book of collected poems, characterized
         by their youthful and romantic spirit as well as
         indicating a concern for black heritage and race in
         such poems as "Heritage" and "The Shroud of Color."

         Reviews: *Akron* (Ohio) *Beacon Journal*, 8 January 1926;
         Baltimore Evening Sun, 19 December 1925; *Birmingham
         Herald*, 29 August 1926; *Birmingham News*, 20 December
         1925; *Booklist*, 22, February 1926, p. 200; *The Bookman*,
         62, December 1925, p. 503: John Farrar; *Boston Evening
         Transcript*, 15 April 1926; *Brooklyn Citizen*, 20 December
         1925: Gremin Zorn; *Brooklyn Daily Eagle*, 14 November
         1925; *Chicago Post*, 24 December 1925: Llewellyn Jones;
         Christian Advocate, 31 December 1925; *Christian Century*,

42, 24 December 1925, p. 1611: Paul Hutchinson;
Cleveland Open Shelf, January 1926, p. 5; *Commonweal*,
3 March 1926, p. 472: Thomas Walsh; *Contemporary Verse*,
January 1926: Madeline Mason-Manheim; *The Crisis*, 31
March 1926, pp. 238-39: Jessie Fauset; *Critical Review*,
March 1926, p. 7: Martin Russak; *Detroit News*, 17
January 1926: Al Weeks; *Dial*, 80, February 1926, p. 161;
Harvard Crimson, 31 October 1925: Cornelius Du Bois;
Independent, 115, 7 November 1925, p. 539; *Indianapolis
News*, 20 January 1926; *International Book Review*, 4
March 1926, p. 252: Jim Tully; *Los Angeles Record*, 4
January 1926; *Lynchburg* (Va.) *News*, 17 January 1926;
Lyric West, 5, n.d., p. 211: Lois Burton Moon; *Nashville
Tennessean*, 11 April 1926; *The Nation*, 121, 30 December
1925, p. 763: Babette Deutsch; *New Republic*, 46, 31
March 1926, p. 179: Eric Walrond; *N.Y. Evening Post*,
30 January 1926: Charles Norman; *N.Y.H.T.*, 10 January
1926: Mark Van Doren; *N.Y. New Leader*, 24 April 1926;
N.Y. Sun, 23 January 1926: Joseph Auslander; *N.Y.T.*,
8 November 1925, sec. 8, p. 15: Herbert S. Gorman;
Newark Evening News, 20 February 1926; *Northwestern
Christian Advocate*, 19 November 1925; *Oklahoma
City Oklahoman*, 11 April 1926: B.A. Botkin; *Opportunity*,
4, January 1926, p. 14: Alain Locke; *Opportunity*, 4,
May 1926, pp. 163-64: Robert T. Kerlin; *Palms*, 3
January 1926, pp. 121-23; *Philadelphia Record*, 26 June
1926: Dorothy Kahn; *Pittsburgh Courier*, 23 January
1926, p. 16: Houron Temple; *Poetry*, 28, April 1926,
pp. 50-53: George H. Dillon; *Pratt Institute
Quarterly Booklist*, Spring 1926, p. 26; *San Francisco
Chronicle*, 13 December 1925; *Saturday Review of
Literature*, 2, 13 February 1926, p. 556; *Times* (London),
21 January 1926; *Toronto Saturday Night*, 27 February
1926; *Tulsa World*, 30 June 1926: Inez Callaway; *Vogue*,
67, May 1926, p. 144: Berenice C. Skidelsky; *World
Tomorrow*, 8, November 1925, p. 353; *Xenia* (Ohio)
Evening Gazette, 10 July 1926; *Yale Review*, 15, July
1926, p. 824: Clement Wood.

222.   *Copper Sun*. New York: Harper & Brothers, 1927.

His second book of poetry, concentrating on the themes
of love, death, or the American racial situation.

Reviews: *Booklist*, 24, November 1927, p. 59; *The
Bookman*, 66, September 1927, p. 103: Emanuel Eisenberg;
Boston Guardian, 29 October 1927; *Boston Transcript*,
27 August 1927, p. 2; *Buffalo Times*, 31 July 1927;

Chicago Defender, 31 December 1927: Blanche Watson;
Chicago Journal of Commerce, 26 November 1927;
Cincinnati Commercial Tribune, 31 July 1927; *Cleveland
Open Shelf*, December 1927, p. 133; *Columbus* (Ohio)
Dispatch, 31 July 1927; *Critical Review*, March 1928,
p. 7: Martin Russak; *Hartford Courant*, 31 July 1927;
Independent, 119, 9 September 1927, pp. 314-15; *The
Nation*, 125, 9 November 1927, p. 518: Herbert S.
Gorman; *New Republic*, 52, 12 October 1927, p. 218:
Harry Alan Potamkin; *N.Y. Amsterdam News*, 26 October
1927: Mary White Ovington; *N.Y.H.T. Books*, 21 August
1927, p. 5: Garreta Busey; *N.Y. Post*, 7 August 1927:
J.M. March; *N.Y.T. Book Review*, 21 August 1927, p. 5:
Herbert S. Gorman; *N.Y. World*, 7 August 1927, p. 6m:
Harry Salpeter; *Opportunity*, 5 September 1927, pp.
270-71: E. Merrill Root; *Pittsburgh Courier*, 27 August
1927, p. 11; *Poetry*, 31, February 1928, pp. 284-86:
Jessica Nelson North; *St. Louis Post-Dispatch*, 17 August
1927; *San Francisco Chronicle*, 7 August 1927; *Springfield*
(Mass.) *Republican*, 4 September 1927, p. 7f; *Survey*,
59, 1 November 1927, p. 184: Gordon Lawrence;
Washington Eagle, 12 August 1927: Alice Dunbar Nelson;
Wichita Beacon, 15 January 1928; *World Tomorrow*, 10,
November 1927, p. 472; *Yale News Literary Supplement*,
2, no. 1, 26 October 1927, p. 4: W.D. Judson, Jr.

223.   *The Medea, And Some Poems*.   New York: Harper &
        Brothers, 1935.

A modern rendition in prose, with the choruses in
verse, of the play by Euripides. The other poems
are sonnets and short lyric verses in traditional form.

Reviews: *Booklist*, 32, October 1935, p. 37; *Christian
Science Monitor*, 4 September 1935, p. 12; *Independent*,
115, November 1935, p. 539; *The Nation*, 141, 18
September 1935, p. 336: Philip Blair Rice; *New .
Republic*, 85, 25 December 1935, p. 207: Horace
Gregory; *N.Y.H.T. Books*, 15 September 1935, p. 27:
Eda Lou Walton; *N.Y. Sun*, 20 .September 1935, p. 28:
P.M. Jack; *N.Y.T. Book Review*, 12 January 1936, p.
15: Peter Monro Jack; *Opportunity*, 13, December 1935,
p. 381.

224.   *On These I Stand: An Anthology of the Best Poems*
         of Countee Cullen. New York: Harper & Brothers,
         1947.

         Posthumous collection of poems Cullen thought to be
         his best--from previous books and six new poems
         "never before published."

         Reviews: *Atlantic Monthly*, 179, March 1947, pp. 144-45:
         John Ciardi; *Booklist*, 43, 1 March 1947, p. 208;
         Bookmark, 8, May 1947, p. 9; *Chicago Sun Book Week*,
         9 March 1947, p. 5: A.J. Green; *Cleveland Open Shelf*,
         May 1947, p. 10; *Library Journal*, 72, 15 February 1947,
         p. 322: Gerald McDonald; *N.Y.H.T. Books*, 31 August
         1947, p. 4: Ruth Lechlitner; *N.Y.T. Book Review*, 23
         February 1947, p. 26: Dudley Fitts; *Opportunity*, 25,
         Summer 1947, p. 170: William Stanley Braithwaite; *PM*,
         10 March 1947: Helen Wolfert; *Poetry*, 70, July 1947,
         pp. 222-25: Harvey Curtis Webster; *San Francisco
         Chronicle*, 27 July 1947, p. 14: George Snell;
         Saturday Review of Literature, 30, 22 March 1947,
         p. 12: Arna Bontemps; *United States Quarterly Book
         List*, 3, September 1947, p. 242; *Virginia Kirkus'
         Bookshop Service*, 15, 1 January 1947, p. 19; *Wisconsin
         Library Bulletin*, 43, April 1947, pp. 64-66: Mary
         Katherine Reely.

225.   *One Way to Heaven.* New York: Harper & Brothers, 1932.

         Cullen's only novel, a romantic social comedy about
         lower-class blacks and the upper bourgeoisie in New
         York City. A con man marries a devout woman (converted
         by his act of false conversion), and their struggle
         to find peace and happiness are played out against
         the shallow world of her black employer, who recognizes
         her inconsequential life but accepts its hollow charms.

         Reviews: *Abbott's Monthly*, June 1932, p. 39; *Baltimore
         Afro-American*, 20 February 1932; *Booklist*, 28, April
         1932, p. 349; *Boston Evening Transcript*, 12 March
         1932, p. 3; *Louisiana Weekly*, 2 April 1932; *N.Y.H.T.
         Books*, 28 February 1932, p. 3: Rudolf Fisher; *N.Y.
         National News*, 18 February 1932; *N.Y. Sun*, 19 February
         1932: Robert Cantwell; *N.Y.T. Book Review*, 28 February
         1932, p. 7: Elizabeth Brown; *Norfolk Journal and Guide*,
         30 April 1932: James G. Fleming; *Philadelphia Tribune*,
         17 March 1932; *Pittsburgh Monthly Bulletin*, 37, May
         1932, p. 35; *Saturday Review of Literature*, 7, 12
         March 1932, p. 585: Martha Gruening; *Southern Workman*,
         61, March 1932, pp. 134-35: George A. Kuyper; *Times*

(London) *Literary Supplement*, 22 December 1932, p. 976; *Wisconsin Library Bulletin*, 28, May 1932, p. 163.

b. Other Writings

*   "The Dark Tower." (See items 559-578.)

*   "Elizabeth Prophet." (See item 579.)

*   "Poet on Poet." (See item 183.)

*   "What Love Meant for Isadora Duncan." (See item 580.)

2. Writings About Him

*   Atlanta University. (See item 780.)

*   Baker, Ruth Taylor. "The Philosophy of the New Negro." (See item 806.)

226. ✓ Bronz, Stephen H. *Roots of Negro Racial Consciousness, the 1920's: Three Harlem Renaissance Authors*. New York: Libra Publishers, 1964.

The three authors are James Weldon Johnson, Countee Cullen, and Claude McKay; they represent different aspects of the Harlem Renaissance in their writings, yet each stressed racial pride and protested against racism. Johnson tried to teach the whites to respect blacks, McKay repudiated America, and Cullen approached race theoretically rather than emotionally, eschewing the directness that was in the writing of McKay. The one thing all of these writers did was to help, like other writers of the Renaissance, to destroy the racial stereotypes of the nineteenth century and to bring greater attention to the real culture of black America.

227. ✓ Canaday, Nicholas, Jr. "Major Themes in the Poetry of Countee Cullen," in *The Harlem Renaissance Remembered*, ed. Arna Bontemps. New York: Dodd, Mead & Co., 1972. Pp. 103-25.

Believes that most of Cullen's themes are found in the poem "Heritage." The themes that are suggested are: doubt and fear in religion, love, death, and color. In particular, sees Cullen as emphasizing the dehumanization of blacks in conjunction with their yearning for total freedom. Finally, generally sees Cullen as an artist seeking to express black experiences in universal, human terms.

*   Christian, Barbara. "Spirit Bloom in Harlem." (See item 822.)

228.   Copeland, Catherine H. "The Unifying Effect of Coupling in Countee Cullen's 'Yet Do I Marvel.'" *CLA Journal*, 28, No. 2 (December 1974), 258-61.

Analyzes this poem from the viewpoint of use of two types of coupling that "derive from both phonic and/or semantic features." Studies such things as verbal constructs, word coupling in series (especially as modifiers), to demonstrate Cullen's skillful employment of such poetic devices to weld a unified sonnet that is clarified in the last two lines.

229. ✓ Daniel, Walter C. "Countee Cullen as Literary Critic." *CLA Journal*, 14, No. 3 (March 1971), 281-90.

Discusses Cullen's comments about literature as well as his own creative philosophy while he was a contributing editor for *Opportunity*. Believes Cullen used this column to encourage writers to display the best side of Negro life in their writings.

230. ✓ Davis, Arthur P. "The Alien-and-Exile Theme in Countee Cullen's Racial Poems." *Phylon*, 14, No. 4 (Fourth Quarter, 1953), 390-400.

Examining only the poems dealing with race, finds the notion of alienation in the United States versus remembrance of past happiness in the African homeland a persistent theme in Cullen's poetry. Believes Cullen espoused the idea that "the Negro is both a geographical and a spiritual exile." Implied in this alien-exile theme is the search for a better world. Cullen's attack on injustices, however, was indirect and gentle and he was therefore a weak protest poet. After *The Black Christ* (1929) he gradually turned from racial poetry, perhaps because he felt this type of poetry was no longer of great interest to readers.

*   Dillard University. (See item 785.)

231. ✓Dorsey, David F., Jr. "Countee Cullen's Use of Greek
      Mythology." *CLA Journal*, 13, No. 1 (September 1969),
      68-77.

      Points out those poems where Cullen refers to mythology,
      commencing with a poem he wrote in high school. He
      uses such allusions to strengthen the meaning of his
      poems within their own contexts.

*   [Editorials] "Countee Cullen." (See item 601.)

*   Fennell, Robert E. "The Death Figure in Countee
      Cullen's Poetry." (See item 840.)

232. Ferguson, Blanche E. *Countee Cullen and the Negro
      Renaissance*. New York: Dodd, Mead & Co., 1966.

      The first and only full-length biography about the
      poet, combining fictional techniques with more reliable
      narrative portions that are based on unadorned fact.
      There are inaccuracies, however; and the book is
      generally poorly written, constructed in a seemingly
      juvenile style that is both cloying and embarrassing
      to read.

*   Hansell, William Howard. "Positive Themes in the
      Poetry of Four Negroes." (See item 847.)

233. Jackson, Blyden. "Largo for Adonais," in his *The
      Waiting Years: Essays on American Negro Literature*.
      Baton Rouge: Louisiana State University Press,
      1976. Pp. 42-62.

      Argues that Countee Cullen's failure as a poet stemmed
      from his inability to see himself clearly--i.e., as
      a black man with a white man's outlook. This led
      Cullen to write tepid, timid poetry and to create
      an Africa that was romantic--a "synthetic continent"
      he could glorify. Analyzes "Heritage" to demonstrate
      the argument that Cullen "never had too much to say"
      in his poetry, even though he wrote pretty verses
      and was an honest, serious artist who did not want
      to exploit his race. Finally, strongly suggests the
      need for a corpus of criticism to precede a literature,
      as a guide for writers, like Cullen, who cannot
      perceive their own weaknesses. (Cullen scholars may
      dismiss this theory; artists surely will.)

      This article originally appeared in *Journal for Negro
      Education* (Winter 1946).

*   Johnson, Charles S. "Countee Cullen Was My Friend."
       (See item 656.)

234.   Kerlin, Robert T. "A Pair of Youthful Negro Poets."
       The Southern Workman, 53, No. 4 (April 1924), 178-81.

       Calls attention to Cullen and Hughes, both of whom
       the author admires--comparing Cullen, e.g., to
       Coleridge and Rossetti. Gives examples of Cullen's
       lyricism. Attempts to demonstrate Hughes's link
       with Africa. Ends with florid praise of both poets.

235.   Larson, Charles R. "Three Novels of the Jazz Age."
       Critique, 11, No. 3 (1969), 66-78.

       Presents the plots of *Home to Harlem* (McKay), *Nigger
       Heaven* (Van Vechten), and *One Way to Heaven* (Cullen)
       to suggest these novels are representative portrayals
       of life as it was in Harlem during the 1920s--complex,
       full of contradictions among its inhabitants who
       were living fully as examples of the New Negro.

236.   Lederer, Richard. "The Didactic and the Literary
       in Four Harlem Renaissance Sonnets." *English
       Journal*, 62, No. 2 (February 1973), 219-23.

       Two poems each by Claude McKay and Countee Cullen
       are examined to argue that Cullen's emotional state
       and personal connections are sensed in his poetry,
       whereas the call-to-action tone of McKay's poems
       seem informed by an intellectual who is personally
       removed from his artistic expression.

*   Miller, Ruth, and Peter J. Katopes. "The Harlem
       Renaissance." (See item 14.)

237.   Mott, Frank Luther. "The Harlem Poets." *The
       Midland: A Magazine of the Middle West*, 12, No. 5
       (May 1927), 121-28.

       Discusses the poetry of McKay, Cullen, and Hughes,
       whom the author calls "Harlem poets." Finds that
       these poets use their own racial materials effectively,
       and suggests that this is what black writers should do
       rather than abandon their race and racial subjects.

*   New York Public Library. (See item 793.)

238.   Perry, Margaret. *A Bio-Bibliography of Countee P. Cullen, 1903-1946*. Westport, Conn.: Greenwood Publishing Corp., 1971.

A brief coverage of the poet's life, description of his poetic interests and influences, and a narrative concerning contemporary reviews of Cullen's work. The bibliography is divided into major writings by Cullen (annotated), writings about him (articles, parts of books, etc.), miscellaneous newspaper references to the poet, and poetry anthologies in which his poems appear. At the end is an index of titles (poetry) appearing in the various anthologies.

239. ✓ Primeau, Ronald. "Countee Cullen and Keats's 'Vale of Soul-Making.'" *Papers on Language & Literature*, 12, No. 1 (Winter 1976), 73-86.

Argues that suffering and pain expressed in poetry are the links that drew Cullen to the poetry of Keats. The Keatsian influence is in Cullen's "non-racial" poetry as well, according to Primeau.

*   Redding, J. Saunders. *To Make a Poet Black*. (See item 46.)

*   Reimherr, Beulah. "Countee Cullen." (See item 886.)

240. ✓ Robb, Izetta Winter. "From the Darker Side." *Opportunity*, 4, No. 48 (December 1926), 381-82.

The sensuous quality of Countee Cullen's verse is discussed mainly in terms of racial elements in language and tone.

*   Singh, Amritjit. *The Novels of the Harlem Renaissance*. (See item 160.)

241. ✓ Smith, Robert A. "The Poetry of Countee Cullen." *Phylon*, 11, No. 3 (Third Quarter, 1950), 216-21.

A summary description of Cullen's poetic publications from *Color* (1925) to *On These I Stand* (1947; posthumous), stating that his best work was lyrical, although he wrote poetry of protest ("blatant, although it never is as intense as that of some of his contemporaries") as well as love lyrics. Believes Cullen's main problem is that he did not "develop a world view" because of shying away in writing from the discrimination he faced.

242. ✓ Turner, Darwin T. "Countee Cullen: The Lost Ariel,"
     in his *In a Minor Chord: Three Afro-American Writers
     and Their Search for Identity*. Carbondale: Southern
     Illinois University Press, 1971. Pp. 60-88.

     Sees Cullen as one who wore blackness like a mask, as
     one who "succumbed" to the prevailing notion of Afro-
     Americans' retaining their African heritage, whether
     or not this was true. Thus, Cullen wrote from an
     emotional distance and concentrated on form and
     conventional poetic modes rather than becoming
     deeply involved in his writing. Biographical
     information is also presented.

243. ✓ Wagner, Jean. "Countee Cullen," in his *Black Poets
     of the United States from Paul Laurence Dunbar to
     Langston Hughes*. Urbana: University of Illinois
     Press, 1973. Pp. 283-347.

     Concentrates on the inner man: sees Cullen as a
     tortured and unstable person, with deep conflicts
     about his sexuality (his homosexuality is assumed
     rather than substantiated here) and his need to
     achieve a Christian ideal. Cullen was never able
     to reconcile his racial and religious self (was
     influenced by pagan Africa), and felt separated--
     because of sin--from Christ. Yet he was finally
     able to reconcile himself with God, the former
     adversary.

     Also addresses Cullen's fascination with death (and
     indicates he once thought of suicide). Sees his
     creative life in two phases: extroverted period,
     when race was a subject but not a deep problem,
     and an introverted phase, the longest, where Cullen
     retreats into himself and becomes the "worrier" that
     Arna Bontemps once described. (See item 224,
     "Reviews.")

244. ✓ Woodruff, Bertram L. "The Poetic Philosophy of
     Countee Cullen." *Phylon*, 1, No. 3 (Third Quarter,
     1940), 213-23.

     Believes Cullen saw life and poetry in terms of life's
     transience and the belief that one has to will oneself
     to live despite life's hardness. Sees Cullen themes
     as "Love, Beauty, Faith in Man, Belief in Christ, and
     Poetry." Love for Cullen was the ideal, and poetry
     itself was healing for him. Some may argue with the

notion that Cullen fully accepted God (p. 219), for
the poet's religious ambivalence has been the subject
of at least one other critic (see item 243).

*   Yale University. (See item 798.)

                    D. Du Bois, W[illiam] E[dward]
                       B[urghardt] (1868-1963)
                       1. His Writings (Selected)
                          a. Novel

245.   *Dark Princess: A Romance*. New York: Harcourt,
        Brace & Co., 1928.

        Matthew Towns, a Negro, leaves medical practice and
        goes to Berlin where he meets Kautilya, an Indian
        princess. He becomes involved in the movement for
        the unification of the dark peoples of the world,
        which takes Towns back to the United States where
        he also becomes involved in Chicago politics.

        Reviews: *Annals of the American Academy*, 140,
        November 1928, p. 347: Jane Reitell; *Boston Transcript*,
        14 July 1928, p. 5; *Cleveland Open Shelf*, September
        1928, p. 105; *The Crisis*, 6, August 1928, p. 244:
        Leon Whipple; *New Republic*, 56, 22 August 1928,
        p. 27: M.P.L.; *N.Y. Evening Post*, 12 May 1928,
        p. 9; *N.Y.H.T. Books*, 20 May 1928: Alain Locke;
        N.Y.T. Book Review, 13 May 1928, p. 19; *Opportunity*,
        35, October 1928, p. 39: Allison Davis; *Springfield*
        (Mass.) *Republican*, 28 May 1928, p. 6: G.H.; *World
        Tomorrow*, 11, November 1928, p. 473.

                       b. Other Writings

*   "The Black Man Brings His Gifts." (See item 588.)

246.   "Criteria of Negro Art." *Crisis*, 32 (October
        1926), 290-97.

        Argues that through truth, beauty, and goodness the
        black writer can use his art to give recognition and
        sympathy to the black race. Here Du Bois expresses
        his major artistic thesis--that is, "all art is
        propaganda."

*   [Editorial] "Mencken." (See item 602.)

*   [Editorial] "The Negro and Radical Thought."
           (See item 603.)

*   [Editorial] "Negro Writers." (See item 604.)

*   [Editorial] "Our Monthly Sermon." (See item 605.)

*   "So The Girl Marries." (See item 589.)

*   "The Younger Literary Movement." (See item 185.)

     2. Writings About Him

*   Atlanta University. (See item 780.)

*   Bone, Robert. *The Negro Novel in America*. (See
           item 32.)

*   Davis, Arthur P. *From the Dark Tower*. (See item 36.)

*   Drake, Mary Mean. "W.E. Burghardt Du Bois." (See
           item 833.)

*   Fisk University. (See item 786.)

247.   Gibson, Lovie N. "W.E.B. Du Bois as a Propaganda
           Novelist." *Negro American Literature Forum*, 10,
           No. 3 (Fall 1976), 75-77, 79-82.

           Du Bois's propagandistic view of art was tempered by
           his belief that even propaganda could not distort
           truth: Du Bois's role as a novelist of this persua-
           sion is important because the artist and sociologist
           merge in his fiction, and his novels illustrate his
           definition of a "good black novel"--one where plot
           and characterization contain a message for blacks as
           well as for whites (which may be why *Dark Princess*
           was his favorite novel). An important part of the
           message was that the positive aspects of the Negro
           character, such as striving for advancement, should
           be emphasized.

*   Gipson, Carolyn R. "Intellectual Dilemmas in the
           Novels of W.E.B. Du Bois." (See item 843.)

Studies of Individual Authors
77

247a.   Kostelanetz, Richard. "Fiction for a Negro Politics:
          Neglected Novels of Du Bois." *Xavier University
          Studies*, 7 (1968), 5-39.

          Article not seen by the author.

*   Littlejohn, David. *Black on White*. (See item 44.)

*   Milandou, David. "L'Afrique et l'âme africaine dans
          l'oeuvre de Richard Wright et dans celle de W.E.B.
          Du Bois." (See item 873.)

*   Newsome, Elaine M. "W.E.B. Du Bois's 'Figure in the
          Carpet.'" (See item 881.)

*   Peronnin, Genevieve. "W.E.B. Du Bois et la prise de
          conscience noire aux États-Unis." (See item 882.)

*   Singh, Amritjit. *The Novels of the Harlem Renaissance*.
          (See item 160.)

*   Tchy, Amon. "La Vie et l'oeuvre de W.E.B. Du Bois."
          (See item 901.)

*   University of Massachusetts. (See item 792.)

*   Williams, Henry C. "An Analogical Study of W.E.B.
          Du Bois." (See item 907.)

                    E. Fauset, Jessie (1882-1961)
                       1. Her Writings (Selected)
                          a. Novels

248.   *Chinaberry Tree*. New York: Frederick A. Stokes, 1931.
          Reprinted, New York: Negro University Press, 1969.

          Romance among young middle-class blacks who live in
          northern New Jersey during the 1920s. A view of
          what the author states is "something of the homelife
          of the colored American."

          Reviews: *Atlanta Bookshelf*, April 1932, p. 16: Mary
          Ross; *Booklist*, 28, February 1932, p. 259; *Boston
          Transcript*, 23 January 1932, p. 3: Frances Bartlett;
          Cleveland Open Shelf, March 1932, p. 8; *The Crisis*,
          39, April 1932: W.E.B. Du Bois; *The Nation*, 135,
          27 July 1932, p. 88; *N.Y.H.T. Books*, 17 January 1932,
          p. 6: Rudolph Fisher; *N.Y.T. Book Review*, 10 January

1932, p. 7; *Opportunity*, 10, March 1932, p. 88: Edwin
Berry Burgum; *Saturday Review of Literature*, 8, 6
February 1932, p. 511; *Saturday Review of Literature*,
8, 5 March 1932, p. 5: M.L. Becker; *The Spectator*,
149, 30 July 1932, p. 163: L.A.G. Strong; *Times*
(London) *Literary Supplement*, 23 June 1932;
Wisconsin Library Bulletin, 28, March 1932, p. 90.

249.   *Comedy American Style*. New York: Frederick A.
         Stokes, 1933.

         A dark child in a light-skinned family that is
         "passing" creates problems for the fanatically
         color-conscious mother.

         Reviews: *Booklist*, 30, December 1933, p. 120; *Boston
         Transcript*, 13 December 1933, p. 3: M.L.S.; *The
         Nation*, 138, 3 January 1934, p. 26; *N.Y.H.T. Books*,
         10 December 1933, p. 6: Mary Ross; *N.Y.T. Book Review*,
         19 November 1933, p. 19; *Springfield* (Mass.)
         Republican, 19 November 1933, p. 7e.

250.   *Plum Bun*. New York: Frederick A. Stokes, 1929.

         Two sisters, one dark and one light, who passes, are
         attracted to the same man, another "passer," without
         each other knowing this. Acceptance of one's race
         at the end is stressed, although the author tends
         to stretch credulity in the personal relationships
         she describes.

         Reviews: *The Crisis*, 36, April 1929, pp. 125, 138;
         New Republic, 10 April 1929: B.K.; *N.Y. News*, 23
         March 1929; *N.Y. Sun*, 9 March 1929: Mary Graham
         Bonner; *N.Y.T. Book Review*, 3 March 1929; *Opportunity*,
         7, September 1929: William Stanley Braithwaite;
         Philadelphia Tribune, 7 March 1929; *Saturday Review
         of Literature*, 6 April 1929.

251.   *There is Confusion*. New York: Boni, 1924.

         A young, bourgeois black woman gives up her career
         as a promising singer to marry the young doctor she
         has always loved but neglected when her career was
         the most important matter in her life.

         Reviews: *Boston Transcript*, 26 April 1924, p. 2:
         B.G.; *Cleveland Open Shelf*, May 1924, p. 35; *The
         Crisis*, 2, June 1924, pp. 181-82: Montgomery Gregory;
         International Book Review, June 1924, p. 555; *Literary
         Review*, 12 April 1924, p. 661; *New Republic*, 39, 9

July 1924, p. 192: E.D.W.; *N.Y. Evening Post*, 9
April 1924: H.B.; *N.Y.T. Book Review*, 13 April 1924,
p. 9; *N.Y. Tribune*, 18 May 1924, p. 23: Eva Goldbeck;
Opportunity, 2, June 1924, pp. 181-82: Montgomery
Gregory; *Springfield* (Mass.) *Republican*, 13 July
1924, p. 5a; *Times* (London) *Literary Supplement*, 4
December 1924, p. 828; *Wilson Library Bulletin*, 20,
October 1924, p. 212.

b. Other Writings

*   Howard University. (See item 789.)

2. Writings About Her

*   Bone, Robert. *The Negro Novel in America*. (See
item 32.)

252.   Braithwaite, William Stanley. "The Novels of Jessie
Fauset." *Opportunity*, 12 (January 1934), 24-28.

A panegyric review where the writer is called "the
potential Jane Austen of Negro literature." Sees
Fauset's primary theme as that of racial solidarity.
Ignores her technical flaws and psychological
weaknesses.

*   Brawley, Benjamin. *The Negro Genius*. (See item 33.)

*   Davis, Arthur P. *From the Dark Tower*. (See item 36.)

*   Du Bois, W.E.B. "The Younger Literary Movement."
(See item 185.)

*   "Facts on Gotham Fascinators." (See item 632.)

253.   Feeney, Joseph J. "Greek Tragic Patterns in a Black
Novel: Jessie Fauset's *The Chinaberry Tree*." *CLA
Journal*, 28, No. 2 (December 1974), 211-15.

Contends that Fauset was able to sustain the tragic
mood of a Greek drama in the subplot romance between
Melissa and Malory in this novel through the use of
suspense, fate, and "the use of recognition scenes."
On the plot level Fauset succeeds, but she fails to
succeed fully as a parallel to Greek tragedy because
it is a domestic novel that concentrates on another

pair (the protagonist, Laurentine, and her lover)
and the novel ends happily.

254.   ————. "A Sardonic, Unconventional Jessie Fauset:
The Double Structure and Double Vision of Her Novels."
CLA Journal, 22, No. 4 (June 1979), 365-82.

Offers a restructuralist view of Fauset's novels,
wherein it is suggested that the darkness of
"frustration of childhood hopes" is expressed in
the novels. Believes that there is more unconvention-
ality in the novels than most critics credit her with;
and that there is an undercurrent of bitterness and
frustration in the novels that reflects Fauset's
double vision of the world both on the surface and
beneath it.

*   Howard University. (See item 789.)

*   Jacobs, George W. "Negro Authors Must Eat." (See
item 651.)

*   "Jessie Fauset Portrays People She Knows." (See
item 653.)

255.   Johnson, Abby Arthur. "Literary Midwife: Jessie
Redmon Fauset and the Harlem Renaissance." *Phylon*,
34, No. 2 (June 1978), 143-53.

Fauset, who received high praise for her fiction
during the Harlem Renaissance, fell into disrepute
and neglect after the thirties. A portrayer of the
"better class" of Negroes she was, however, a
champion of young black writers—like McKay—who
wrote more experimentally. There was conflict, then,
between what she wrote and what she expressed as a
critic. She had a fervent interest in Pan-Africanism
at one time; even after she lessened her interest
she retained her belief in the existence of a special
bond between blacks of all nations. Therefore, there
is a meshing of Fauset's work as critic and creative
writer: she wrote about the world she knew best
(middle-class life), but she emphasized her racial
pride through such methods as opposing passing.
She attempted to bridge the chasm between the masses
and middle- and upper-class blacks, and through her
work as an editor on *The Crisis*, she helped raise the
consciousness of blacks and whites about the black
race and its artistic and cultural achievements.

255a.   McDowell, Deborah E.   "The Neglected Dimension of
          Jessie Redmon Fauset."   *Afro-Americans in New York
          Life and History*, 5, No. 2 (July 1981), 33-49.

          A revision of a talk, "Black Women Writers of the
          Harlem Renaissance," presented on 18 April 1980 at
          the 6th Annual BFSA Symposium in Buffalo, New York.

          Argues that Fauset brought up subjects that were
          daring for a black female writer of her time (e.g.,
          illegitimacy), and that she made more significant
          contribution to literature than male critics especially
          give her credit for (e.g., Bone, item 32).

*   Redding, J. Saunders. *To Make a Poet Black*.
          (See item 46.)

*   Royster, Beatrice Horn.   "The Ironic Vision of Four
          Black Women Novelists."   (See item 889.)

256.   Sato, Hiroko. "Under the Harlem Shadow: A Study of
          Jessie Fauset and Nella Larsen," in *The Harlem
          Renaissance Remembered*, ed. Arna Bontemps.   New
          York: Dodd, Mead & Co., 1972. Pp. 63-89.

          Sees Fauset writing in the mode of the novel of
          manners, wherein she emphasizes likenesses of the
          black and white races rather than their differences.
          Even though she seems to extol blacks who have white
          habits and values, Fauset is also seen as a novelist
          of social protest because she clearly places the blame
          for prejudice and hatred against Negroes upon the
          white race.   Finally, Fauset "was not a great writer.
          She was not even a good writer," a summation agreed
          upon by modern critics, despite the early, excessive
          praise of Braithwaite. (See item 252.)

          Larsen, on the other hand, is cited as understanding
          the craft of fiction.   Does not see Larsen as glorifying
          blackness because race problems are not her main
          concern: instead, she emphasizes the overall concept
          of the modern person's search for identity in a
          materialistic society.

*   Singh, Amritjit. *The Novels of the Harlem Renaissance*.
          (See item 160.)

257.   Starkey, Marion L. "Jessie Fauset." *The Southern
           Workman*, 61, No. 5 (May 1932), 217-20.

           Interview with and biographic sketch of Fauset,
           emphasizing her devotion to work and the inspiration
           that led her to writing (a novel by T.S. Stribling
           made her decide to write an authentic novel about
           blacks). Fauset points out the difficulties she
           encounters with readers who do not believe her type
           of Negro characters (educated blacks). Does not see
           the "problem story" as her genre. Ends by stating
           a need for more biographies about black people.

257a.   Sylvander, Carolyn Wedin. *Jessie Redmon Fauset,
           Black American Writer*. Troy, N.Y.: Whitston Pub.
           Co., 1981.

           An apologia for a prolific and personally well-
           regarded writer who Sylvander feels has never been
           treated fairly or seriously in a critical manner
           (except, it is suggested, in item 255). Covers
           Fauset's early life and up to her death, and discusses
           all of her novels, granting weaknesses but in strong
           sympathy with her, nevertheless. Therefore, the
           criticism lacks the sharp edge of assessment one
           might bring to bear upon a real master of creativity.
           This is the only full-length study devoted to Fauset,
           however, and it is well researched Bibliography,
           extensive notes, and a valuable listing of letters
           related to Fauset that can be found in various
           special collections.

*   Thompson, Enola. "Jessie Fauset As Interpreter of
           Negro Life." (See item 903.)

*   Wood, Darlene Iva. "The Fictional Writings of Jessie
           Fauset." (See item 910.)

F. Fisher, Rudolph (1897-1934)
1. His Writings
a. Novels

258. *The Conjure-Man Dies: A Mystery Tale of Dark Harlem.* New York: Covici, Friede, 1932.

The first black detective novel published in the United States--the story of a murder in Harlem, in the business-place of an African conjurer. Detective Dart and Doctor Archer join forces to solve this mystery, aided and hindered by two comic characters (Jinx and Bubber) who appear in Fisher's first novel, *The Walls of Jericho.*

Reviews: Booklist, 29, November 1932, p. 76; *Boston Transcript,* 3 August 1932, p. 3; *N.Y. Evening Post,* 30 July 1932, p. 7: William Soskin; *N.Y. H.T. Books,* 14 August 1932, p. 8: Will Cuppy; *N.Y.T. Book Review,* 31 July 1932, p. 13: Isaac Anderson; *Opportunity,* 10, October 1932, p. 320: Arthur P. Davis; *Time,* 20, 1 August 1932, p. 39.

259. *The Walls of Jericho.* New York: Alfred A. Knopf, 1928. Reprinted, New York: Arno Press, 1969.

All strata of Negro society are examined through stories centered on romance in the lower classes and racial and social conflict among upper-class blacks: the latter conflict is double-edged, because blacks are presented in opposition to one another until the "walls" of self-delusion are broken down.

Reviews: Cleveland Open Shelf, December 1928, p. 136; *The Crisis,* 35, November 1928, p. 374; *Harlem,* 1, 1928: Wallace Thurman; *New Statesman,* 31, 15 September 1928, p. 704; *N.Y.H.T. Books,* 26 August 1928, p. 5: Eric Walrond; *N.Y.T. Book Review,* 5 August 1928, p. 6; *N.Y. World,* 5 August 1928, p. 7m: W.F. White; *Opportunity,* 6, November 1928, p. 346: B.A. Botkin; *Saturday Review,* 146, 25 August 1928, p. 250; *Saturday Review of Literature,* 5, 8 September 1928, p. 110; *Spectator,* 141, 25 August 1928, p. 252; *Times* (London) *Literary Supplement,* 6 September 1928, p. 630.

b. Short Stories/Other Writings

260.   "The Backslider." *McClure's Magazine*, 59, No. 2
        (August 1927), 16-17, 101-04.

261.   "Blades of Steel." *Atlantic Monthly*, 140 (August
        1925), 183-92.

*   Brown University. (See item 782.)

*   "The Caucasian Storms Harlem." (See item 635.)

262.   "The City of Refuge." *Atlantic Monthly*, 135
        (February 1925), 178-87.

263.   "Common Meter," Part 1. *Baltimore Afro-American*
        (8 February 1930), 11. Part 2. *Baltimore Afro-
        American* (15 February 1930), 11.

264.   "Dust." *Opportunity*, 9, No. 2 (February 1931),
        46-47.

265.   "Ezekiel." *Junior Red Cross News*, 13 (March 1932),
        151-53.

266.   "Ezekiel Learns." *Junior Red Cross News*, 14, No. 6
        (February 1933), 123-35.

267.   "Fire by Night." *McClure's Magazine*, 59, No. 6
        (December 1927), 64-67, 98-102.

268.   "Guardian of the Law." *Opportunity*, 11, No. 3
        (March 1933), 82-85, 90.

269.   "High Yaller," Part 1. *Crisis*, 30, No. 6 (October
        1925), 281-86. Part 2. *Crisis*, 31, No. 1 (November
        1925), 33-38.

270.   "John Archer's Nose." *The Metropolitan: A Monthly
        Review*, 1, No. 1 (January 1935), 10-12, 47-50, 52,
        67, 69-71, 73-75, 80.

271.   "Miss Cynthie." *Story*, 3, No. 13 (June 1933), 3-15.

272.   "The Promised Land." *Atlantic Monthly*, 139
        (January 1927), 37-45.

273.   "Ringtail." *Atlantic Monthly,* 135 (May 1925), 652-60.

274.   "The South Lingers On." *Survey Graphic,* 53, No. 11 (1 March 1925), 644-47.

These sketches in this special issue devoted to the Negro, minus one, also appeared in Alain Locke's *The New Negro* under the title of "Vestiges." (See item 772.)

2. Writings About Him

*   Davis, Arthur P. *From the Dark Tower.* (See item 36.)

275.   Friedmann, Thomas, "The Good Guys in the Black Hats: Color Coding in Rudolf [sic] Fisher's 'Common Meter.'" *Studies in Black Literature,* 7, No. 1 (Winter 1976), 8-9.

Through the color of the characters in Fisher's stories, one can assess the character of the individual: the darkest black possesses wholeness in racial as well as in social and moral definitions, whereas the yellow-skinned blacks demonstrate weaker moral character, display the ambivalence of a dual heritage. In this way, Fisher demonstrates a spiritual as well as physical acceptance of blackness.

*   Gross, Theodofe. "The Negro Awakening." (See item 101.)

276.   Henry, Oliver Louis. "Rudolph Fisher: An Evaluation." *Crisis,* 78, No. 5 (July 1971), 149-54.

Thinks Fisher should be evaluated primarily on his short stories because this was the genre in which he concentrated. Sees "class consciousness" as Fisher's major theme. Believes Fisher captures black life but writes in a manner that exposes basic human features within the racial context.

*   Ivy, James W. "Écrits Nègres aux États-Unis." (See item 116.)

*   Perry, Margaret. *Silence to the Drums.* (See item 153.)

* Queen, Eleanor Claudine. "A Study of Rudolph Fisher's Prose Fiction." (See item 884.)

* Redding, J. Saunders. *To Make a Poet Black.* (See item 46.)

* Seydi, Souleymane. "Rudolph Fisher." (See item 890.)

* Singh, Amritjit. *The Novels of the Harlem Renaissance.* (See item 160.)

* Tignor, Eleanor Q. "Rudolph Fisher: 'This is Harlem'--1920's." (See item 731.)

277.   Turpin, Waters E. "Four Short Fiction Writers of the Harlem Renaissance--Their Legacy of Achievement." *CLA Journal*, 11 (September 1967), 59-72.

Stresses "positive achievements" of the following writers: Jean Toomer, Rudolph Fisher, Langston Hughes, and Claude McKay. Considers Toomer's style poetic and cites his ability to evoke the atmosphere of small Southern places. Analyzes Hughes's story "Slave on the Block," which is described as a satire in which Hughes succeeds admirably in his characterizations. Fisher's "Miss Cynthie" represents the truisms between the conflicts of age and youth, and McKay's "Truant" is felt to present the true conflicts of marriage. Praises the writing style of each author also. A didactic and descriptive approach to these stories.

G. Grimké, Angelina Weld (1887-1958)
1. Her Writings (Selected)

278.   *Rachel--A Play of Protest.* Boston: Cornhill, 1920.

Sorrow and sacrifice occur in the family of Rachel, stemming from prejudice.

Reviews: *Baltimore Afro-American*, 20 September 1920; *Buffalo Commercial*, 4 September 1920; *Buffalo Courier*, 3 October 1920; *Catholic World*, December 1920; *Detroit Free Press*, 12 September 1920; *Detroit News*, 12 September 1920; *The Dispatch* (Columbus, Ohio), 26 September 1920; *Grinnell Review* (Iowa), January 1921; *Journal of Negro History*, 6, April 1921, pp. 248-54: Lillie B.C. Wyman; *Mirror-American* (Manchester, N.H.),

4 September 1920; *N.Y.H.T. Books*, 3 October 1920;
Post-Express (Rochester, N.Y.), 14 September 1920;
The Star (Washington, D.C.), 5 December 1920; *Utica Daily Press*, 8 October 1920.

2. Writings About Her

*   Howard University. (See item 789.)

*   Hull, Gloria T. "Black Women Poets." (See item 112.)

*   ————. "Rewriting Afro-American Literature."
(See item 113.)

*   Kerlin, Robert T. *Negro Poets and Their Poems*.
(See item 43.)

279.   Miller, Jeanne-Marie A. "Angelina Weld Grimké:
Playwright and Poet." *CLA Journal*, 21, No. 4 (June
1978), 513-24.

Explication of Grimké's plays *Rachel* and *Mara*, which
can be seen as protest plays by example of the fate
meted out to the genteel, well-deserving Negro
characters. Both plays have a main character with
a biblical name, as if to emphasize Grimké's
denouncement against God letting such grief come
to her good characters. Her poetry was introspective,
concerned with "life, love and death." In both her
plays and poetry she joins other Renaissance writers
in protesting against racial prejudice as well as
demonstrating pride in the black race.

H. Hughes, Langston (1902-1967)
1. His Writings (Selected)
a. Poetry

280.   *Dear Lovely Death*. Amenia, N.Y.: Troutbeck Press,
1931.

A dozen poems that express some disillusionment.

281.   *Fine Clothes to the Jew*. New York: Alfred A.
Knopf, 1927.

The poet's second book of poetry, concentrating on
blues poetry.

Reviews: *Bookman*, 65, April 1927, p. 221: Babette
Deutsch; *Boston Transcript*, 2 March 1927, p. 4;
Carolina Magazine, 57, May 1927, pp. 41-44: Lewis
Alexander; *Cleveland Open Shelf*, April 1927, p. 51;
The Crisis, 34, March 1927, p. 20; *Literary Review*,
12 February 1927, p. 4: J.M.M.; *The Nation*, 124, 13
April 1927, p. 403: H.A. Potamkin; *New Republic*, 51,
8 June 1927, p. 77: Abbe Niles; *N.Y.H.T. Books*, 20
February 1927, p. 5: DuBose Heyward; *N.Y.T. Book
Review*, 27 March 1927, p. 2: H.S. Gorman; *N.Y.
World*, 5 February 1927, p. 9m: W.F. White; *Opportunity*,
5, March 1927, pp. 84-85: Margaret Larkin; *Saturday
Review of Literature*, 3, 9 April 1927, p. 112: Alain
Locke; *Times* (London) *Literary Supplement*, 19 May
1927, p. 358.

282.   *Scottsboro Limited*. New York: Golden Stair Press,
        1932.

        Four poems and a play concerning this *cause célèbre*.

283.   *The Weary Blues*. New York: Alfred A. Knopf, 1926.

        The first collection of the poet's work, containing
        jazz and cabaret poems but also featuring his famous
        "The Negro Speaks of Rivers" and "Mother to Son."

        Reviews: *Booklist*, 22, July 1926, p. 410; *Boston
        Transcript*, 15 May 1926, p. 2; *Cleveland Open Shelf*,
        April 1926, p. 45; *Independent*, 116, 3 April 1926,
        p. 404; *New Republic*, 46, 12 May 1926, p. 371: E.S.
        Sergeant; *N.Y.H.T. Books*, 1 August 1926, p. 4: DuBose
        Heyward; *N.Y.T. Book Review*, 21 March 1926, p. 6;
        Opportunity, 4, February 1926, pp. 73-74: Countee
        Cullen; *Palms*, 4, No. 1 (1926); *Times* (London)
        Literary Supplement, 29 July 1926, p. 515; *World
        Tomorrow*, 9, April 1926, p. 131.

                        b. Fiction

284.   *Not Without Laughter*. New York: Alfred A. Knopf, 1930.

        Story of Sandy, a black boy living in the Midwest, of
        his grandmother, Aunt Hagar, and the rest of his
        family, where the boy gradually learns to perceive
        what is important in life for self-development and
        fulfillment.

Reviews: *Booklist*, 27, December 1930, p. 160;
Cleveland Open Shelf, December 1930, p. 148; *The*
Nation, 131, 6 August 1930, p. 157: V.F. Calverton;
N.Y.H.T. Books, 27 July 1930, p. 5: Mary Ross; *N.Y.T.*
Book Review, 3 August 1930, p. 6; *Opportunity*, 8,
September 1930, pp. 279-80: Sterling A. Brown;
Pittsburgh (Mo.) *Bulletin*, 35, October 1930, p. 70;
Saturday Review of Literature, 7, 23 August 1930,
p. 69: Herschel Brickell; *Times* (London) *Literary*
Supplement, 2 October 1930, p. 778; *World Tomorrow*,
13, December 1930, p. 520.

285.   *The Ways of White Folks*.   New York: Alfred A.
       Knopf, 1934.

       A collection of short stories (his first), including
       the bitter "Cora Unashamed" and 'the poignant "Little
       Dog." Generally, the stories are satiric.

       Reviews: *Booklist*, 30, July 1934, p. 351; *Boston*
       Transcript, 30 June 1934, p. 3: C.F.; *Cleveland Open*
       Shelf, July 1934, p. 6; *The Nation*, 139, 11 July
       1934, p. 49: Sherwood Anderson; *New Republic*, 80,
       5 September 1934, p. 108: Martha Gruening; *N.Y.H.T.*,
       27 June 1934, p. 15: Lewis Gannett; *N.Y.H.T. Books*,
       1 July 1934, p. 4: Horace Gregory; *N.Y.T. Book Review*,
       1 July 1934, p. 6: Leane Zugsmith; *North American*
       Review, 238, September 1934, p. 286: Herschel
       Brickell; *Opportunity*, 12, September 1934, pp. 283-84:
       E.C. Holmes; *Saturday Review of Literature*, 10, 14
       July 1934, p. 805: Vernon Loggins; *Spectator*, 154, 4
       January 1935, p. 25: William Plomer; *Survey Graphic*,
       23, November 1934, p. 565: Alain Locke; *Times* (London)
       Literary Supplement, 25 October 1934, p. 736.

                    c. Other Writings

*   *Arna Bontemps - Langston Hughes Letters, 1925-1967.*
       (See item 210.)

286.   *The Big Sea: An Autobiography*.   New York: Hill and
       Wang, 1963, c1940.

       Captures the tone and temper of the 1920s when "the
       Negro was in vogue." His portraits of his contemporary
       writers are enlightening and vivid, but the true
       Langston Hughes remains elusive.

*   Chicago Public Library. (See item 783.)

*   Fisk University. (See item 786.)

287.   "Harlem Literati in the Twenties." *The Saturday
          Review* (22 June 1940), 13-14.

          In Hughes's self-deprecating, very studied "light
          touch," reminiscences about artists and intellectuals
          he knew during the 1920s. An incisive characterization,
          nevertheless, of personages such as Wallace Thurman
          and Alain Locke. Other writers he etches are
          Hurston and Fisher. Relates the story of the short-
          lived periodical *Fire*, which the young writers
          hoped would be a genuine Negro literary magazine.

          This piece appears in a longer, slightly different
          version in Hughes's autobiography, *The Big Sea*.

*   [Letter to the Editor.] (See item 647.)

288.   "My Early Days in Harlem." *Freedomways*, 3, No. 3
          (Summer 1963), 312-14.

          An infectious, wide-ranging memoir of Hughes's very
          first days in his spiritual home town. Says he was
          in love with Harlem before he arrived and his
          admiration continues to shine through this brief
          reminiscence. Sometimes syncopated in style--in the
          mode of his jazz poetry.

289.   "The Negro Artist and the Racial Mountain." *The
          Nation*, 122 (23 June 1926), 692-94.

          A personal manifesto of belief in his own race as
          material to be used as inspiration for black writing.
          Sees the "racial mountain" as the desire to be
          raceless, to suppress the Afro part of the black
          writer's Americanism, to write as if one were white.
          Believes the black artist suffers from misunderstanding
          by blacks as well as by whites because of the pre-
          vailing notion of "White is best." Rejects this idea
          and states he doesn't care if his work is rejected--
          he'll write as he pleases and remain free inside.

          The best-known, perhaps the only statement about the
          aesthetics of black writing during the 1920s. A
          reply to Schuyler's attack on Negro artists (see
          item 416).

290.   "The Twenties: Harlem and Its Negritude." *African
         Forum*, 1 (1966), 11-20.

         Reminiscences about the past and persons Hughes knew,
         related in his easy-going, colloquial style. Finally
         suggests the poets of the Harlem Renaissance influenced
         African and West Indian black writers, like Césaire
         and Senghor, because there was pride of heritage and
         race consciousness in their poetry. Also relates the
         story of the venture of producing the literary maga-
         zine *Fire*. Ends nostalgically by noting that the
         writers of the 1920s did not take themselves as
         seriously as the black writers who followed them.

*   "When I worked for Dr. Woodson." (See item 648.)

*   Yale University. (See item 798.)

                   2. Writings About Him

*   Akinkoye, Ajibike. "La Voix des Éxiles." (See
         item 801.)

*   Armstead, T.J. "The Social Realism of Langston
         Hughes." (See item 804.)

*   Baker, Ruth Taylor. "The Philosophy of the New
         Negro." (See item 806.)

291.   Barksdale, Richard K. *Langston Hughes: The Poet and
         His Critics*. Chicago: American Library Association,
         1977.

         A review of criticism of Hughes's poetry. Argues
         with many of the critics; in particular, reproaches
         critics who seemed to have dismissed Hughes's social
         poetry of the 1930s.

*   Blue, Ila J. "A Study of the Poetry of Langston
         Hughes." (See item 814.)

*   Bouachrine, Assila. "Le Noir Americain dans l'oeuvre
         de Langston Hughes." (See item 816.)

*   Burns, Loretta S. "The Black Metropolis in the Poetry
         of Langston Hughes." (See item 820.)

292.   Cartey, Wilfred. "Four Shadows of Harlem." *Negro Digest*, 18, No. 10 (August 1969), 22-25, 83-92.

Examines the views of Harlem and New York City of Federico Garcia Lorca, Langston Hughes, Claude McKay, and Leopold Senghor: all four see some influence of one section upon the other, and individual poems are used to demonstrate such notions as "the dream deferred" or the exoticism of the nights in both Harlem and Manhattan.

293.   Cobb, Martha K. "Concepts of Blackness in the Poetry of Nicolás Guillén, Jacques Roumain and Langston Hughes." *CLA Journal*, 28, No. 2 (December 1974), 262-72.

Sees a connection between these writers, who were contemporaries, and believes they helped to move black writers towards formulating a black aesthetics of literature. The Harlem Renaissance was an influence on the Caribbean writers, who developed the concept of Negritude in the 1930s. These three writers are similar in that the same themes appear in their poetry--e.g., struggle in an alien society, dualism, the quest for identity--and Hughes and Guillén both experimented with language, sounds, and rhythms that derived from the city and the common people.

*   Davis, Arthur P. *From the Dark Tower*. (See item 36.)

294.   ———. "The Harlem of Langston Hughes' Poetry." *Phylon*, 13 (Fourth Quarter, 1952), 276-83.

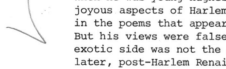

When he was young Hughes celebrated the jazzy and joyous aspects of Harlem in his poetry, especially in the poems that appeared in *The Weary Blues* (1926). But his views were false in great part because this exotic side was not the real Harlem; however, in his later, post-Harlem Renaissance work (1940s) he presents a more balanced portrait of *his* city. Ultimately, all of his work uses Harlem poetically to project the fears and aspirations, the sorrows and the joys of black people who want a place in the American dream.

295.   ————. "Langston Hughes: Cool Poet," in *Langston
         Hughes, Black Genius: A Critical Evaluation*, ed.
         Therman B. O'Daniel. New York: William Morrow &
         Co., 1971. Pp. 18-38.

         Hughes experimented with form and rhythms--but he
         consistently wrote about the race issue, not bitterly
         but in wonderment about white racist attitudes towards
         Negroes. His style is *"deceptively"* simple--for
         there is often a second level of meaning to his poems.

296.   ————. "The Tragic Mulatto Theme in Six Works of
         Langston Hughes." *Phylon*, 16, No. 2 (Second Quarter,
         1955), 195-204.

         From his earliest writings Hughes used the theme of
         the tragic mulatto, used it primarily to display
         rejection in the lives of his characters. This may
         be connected with his personal life and the negative
         feelings he had for his own father.

297.   Diakhate, Lamine. "Langston Hughes, conquerant de
         l'espoir." *Présence Africaine*, 64, 4th Quarterly
         (1967), 38-46.

         Early in his writing Hughes affirmed his black identity
         in the face of the absurdity of America's racial
         prejudices. His famous essay "The Negro Artist and
         the Racial Mountain" (see item 289) was not a
         manifesto or even a profession of faith: it was a
         statement of action--the active man conquering life.
         A believer in principles and a man of dignity, Hughes
         never lost hope that shattered dreams and difficulties
         in life were conquerable. It is suggested that he
         did just this in his own life--found the dreams and
         aspirations of his youth and found meaning and
         direction in his life.

298.   Dickinson, Donald C. *A Bio-Bibliography of Langston
         Hughes, 1902-1967*. Hamden, Conn.: Archon Books, 1967.

         A five-chapter biographical section, detailing not
         only events in the poet's life but literary publica-
         tions and general discussion of Hughes's writings.
         The bibliography "includes all publications in
         English and foreign languages up to 1965.... It
         does not include his publications in newspapers, his
         lyrics for published music, or his readings on
         phonograph recordings." Does include his edited
         books and works about Hughes. The author had the
         help of Hughes in the early days of this project.

299.   Emanuel, James A. *Langston Hughes*. New Haven,
        Conn: College & University Press, 1967. (Twayne's
        United States Authors Series.)

        After a brief biographical introduction and an
        overall literary picture of Hughes's career, presents
        studies of all genres in which Hughes wrote. Groups
        his work thematically, to demonstrate the continuity
        of his work in terms of his subject interests and
        stylistic experiments. A selected bibliography is
        at the end, some of it annotated.

300.   ————. "The Literary Experiments of Langston
        Hughes," in his *Langston Hughes, Black Genius: A
        Critical Evaluation*. New York: William Morrow &
        Co., 1971. Pp. 171-82.

        Discusses stylistic ventures Hughes tried in his
        poetry--"topographical and emblematic experiments,"
        such as the use of headlines, Harlem bars and
        night clubs as a complete poem.

*   Etonde-Ekoto, Grace. "Langston Hughes." (See
        item 839.)

301.   Farrison, W. Edward. "Langston Hughes: Poet of the
        Negro Renaissance." *CLA Journal*, 15, No. 4 (June
        1972), 401-10.

        Narrates details about Hughes's personal life (the
        author and Hughes were at Lincoln University at the
        same time), and believes that *The Weary Blues*
        contains probably the best blues poetry Hughes
        wrote. Suggests that Hughes always maintained the
        ideals of the Renaissance, such as pride in black
        heritage and the desirability of integrating into
        the mainstream of America.

302.   ————. "Not Without Laughter But Without Tears,"
        in *Langston Hughes, Black Genius: A Critical
        Evaluation*, ed. Therman B. O'Daniel. New York:
        William Morrow & Co., 1971. Pp. 96-109.

        Describes reviews of *Not Without Laughter*, then
        explores special features of the book--the language
        and the social situations, which give it a claim to
        being "an important social document as well as a
        literary work."

303.   Garber, Earlene D. "Form as a Complement to Content
        in Three of Langston Hughes' Poems." *Negro American
        Literature Forum*, 5 (1971), 137-39.

        Examines "Border Line," "Dream," and "Dreams," to
        demonstrate the technical methods Hughes used to
        forge unity between theme and structure in some of
        his poetry. Believes the logical structure of the
        poem is enhanced by the awareness of poetic techniques
        in the use of rhythm and poetic stresses.

304.   Gibson, Donald B. "The Good Black Poet and the Good
        Gray Poet: The Poetry of Hughes and Whitman," in
        Langston Hughes: Black Genius, ed. Therman B. O'Daniel.
        New York: William Morrow & Co., 1971. Pp. 65-80.

        Hughes acknowledged a kinship with Whitman, and their
        poetry bears a resemblance because of the following
        factors: both believed in the American ideal, both
        were more frequently cheerful than not, their writing
        was often in a non-traditional fashion, and they both
        felt free in their choice of subject for poetry.

*   Gross, Theodore. "The Negro Awakening." (See
        item 101.)

305.   Guillén, Nicolas. "Le Souvenir de Langston Hughes."
        Présence Africaine, 64, 4th Quarterly (1967), 34-37.

        A warm remembrance of Hughes, who told this Cuban
        poet during a visit to Havana in 1930 that he wished
        he were not a mulatto, that he would rather be black.

*   Hall, Rubye M. "Realism in the Poetry of Langston
        Hughes." (See item 846.)

*   Hansell, William Howard. "Positive Themes in the
        Poetry of Four Negroes." (See item 847.)

*   Harrington, Donald S. "Langston Hughes." (See
        item 643.)

*   Harris, Carol Ann. "Black Women in Langston Hughes'
        Poetry and Short Fiction." (See item 849.)

*   Hill, Eloise H. "Langston Hughes." (See item 853.)

*   Hudson, Theodore R. "An Analysis of the Poetry of
        Langston Hughes." (See item 855.)

306.   ————. "Technical Aspects of the Poetry of
            Langston Hughes." *Black World*, 22, No. 11 (September
            1973), 24-25.

            Contends that Hughes wrote with conscious forms and
            techniques in mind. He was influenced chiefly by
            free verse writers and African and Afro-American oral
            and literary tradition. The three most pervasive
            patterns seen in his poetry are: use of music--the
            blues, jazz, spirituals, gospel songs; the ballad;
            and free verse. In his diction he was aware also
            of borrowing such techniques as call-and-response,
            exclamation--devices for emphasis and special
            effects. Thus, he was well aware of technique,
            and one must study his methods and preoccupations
            in order to fully comprehend his poetry.

307.   Isaacs, Harold R. "Five Writers and Their African
            Ancestors." *Phylon*, 21, No. 3 (Third Quarter, 1960),
            243-65, 317-36.

            Believes Langston Hughes did not see Africa in a
            romantic light, but wanted to demonstrate a connection
            between the peoples of Africa and the blacks of
            America. He could not be African, nor did he wish
            to be; but some of his work shows the influence of
            his thinking about and coming into contact with
            Africa. Langston Hughes is the only Harlem Renaissance
            writer discussed here, in the pages listed above, in
            Part I of the article.

*   Jackson, Blyden. "Harlem Renaissance in the
            Twenties." (See item 117.)

*   ————. "Langston Hughes." (See item 6.)

308.   Jemie, Onwuchekwa. *Langston Hughes: An Introduction
            to the Poetry*. New York: Columbia University Press,
            1976.

            Stresses Hughes's devotion to and inspiration from
            the black masses and black folk heritage. Compares
            him with other Harlem Renaissance poets, such as
            Cullen and McKay. Details subject and style of his
            major poetic collections, and presents Hughes's
            opinions about the aims of the young Negro artists
            during the 1920s. Included is a chronology of his
            life and publications, and a generic bibliography
            of books by and about Hughes.

309.   Kent, George E.   "Langston Hughes and Afro-American
         Folk and Cultural Tradition," in his *Blackness and
         the Adventure of Western Culture*.   Chicago: Third
         World Press, 1972.   Pp. 53-75.

         Hughes, who is "full of the folk," has to be understood
         outside of conventional Western terms of reconciling
         contradictions neatly.   Hughes relies on instinct
         more than intellect.   There is a protean quality to
         the folk tradition that permits Hughes (and all
         blacks) to face the problems of life.   Therefore,
         Hughes's personal relationship to the Afro-American
         folk tradition is an integral part of his work, which
         is not large in vision but close to the "souls and
         strivings of black folks."

*   Kerlin, Robert T.   "A Pair of Youthful Poets."
         (See item 234.)

*   Kitamura, Takao.   "Langston Hughes."   (See item 864.)

*   "Langston Hughes, 1902-1967."   (See item 9.)

310.   McGhee, Nancy B.   "Langston Hughes: Poet in the Folk
         Manner," in *Langston Hughes, Black Genius: A Critical
         Evaluation*, ed. Therman B. O'Daniel.   New York:
         William Morrow & Co., 1971.   Pp. 39-64.

         His interest in folk subjects and the folk idiom
         render his poetry accessible to readers, for he
         uses universal truth and wisdom in this style of
         writing.

*   Mandelik, Peter, and Stanley Schatt, comps.   "A
         concordance to the Poetry of Langston Hughes."
         (See item 12.)

311.   Martin, Dellita.   "Langston Hughes's Use of the Blues."
         CLA Journal, 22, No. 2 (December 1978), 151-59.

         Examines poems from *Fine Clothes to the Jew* (1927) in
         order to illustrate the unity of Hughes's verse
         patterns when he writes blues poetry--the antiphonal
         structure, the call and response motif, and the
         thematic emphasis on love, loss of love, and loneli-
         ness.   This unity of form and substance creates a
         mood akin to the blues music.

312.   Miller, R. Baxter. "'Even After I Was Dead': *The
         Big Sea*--Paradox, Preservation, and Holistic Time."
         Black American Literature Forum, 11, No. 2 (Summer
         1977), 39-45.

         States that Hughes's personality is submerged in his
         concentrating on others he knew--in particular,
         persons who were involved in the Harlem Renaissance.
         It does not appear that he has a direct plan in whom
         he describes or in what manner: he does not elaborate
         on his good friend Arna Bontemps, and he gives only
         a superficial glimpse of Carl Van Vechten. His
         portrayals of Wallace Thurman and Zora Neale Hurston
         are full and colorful. The Renaissance period is
         vivified by his descriptions in a total manner, but
         there emerges from this book a man who does not show
         himself engaged in the very period that both shaped
         and fascinated him. The private Hughes remains as
         private as ever.

*   Mott, Frank Luther. "The Harlem Poets." (See
         item 237.)

*   New York Public Library. (See item 793.)

*   O'Daniel, Therman B. "Langston Hughes: A Selected
         Classified Bibliography." (See item 17.)

313.   ———, ed. *Langston Hughes, Black Genius: A
         Critical Evaluation*. New York: William Morrow
         & Co., 1971.

         A collection of essays (see items 295, 300, 302,
         304, 310), followed by a selected classified
         bibliography. O'Daniel presents a bio-bibliographical
         introduction.

*   Pinkston, Annette Earline. "The Literary Career
         of Langston Hughes." (See item 883.)

314.   Prowle, Allen D. "Langston Hughes," in *The Black
         American Writer*. Volume II: *Poetry and Drama*.
         Edited by C.W.E. Bigsby. Deland, Fla.: Everett
         Edwards, 1969. Reprinted, Baltimore: Penguin
         Books, 1971. Pp. 77-87.

         Characterizes Hughes's poetry, especially that
         written in the 1920s, as possessing race pride,
         protest, language in the Negro's own idiom, irony

and understatement, and fundamental optimism. Gives
specific examples to illustrate his analysis.

* Redding, J. Saunders. *To Make a Poet Black*.
  (See item 46.)

* Rosenblatt, Roger. *Black Fiction*. (See item 47.)

* Singh, Amritjit. *The Novels of the Harlem
  Renaissance*. (See item 160.)

* Souffrant, Marcel. "La Culture et la culture anglaise
  chez ... Langston Hughes." (See item 896.)

315. Taylor, Patricia E. "Langston Hughes and the Harlem
     Renaissance, 1921-1931: Major Events and Publications,"
     in *The Harlem Renaissance Remembered*, ed. Arna
     Bontemps. New York: Dodd, Mead & Co., 1972.
     Pp. 90-102.

     A description of events attended by Langston Hughes,
     his publications by genre, and information about his
     personal life, such as his relationship with his
     patron and his experiences with the short-lived
     magazine *Fire!!* A straightforward chronological
     narration about his major works and some events
     in his life.

316. Turner, Darwin T. "Langston Hughes as Playwright."
     CLA Journal, 11, No. 8 (June 1968), 297-309.

     Relates the long career of Hughes as a dramatist,
     from *Mulatto* (1930, produced in 1935) to his death.
     Believes Hughes was a strong delineator of character.

* Turpin, Waters E. "Four Short Fiction Writers of
  the Harlem Renaissance." (See item 277.)

317. Wagner, Jean. "Langston Hughes," in his *Black Poets
     of the United States from Paul Laurence Dunbar to
     Langston Hughes*. Urbana: University of Illinois
     Press, 1973. Pp. 385-474.

     States that Hughes was the most productive poet of
     the Harlem Renaissance, that Hughes identifies with
     the black masses and believes in the black collective
     spirit: there is a mystical union between blacks of
     all times. Yet he does not idealize Africa. Stresses
     the importance of jazz as a reality in black life and

Harlem. Says that "Hughes feels how, in genuine jazz,
the whole soul of his race finds expression."

Many poems are analyzed to relate to discussion
concerning Hughes's themes and interests--such as
glorification of blackness, class consciousness, and
the promises of American democracy.

318.   Waldron, Edward E. "The Blues Poetry of Langston
         Hughes." *Negro American Literature Forum*, 5 (1971),
         140-49.

         Hughes places the essence of blues into his poetry,
         writing about the duality of black life--the sorrow
         and the joy. He is aware of the varying patterns of
         the blues and employs them consciously--e.g., definite
         stresses or the use of repetition.

*   Wilson, Ronald H. "The Prose of Langston Hughes."
         (See item 908.)

*   Zeidman, Nathalie. "The Image of the Negro Through
         the Eyes of Langston Hughes." (See item 913.)

                I. Hurston, Zora Neale (1903-1960)
                   1. Her Writings (Selected)
                      a. Novels

319.   *Jonah's Gourd Vine*. Philadelphia: J.B. Lippincott
         Co., 1934. Reprinted, with an introduction by
         Larry Neal, Philadelphia: J.B. Lippincott, 1971.

         John Buddy Pearson, son of a white tenant farmer
         and Negro woman, makes his way in the world as a
         preacher but becomes embroiled in too many illicit
         love affairs.

         Reviews: *Booklist*, 30, July 1934, p. 351; *Boston
         Chronicle*, 5 May 1934: R.E.M.J.; *The Crisis*, 41,
         June 1934: Andrew Burris; *Louisiana Weekly*, 15
         September 1934: Odile Mouton; *The Nation*, 138, 13
         June 1934, p. 683; *New Republic*, 79, 11 July 1934,
         p. 244: Martha Gruening; *N.Y. Age*, 5 May 1934: Mary
         White Ovington; *N.Y.H.T. Books*, 6 May 1934, p. 7:
         Josephine Pinckney; *N.Y. Post*, 5 May 1934, p. 13:
         Herschel Brickell; *N.Y.T. Book Review*, 6 May 1934,
         p. 6: Margaret Wallace; *North American Review*, 238,
         July 1934, p. 95: Herschel Brickell; *Spectator*, 154,
         4 January 1935, p. 25: William Plomer; *Times* (London)
         Literary Supplement, 18 October 1934, p. 716.

320.   *Their Eyes Were Watching God.* Philadelphia: J.B.
        Lippincott, 1937. Reprinted, Greenwich, Conn.:
        Fawcett Publications, 1965. Reprinted, New York:
        Negro Universities Press, 1969. Reprinted, Urbana:
        University of Illinois Press, 1978.

        A woman, Janie, searches for love and eventually
        finds it with her third husband--a man who is happy-
        go-lucky but who knows how to share his life with her,
        in order to create a wholeness both feel together.

        Reviews: *Booklist*, 34, 15 October 1937, p. 71; *The
        Nation*, 16 October 1937, p. 409: Sterling A. Brown;
        New Republic, 92, 13 October 1937, p. 276: Otis
        Ferguson; *N.Y.H.T. Books*, 26 September 1937, p. 2:
        Sheila Hibben; *N.Y. Post*, 14 September 1937: Herschel
        Brickell; *N.Y.T. Book Review*, 26 September 1937, p.
        29: Lucy Thompkins; *Saturday Review of Literature*, 16,
        18 September 1937, p. 3: George Stevens; *Time*, 30,
        20 September 1937, p. 71.

                        b. Short Stories

321.   "Drenched in Light." *Opportunity*, 2 (December 1924),
        171-74.

322.   "The Gilded Six Bits," in *Story in America*, ed.
        Whit Burnett and Martha Foley. New York: Vanguard,
        1034. Pp. 73-84.

323.   "John Redding Goes to Sea." *Opportunity*, 4
        (January 1926), 16-21.

324.   "Sweat." *Fire!!*, No. 1 (December 1926).

                        c. Other Writings

325.   "Characteristics of Negro Expression," in *Negro: An
        Anthology*, ed. Nancy Cunard. London: Wishart,
        1934. Pp. 39-46.

        A disjointed yet highly descriptive analysis of
        elements in black speech and writing. States that
        black expressions are dramatic, ornamental, use
        folklore, are very original, employ mimicry, display
        community spirit, and, finally, use dialect
        effectively. The explication of different features

in the black idiom is supported by examples. A
celebration of black-white linguistic differences.

326.   *Mules and Men*. Philadelphia: J.B. Lippincott Co.,
         1935. Reprinted, New York: Negro Universities Press,
         1969. Reprinted, with an introduction by Darwin T.
         Turner, New York: Harper & Row, 1970.

         A collection of black folktales and Voodoo practices
         in the South collected by Hurston during visits for
         this purpose.

         Reviews: *Booklist*, 32, November 1935, p. 54; *Boston
         Transcript*, 16 October 1935, p. 2; *New Republic*, 11
         December 1935, p. 143: Henry Lee Moon; *N.Y.H.T. Books*,
         13 October 1935, p. 7: Samuel Gaillard Stoney; *N.Y.
         Post*, 26 October 1935, p. 7; *N.Y.T. Book Review*, 10
         November 1935, p. 4: H.I. Brock; *Saturday Review of
         Literature*, 19 October 1935, p. 12: Jonathan Daniels.

*   University of Florida Libraries. (See item 787.)

*   Yale University. (See item 798.)

                    2. Writings About Her

327.   Blake, Emma L. "Zora Neale Hurston: Author and
         Folklorist." *Negro History Bulletin*, 29 (April
         1966), 149-50, 165-66.

         A brief recounting of Hurston's life and summaries of
         her writings in all genres. Does not go into precise
         detail about her economic struggles (or physical
         ones), although she alludes to them.

*   Bone, Robert. *The Negro Novel in America*. (See
         item 32.)

328.   Burke, Virginia M. "Zora Neale Hurston and Fannie
         Hurst As They Saw Each Other." *CLA Journal*, 20,
         No. 4 (June 1977), 435-47.

         Exploration of the Hurst-Hurston relationship, which
         lasted for two years when Hurston was in the other
         writer's employ. Their backgrounds have some
         psychological parallels, and they were both tough,
         independent women. Hurston understood Hurst the
         best, because Hurst "ran afoul of stereotypes ...
         created by whites during the Harlem Renaissance --

the exotic primitive...." Still, Hurst recognized
the talent of Hurston.

Hurst was an important figure in the life of Hurston,
and this can be seen in her autobiography. Con-
versely, Hurston was a brief episode in Hurst's life,
and is not even mentioned in her autobiography.

329.   Gloster, Hugh M. "Zora Neale Hurston: Novelist and
        Folklorist." *Phylon*, 4 (2nd Quarter, 1943), 153-59.

        All of Hurston's books are influenced greatly by her
        interest and work in anthropology. In blending
        folklore and fiction, Hurston--despite technical
        flaws--achieves success in creating literature that
        is rich in folkways and the idiomatic language of
        the rural South.

*   Hemenway, Robert. (See item 788.)

330.   ————. "Folktale Field Notes from Zora Neale
        Hurston." *The Black Scholar*, 7, No. 7 (April
        1976), 39-46.

        Hurston was a sociologist as well as an anthropologist,
        and the fact of not pursuing a doctorate in anthro-
        pology freed her to approach her study of black
        culture openly, without preconceived theories. She
        emphasized the relationship between race and culture,
        and documented the influence of the black oral
        tradition upon behavior. Her book *The Negro in
        Florida* was never published; but notes collected for
        the book are presented at the end of this paper.

331.   ————. *Zora Neale Hurston: A Literary Biography*.
        Urbana: University of Illinois Press, 1977.

        The fullest treatment of Hurston--her life, her
        writings, her personality. Documentation concerning
        her literary and anthropological careers places
        Hurston within the context of the period when interest
        in one's heritage was great but not always factually
        understood. Hurston's knowledge was both academic and
        intuitive: she chafed under the restrictions of
        academe, and it was in her folkloric writing that
        she found herself artistically. The controversy she
        and Hughes had over the play *Mule Bone* is scrupulously
        investigated and explained. Footnotes provide
        valuable information also.

332.   ————.   "Zora Neale Hurston and the Eatonville
            Anthropology," in *The Harlem Renaissance Remembered*,
            ed. Arna Bontemps. New York: Dodd, Mead & Co.,
            1972. Pp. 190-214.

            Relates Hurston's career and sees her as "an important
            contributor to the Renaissance spirit," even though
            anthropology was her main interest during many of
            the Renaissance years. Suggests her interest in the
            scientific side of exploring her race stemmed from a
            desire to have a solid structure behind what black
            folk literature demonstrated--affirmation of the
            black person's humanity.

333.   Howard, Lillie P.   "Marriage: Zora Neale Hurston's
            Systems of Values." *CLA Journal*, 21, No. 2 (December
            1977), 256-68.

            Hurston's interest in exploring the marriage relationship
            can be found in four short stories and in three of
            her novels. She does not romanticize it; indeed,
            there are violence and hatred in some of the marriages
            she portrays--and only three of the eleven marriages
            she describes work. They work because they possess
            the qualities Hurston deemed necessary for a good
            marriage (her own did not succeed): "courage,
            honesty, love, trust, respect, understanding, and
            a willingness to work together." Also describes
            Hurston's fictional married couples and concludes
            she was a strong advocate of marriage because this
            belief stemmed from her system of personal values.

*   ————.   "Zora Neale Hurston." (See item 854.)

*   Howard University. Locke Papers. (See item 789.)

334.   Hurst, Fannie. "Zora Hurston: A Personality Sketch."
            Yale University Library Gazette, 35, No. 1 (July
            1960), 17-22.

            At the death of Hurston, reminisces about Hurst's first
            meeting with Hurston; views this as one of those
            quaint moments in life. Hurst was fascinated with
            the other woman's zest for life. Hurston's ability
            to appear unworried about racial abuse and rebuffs,
            as well as her own studied interest in her own
            culture, makes Hurst see the writer as a cross
            between the happy-go-lucky innocent and the scholar.
            Therefore, Hurst says of Hurston that she possessed

"vividness, both vulgar and exquisite." It is as a recorder of Negro Americana, however, that Hurst remembers her most--a person, even to the end, who was a woman "half in shadow."

At end of article is a list of books, manuscripts, and letters in the James Weldon Johnson Collection at Yale by 1960. (See also item 798.)

*   Johnson, Gloria J. "Hurston's Folk." (See item 860.)

335.   Jordan, June. "On Richard Wright and Zora Neale Hurston: Notes Toward a Balancing of Love and Hatred." *Black World*, 23, No. 10 (August 1974), 4-8.

Believes that Wright's status as a literary giant does not separate him that greatly from Hurston who wrote, in *Their Eyes Were Watching God*, a novel of affirmation. Her work is not antipathetic to Wright's *Native Son*, which conforms to white standards (while Hurston creates her own). But both novels reveal black life and, therefore, one should not attempt to choose between the two since black protest (Wright) and black affirmation (Hurston) are both a part of black life.

336.   Love, Theresa R. "Zora Neale Hurston's America." *Papers on Language & Literature*, 12, No. 4 (Fall 1976), 422-37.

Hurston's use of folk tales, black dialect, and legends from the Caribbean are examined--stressing Hurston's belief that the black past and present were fused through a commonality of feeling, belief, and vision. Although it is stressed that Hurston was well grounded in anthropology and had an academic background in folklore in addition to her personal one, it is suggested that Hurston emphasized the artistic, imaginative side of her nature rather than the intellectual.

337.   Neal, Larry. "Eatonville's Zora Neale Hurston: A Profile." *Black Review No. 2*. New York: William Morrow, 1972. Pp. 11-24.

Deplores the lack of recognition Hurston was receiving, especially in view of her authentic use of folklore and the influence of the black church in her writing, which "gave her a slight edge on some of her contemporaries."

This article also appeared in *Southern Exposure*
(Winter 1974).

338.   Pratt, Theodore. "A Memoir--Zora Neale Hurston--
         Florida's First Distinguished Author." *Negro
         Digest* (February 1962), 52-56.

         Praises her personality and writing. Emphasizes her
         personality traits, although one is suspicious of his
         knowledge since he describes her as "black as coal,"
         which the picture accompanying the article disproves.
         Still, this is one of the earliest reappraisals of
         Hurston, at a time when she had fallen into oblivion
         with other Renaissance writers.

339.   Rambeau, James. "The Fiction of Zora Neale Hurston."
         The Markham Review, 5 (Summer 1976), 61-64.

         Describes the life of Hurston and her writings,
         indicating that her experiences--especially her early
         life in the all-Negro town of Eatonville, Florida--
         made her writing dramatically different from the more
         numerous urban-oriented black writers of the 1920s.
         Also sees Hurston as avoiding the pitfalls of a black
         aestheticism that homogenized the race and imitated
         white life, by her skillful adaptation of the unique
         black idiom to normal human situations.

*   Rollins College. (See item 795.)

*   Rosenblatt, Roger. *Black Fiction*. (See item 47.)

*   Royster, Beatrice Horn. "The Ironic Vision of Four
         Black Women Novelists." (See item 889.)

340.   Schwalbenberg, Peter. "Time As Point of View in
         Zora Neale Hurston's *Their Eyes Were Watching God*."
         Negro American Literature Forum, 10, No. 3 (Fall
         1976), 104-05, 107-08.

         Asserts that time, just as speech and description,
         creates a point of view in this novel. Hurston in
         this novel presents time as the rhythm of change--
         not a chronological phenomenon but something in
         terms of Janie's (the protagonist's) growing inner
         consciousness: she notes the passage of "real" time
         but senses the difference between time as event and
         time as experience. That is why time does not, in
         the end, make her old but young--because she is filled
         with an internal sense of energy and optimism.

*   Sheffey, Ruthe T. "Zora Neale Hurston." (See item 718.)

341.   Southerland, Ellease. "The Novelist-Anthropologist's Life/Words: Zora Neale Hurston." *Black World*, 23, No. 10 (August 1974), 20-30.

      Relates the details of Hurston's life, followed by a synopsis-description of each of Hurston's books.

      An article written to interest the reader in discovering the life and works of Hurston--not a critical assessment.

342.   Turner, Darwin T. "Zora Neale Hurston: The Wandering Minstrel," in his *In a Minor Chord: Three Afro-American Writers and Their Search for Identity*. Carbondale: Southern Illinois University Press, 1971. Pp. 89-120.

      Stresses how the personal life of Hurston--e.g., the white patronage, her political conservatism--adversely affected the quality of her writing. Because Hurston was restless, she failed to concentrate on her art as well as on her academic studies; thus, according to Turner, "she became neither an impeccable raconteur nor a scholar," although she deserves to be recognized for her humor and use of folklore in her works. The enigmatic quality of her personality is explored, but no definite assertion about the conflicting patterns of her conduct is given.

343.   Walker, Alice. "In Search of Zora Neale Hurston." *Ms.*, 3 (March 1975), 74-79, 85-87.

      Narrated in story-form, the search by this young writer for Hurston's unmarked grave displays humor, sorrow, love, and joy for Hurston and her spirit.

344.   Washington, Mary Helen. "The Black Woman's Search for Identity." *Black World* (August 1972), 68-75.

      Demonstrates how Janie, in Hurston's *Their Eyes Were Watching God*, has relationships with men that eventually lead her to find her true self and self-fulfillment through understanding her blackness and coming to terms with this primary aspect of her life.

J. Johnson, James Weldon (1871-1938)
  1. His Writings
    a. Novel

345.   *The Autobiography of an Ex-Coloured Man.* Boston:
Sherman, French & Co., 1912. Reprinted, with an
introduction by Carl Van Vechten, New York: Alfred
A. Knopf, 1927. Reprinted, New York: Alfred A.
Knopf, 1955, 1961. Reprinted, with an introduction
by John Hope Franklin, *Three Negro Classics*, New
York: Avon Books, 1965.

A mulatto narrates his own story about life among
both whites and blacks. He never demonstrates
traits of blackness, although he evinces some
desire in remaining in the Negro race because of
his interest in its folk music. He decides to pass,
however, when it is clear that he cannot stand the
pressure of belonging to an oppressed race.

Reviews: *Booklist*, 24 January 1928, p. 174; *The
Crisis*, 34, November 1927, p. 308: W.E.B. Du Bois;
The Dial, 84, February 1928, p. 163; *New Republic*,
53, 1 February 1928, p. 303; *N.Y.T. Book Review*, 16
October 1927, p. 14; *Opportunity*, 5, November 1927,
pp. 337-38: Alice Dunbar Nelson; *Pittsburgh* (Mo.)
Bulletin, 32, December 1927, p. 627; *The Spectator*,
140, 15 February 1928, p. 267; *Survey*, 59, 1 November
1927, p. 164; *Times* (London) *Literary Supplement*, 22
March 1928, p. 207.

b. Poetry

346.   *God's Trombones: Seven Negro Sermons in Verse.* New
York: Viking Press, 1927. Viking Compass Edition:
1969.

The poems Johnson used to demonstrate use of Negro
idiom in place of dialect, as well as to capture the
spirit of the "old-time Negro preacher," who Johnson
felt was passing into history. Contains the two
best-known of Johnson's poems--"The Creation" and
"Go Down Death."

Reviews: *Booklist*, 24, December 1927, p. 110; *Bookman*,
65, August 1927, p. 718: H.B. Benjamin; *Bookman*, 66,
October 1927, p. 221: Countee Cullen; *Boston
Transcript*, 30 July 1927, p. 2; *Catholic World*, 126,

November 1927: C.J.Q.; *Chicago Defender*, 25 June 1927:
Elmer Gertz; *Chicago Defender*, 6 August 1927: Mary
White Ovington; *Cleveland Open Shelf*, December 1927,
p. 133; *The Crisis*, 34, July 1927, p. 159: W.E.B.
Du Bois; *The Nation*, 124, 29 June 1927, p. 721:
H.A. Potamkin; *N.Y. Evening Post*, 6 August 1927,
p. 9: J.M. March; *N.Y.H.T. Books*, 5 June 1927, p. 3:
T. Munroe; *N.Y.T. Book Review*, 19 June 1927, p. 11;
N.Y. World, 19 June 1927, p. 8m; *Outlook*, 146, 6
July 1927, p. 319: Arthur Guiterman; *Pittsburgh* (Mo.)
Bulletin, 32, November 1927, p. 590; *Saturday Review of
Literature*, 3, 11 June 1927, p. 904; *Survey*, 58, 1
August 1927, p. 473; *Wisconsin Library Bulletin*, 23,
October 1927, p. 223; *World Tomorrow*, 10, October
1927, p. 427.

c. Other Writings

347.　*Along This Way*. New York: Viking Press, 1933, c1961.

The autobiography of Johnson, reflecting his genteel,
gentle, and overly-modest manner, is a history, in
great part, of his times--although the Harlem
Renaissance period does not occupy much space here.
Talks about *Nigger Heaven*, and his opinion of Van
Vechten. Also writes about McKay, and mentions
other Renaissance artists, such as Nella Larsen
and Jessie Fauset.

Reviews: *American Journal of Sociology*, May 1935:
Robert E. Park; *Chicago Defender*, 27 January 1934:
Dewey R. Jones; *Greenwich Villager*, 1 December 1933:
Joe Gould; *Kansas City American*, 12 October 1933: Mary
White Ovington; *N.Y. Amsterdam News*, 1 November 1933:
Theophilus Lewis; *N.Y. Herald Tribune*, 2 October 1933;
N.Y.H.T. Books, 1 October 1933; *N.Y.T. Book Review*,
15 October 1933; *N.Y. World Telegram*, 2 October 1933:
Harry Hansen; *Norfolk Journal and Guide*, 17 March
1934: D.A. Steward; *Saturday Review of Literature*,
23 December 1933: Oswald Garrison Villard.

*　Atlanta University. (See item 780.)

348.　*Black Manhattan*. New York: Alfred Knopf, 1930.
Reprinted, New York: Atheneum, 1968.

A full history of Harlem: the Renaissance is
discussed in Chapter 19, although from Chapter 14

on pertinent information about its setting and
social situation is given. Is favorable and
optimistic toward artists like McKay and Cullen,
and clearly applauds the interest writers have in
racial experiences. States pride in the number of
books that have been produced by "writers of the
Harlem group." General tone of optimism ignores the
slum that was developing during the late 1920s.

Reviews: *Bookman*, 30 August 1930: Louise Rich; *Boston
Chronicle*, 26 July 1930; *Boston Herald*, 19 July 1930;
N.Y.T. Book Review, 27 July 1930: John Chamberlain.

*   *The Book of American Negro Poetry*. (See item 771.)

*   "The Dilemma of the Negro Author." (See item 129.)

*   "Harlem: The Cultural Capital." (See item 130.)

*   "Negro Authors and White Publishers." (See item 661.)

349.   "Race Prejudice and the Negro Artist." *Harper's
         Magazine*, 157 (November 1928), 769-76.

         States that opinions about Negroes have always
         shifted with the times. Believes there is a new
         attitude of openness to Negro culture--for example,
         its music (the spirituals as well as jazz). There
         is a great awakening to what Negroes have to offer.
         The significance of this is two-fold: the Negro is
         making a different and distinctive contribution to
         American culture, and the status of the Negro has
         changed. Because Negroes have achieved real changes
         in their condition, attitudes should change (and
         most likely will, because of the new interest in
         black culture).

                    2. Writings About Him

350.   Adelman, Lynn. "A Study of James Weldon Johnson."
         The Journal of Negro History, 52, No. 2 (April
         1967), 128-45.

         Substantial biographical information, chronological
         in order, concentrating on social and political
         activities, although his literature is discussed
         briefly and his theory concerning the use of dialect
         in creative literature is explained.

351.   Baker, Houston [A.].   "A Forgotten Prototype: *The
         Autobiography of an Ex-Colored* [sic] *Man* and
         Invisible Man," in his *Singers of Daybreak.*
         Washington, D.C.: Howard University Press,
         1974. Pp. 17-31.

         Sees parallels between Johnson's early novel (1912;
         reissued 1927) and Ellison's in terms of the narrators'
         sensibilities and their search for freedom in a
         white-controlled world. Some symbols parallel one
         another as well--such as the gold piece in *Auto-
         biography* and the briefcase in *Invisible.*

         This article appeared originally in *Virginia Quarterly
         Review* (Summer 1973).

*   Baker, Ruth Taylor.   "The Philosophy of the New Negro."
         (See item 806.)

*   Barksdale, Howard Reed.   "James Weldon Johnson as a
         Man of Letters."   (See item 808.)

*   Bronz, Stephen.   *Roots of Negro Racial Consciousness.*
         (See item 226.)

352.   Carroll, Richard A.   "Black Racial Spirit: An Analysis
         of James Weldon Johnson's Critical Perspective."
         Phylon, 32 (Winter 1971), 344-64.

         Although Johnson was accused of being "chauvinistic"
         and exaggerated in his praise of black artists, his
         integrity was never questioned. He felt blacks had
         made significant contributions to American culture
         and had unique features to contribute to forms of
         literature yet to be developed by black writers.
         The racial spirit had to be expressed, but in
         language and in form that would free it from
         restrictions and give the literature greater range
         in emotion and readership appeal.

*   Clark, Peter W.   "A Study of the Poetry of James
         Weldon Johnson."   (See item 823.)

353.   Collier, Eugenia [W.].   "The Endless Journey of an
         Ex-Coloured Man."   *Phylon*, 32 (Winter 1971), 365-73.

         Johnson's novel penetrates but does not solve
         ("literature does not solve problems") the theme of
         the dual heritage of black Americans. He does lay
         bare the frequent desire of blacks to escape their

blackness. As such, the story is psychologically strong and valid, inasmuch as the novel transcends the time in which it was written.

354.   ————. "James Weldon Johnson: Mirror of Change." *Phylon*, 21, No. 4 (Fourth Quarter 1960), 351-59.

Traces Johnson's influence in advancing the change in literature from dialect to idiomatic language that captured the sound and spirit of common black folk.

355.   Copans, Sim J. "James Weldon Johnson et le patrimoine culturel des noirs africains." *Cahiers de la Compagnie Madeleine Renaud-Jean Louis Barrault*, 61 (1967), 42-48.

Article not seen by author.

*   Copeland, George Edward. "James Weldon Johnson." (See item 827.)

*   Crawford, Lucille Hayes. "Musical Activities of James Weldon Johnson." (See item 829.)

*   Davis, Arthur P. *From the Dark Tower*. (See item 36.)

356.   Davis, Charles T. "The Heavenly Voice of the Black American," in *Anagogic Qualities of Literature*, ed. Joseph P. Strelka. University Park: Pennsylvania State University Press, 1971. Pp. 107-19.

Contends that the folk sermon is an art form and demonstrates how James Weldon Johnson adopts this form to produce his group of poems, *God's Trombones*. He moves close to the emotional center, however, by eliminating some of the framework the real preacher would use in a sermon.

357.   Fleming, Robert E. "Contemporary Themes in Johnson's *Autobiography of an Ex-Coloured Man*." *Negro American Literature Forum*, 4 (Winter 1970), 120-24, 141.

Johnson established the use of the blues in fiction, used by such later novelists as Ellison and Baldwin. He used other subjects and devices that also become part of the Afro-American literary tradition (e.g., "the nameless protagonist, racial self-hatred, the black mother, and the white patron/white liberal."

358.   ————. "Irony as a Key to Johnson's *The Autobiography*
            of an Ex-Coloured Man." *American Literature,* 43
            (March 1971), 83-96.

            Too often a sociological rather than literary reading
            is given this book: there is a dual level of meaning
            in the narrator's story, for what he says and what
            he reveals about his character are subtly different
            because of Johnson's perceptive art. The narrator
            is naive and misinterprets the significance of his
            actions. Johnson points the way toward developing
            the tradition of a more complex Afro-American novel.

359.   Gallagher, Buell G. "James Weldon Johnson: Man of
            Letters." *Crisis,* 78, No. 4 (Winter 682) (June
            1971), 119-22.

            Called a realist as well as a poet, James Weldon
            Johnson is described as a man whose writing reveals
            his personal integrity. Describes very briefly
            rather than assesses his major creative works--
            God's Trombones and *Autobiography of an Ex-Coloured
            Man.*

360.   Garrett, Marvin P. "Early Recollections and
            Structural Irony in *The Autobiography of an Ex-
            Colored* [sic] *Man.*" *Critique,* 13, No. 2 (1971), 5-14.

            Explores the behavioral pattern of the unnamed
            protagonist and concludes he was untrustworthy,
            self-centered, and that his behavior is part of the
            irony intended by the author.

*   Gear, Alice J. "Career and Writing of James Weldon
            Johnson." (See item 842.)

*   Graham, James D. "Negro Protest in America."
            (See item 642.)

*   Grissom, Ruby M. "Contribution of the Negro to
            American Literature." (See item 845.)

361.   Jackson, Miles, Jr. "James Weldon Johnson." *Black
            World,* 19, No. 8 (June 1970), 32-34.

            Chronicles Johnson's life as a writer, excerpting at
            length his personal letters.

362.   ————. "Literary History: Documentary Sidelights:
            James Weldon Johnson and Claude McKay." *Negro*
            Digest, 17 (June 1968), 25-29.

            Cites J.W. Johnson's interest in the work of McKay
            and his help to the writer--monetarily and also in
            helping McKay to get back into the United States
            when he was having difficulties with American
            officials over his status. Includes many letters
            from Johnson to McKay, revealing Johnson's view of
            McKay's work as well as discussing Johnson's efforts
            to keep the author in the public view.

363.   Kostelanetz, Richard. "The Politics of Passing:
            The Fiction of James Weldon Johnson." *Negro American*
            Literature Forum, 3 (March 1969), 22-24, 29.

            Although Johnson uses the old theme of the fate of
            the tragic mulatto he adds to the tradition by
            utilizing black music--the blues, which symbolizes
            the plight of the black person who appears to be white.

364.   Long, Richard A. "A Weapon of My Song: The Poetry of
            James Weldon Johnson." *Phylon*, 32 (Winter 1971),
            374-82.

            States that Johnson's poetry falls into four group-
            ings: standard English, dialect tradition, "folk-
            inspired free verse, and a long satirical poem."
            Because Johnson revised his poetry, one must study
            various texts and publications of his poems. Also
            sees Johnson as advancing from a more timid,
            accommodationist tone to one of some militancy,
            with propagandistic overtones.

*   Miller, Ruth, and Peter J. Katopes. "The Harlem
            Renaissance." (See item 14.)

*   Newman, Anne E. "Contemporary Southern Literature."
            (See item 880.)

365.   O'Sullivan, Maurice J. "Of Souls and Pottage: James
            Weldon Johnson's *The Autobiography of an Ex-Coloured*
            Man." *CLA Journal*, 23, No. 1 (September 1979), 60-70.

            Sees a resolution to the protagonist's character and
            the choice he makes at the end of the novel as both
            impossible to judge: the unnatural protagonist found
            his state of existence "belittling"; however, Johnson
            also narrates the story in a manner that discourages

the reader from judging the ex-coloured man. The
ambivalence with which the reader and narrator are
faced comes from "the fear of self-knowledge" on the
part of the narrator, whose final choice does not
resolve this problem either for himself or the reader.

*   Redding, J. Saunders. *To Make a Poet Black*. (See
item 46.)

*   Rosenberg, Harold. "Truth and the Academic Style."
(See item 205.)

*   Rosenblatt, Roger. *Black Fiction*. (See item 47.)

366.   Ross, Stephen M. "Audience and Irony in Johnson's
The Autobiography of an Ex-Coloured Man." *CLA
Journal*, 28, No. 2 (December 1974), 198-210.

Suggests that Johnson's ironic story is directed at
the white audience in order to stress betrayal by the
white system of values that the hero finds impossible
to give up. Thus, the reader as well as the narrator
is faced with his tragedy of the divided self, the
"genuine tragedy ... [of a] mulatto trapped by
white values."

*   Sukho, Emilie. "Les Afro-Americains à la recherche
de leur identité." (See item 899.)

367.   Vauthier, Simone. "The Interplay of Narrative Modes
in James Weldon Johnson's *The Autobiography of an
Ex-Coloured Man*." *Jahrbuch für Amerikastudien*, 10
(1973), [173]-81.

Article not seen. Mentioned in Fleming book (see
item 1).

368.   Wagner, Jean. "James Weldon Johnson," in his *Black
Poets of the United States from Paul Laurence Dunbar
to Langston Hughes*. Urbana: University of Illinois
Press, 1973. Pp. 351-84.

Believes that most of Johnson's poetry is marked by
convention and is not in concert with the spirit of
the Renaissance. Only *God's Trombones* rises above
the ordinary; it is a set of verses where he
experiments with the English language, in the manner
of the Irish nationalist John M. Synge. Here, Johnson
succeeds in eschewing black dialect but still creates
in standard English the tone and feeling of the
black preacher.

369.   Wohlforth, Robert.   "Profiles: Dark Leader--James
        Weldon Johnson." *New Yorker*, 9 (30 September
        1933), 21-26.

        Describes Johnson's occupations, achievements, and
        other biographical information, but does mention
        literary pursuits and calls *The Autobiography of an
        Ex-Coloured Man* "the forerunner of the renaissance
        in colored literature."

*   Yale University. (See item 798.)

                K. Larsen, Nella (?1893-?1963)
                1. Her Writings (Selected)
                   a. Novels

370.   *Passing*. New York: Alfred A. Knopf, 1929.   Reprinted,
        New York: Macmillan, 1971.

        Story of Clare Kendry, a woman who passes, and of
        her double life among friends in Harlem and with her
        husband, who despises Negroes and who jokingly calls
        her "Nig," because of her swarthy complexion. The
        conflicts of Clare's life come to a dramatic end
        when these two worlds come face to face.

        Reviews: *Bookman*, June 1929: Esther Hyman; *The Crisis*,
        36, July 1929, p. 234: W.E.B. Du Bois; *N.Y. Amsterdam
        News*, 5 June 1929: Aubrey Bowser; *N.Y. News*, 28
        September 1929; *N.Y. Sun*, 1 May 1929; *Opportunity*, 7
        August 1929, p. 255: Mary Fleming Labaree; *Saturday
        Review of Literature*, 18 May 1929: W.B. Seabrook;
        Wilson Library Bulletin, December 1929: M.L.H.

371.   *Quicksand*. New York: Alfred A. Knopf, 1929.
        Reprinted, New York: Macmillan, 1971.

        A "tragic mulatto" story about Helga Crane who
        searches for happiness in Harlem and Denmark and
        then decides--precipitously--that religion and a
        greasy minister are what will give her this happiness.
        The sensual side of this woman's nature is emphasized
        in this novel, unlike most of the Harlem Renaissance
        novels which treat bourgeoise women with idealistic
        reverence.

        Reviews: *Annals of the American Academy of Social
        and Political Science*, 140, November 1928, p. 345:
        K.S. Hayden; *Boston Transcript*, 20 June 1928, p. 2;

Chicago Defender, 25 August 1928: Barefield Gordon;
Christian Century, 18 October 1928: E. Merrill Root;
Cleveland Open Shelf, July 1928, p. 91; *The Crisis*,
35, June 1928, p. 202: W.E.B. Du Bois; *Harlem*, 1,
1928: Wallace Thurman; *The Nation*, 126, 9 May 1928,
p. 540: A.B. Parsons; *The Nation and Athenaeum*, 43,
23 June 1928, p. 397: Raymond Mortimer; *New Republic*,
55, 30 May 1928, p. 50: T.S. Matthews; *New Statesman*,
31, 2 June 1928, p. 260: G.W.K.; *N.Y. Amsterdam
News*, 16 May 1928; *N.Y.H.T. Books*, 13 May 1928, p 22:
Roark Bradford; *N.Y.T. Book Review*, 8 April 1928,
p. 16; *Pittsburgh* (Mo.) *Bulletin*, 33, June 1928,
p. 321; *Pittsburgh Courier*, 26 May 1928: Ruth L.
Yates; *Saturday Review of Literature*, 4, 19 May 1928,
p. 896; *Times* (London) *Literary Supplement*, 26 July
1928, p. 553; *World Tomorrow*, 11, November 1928,
p. 474.

b. Short Story

372.   "Sanctuary." *Forum*, 83 (January 1930), 15-18.

Short story, which she was later accused of having
plagiarized. (This was not the case, and an explanation appeared in a later edition of the magazine in
April 1930.)

2. Writings About Her

*   Bone, Robert. *The Negro Novel in America*. (See
         item 32.)

*   Davis, Arthur P. *From the Dark Tower*. (See item 36.)

*   Jacobs, George W. "Negro Authors Must Eat."
         (See item 651.)

*   Mootry, Maria Katella. "Studies in Black Pastoral."
         (See item 876.)

*   Perry, Margaret. *Silence to the Drums*. (See item 153.)

*   Sato, Hiroko. "Under the Harlem Shadow." (See
         item 256.)

*   Singh, Amritjit. *The Novels of the Harlem
         Renaissance*. (See item 160.)

373.   Thornton, Hortense E. "Sexism and Quagmire: Nella
        Larsen's *Quicksand.*" *CLA Journal*, 16, No. 3
        (March 1973), 285-301.

        Argues that the tragic mulatto aspect of this novel
        has been stressed too much and that the issue of
        sexism is also important, perhaps more so than the
        racial problems that are in the novel. Most male
        critics have not been aware of this (cites Du Bois
        as an exception). Therefore, the main character of
        Quicksand, Helga Crane, is really oppressed by sexual
        exploitation in addition to suffering within the racist
        system faced by all blacks at that time.

374.   Youman, Mary Mabel. "Nella Larsen's *Passing*: A Study
        in Irony." *CLA Journal*, 28, No. 2 (December 1974),
        235-41.

        Provides the theory that this novel is really about
        the rejection of black values by a black living in
        her own world, Irene Redfield. The book is narrated
        by Irene and is therefore the story of her loss of
        black values and traits rather than Clare Kendry's
        story of passing, as most would have it.

                L. McKay, Claude (1890-1948)
                    1. His Writings (Selected)
                        a. Poetry

375.   *Harlem Shadows*. New York: Harcourt, Brace & Co., 1922.

        His first book of poetry to be published in the U.S.,
        and containing most of the poems from his *Spring in
        New Hampshire and Other Poems*. His themes of
        nostalgia and his anti-metropolis spirit are displayed
        in these verses.

        Reviews: *Booklist*, 18, July 1922, p. 357; *Bookman*,
        July 1922, p. 531: W.F. White; *Detroit News*, 16 July
        1922, p. 7: Stirling Rowen; *Independent*, 109, 5
        August 1922, p. 54: Arthur Guiterman; *Literary
        Review*, 21 October 1922, p. 127: Clement Wood; *The
        Nation*, 114, 7 June 1922, p. 694: W.F. White; *New
        Republic*, 31, 12 July 1922, p. 196: Robert Littell;
        N.Y.H.T. Books, 7 May 1922, p. 8: Rex Hunter; *N.Y.T.
        Book Review*, 14 May 1922, p. 17; *Pratt Institute
        Quarterly*, Winter 1923, p. 27; *Wisconsin Library
        Bulletin*, 18, July 1922, p. 182.

b. Fiction

376.   *Banana Bottom.* New York: Harper & Bros., 1933.

Placed in Jamaica, story of Bita, a native girl who is
put in the care of white missionaries. Despite their
educating her to English ways, she chooses to marry
a native and live as one (symbolizing the primitive
life over one that adopts Western ways).

Reviews: *Boston Transcript*, 5 April 1933, p. 2;
The Nation, 136, 17 May 1933, p. 564; *N.Y. Amsterdam
News*, 22 March 1933: N.A.G.; *N.Y.H.T. Books*, 2
April 1933, p. 5: Mary Ross; *N.Y.T. Book Review*, 2
April 1933, p. 16; *N.Y. World Telegram*, 30 March
1933: C. Hartley Grattan; *Opportunity*, 11, July 1933,
pp. 217, 222: Sterling A. Brown; *Saturday Review of
Literature*, 9, 8 April 1933, p. 529.

377.   *Banjo: A Story Without a Plot.* New York: Harper &
Bros., 1929. Reprinted, New York: Harcourt Brace
and Co., 1957.

Story of a black, happy-go-lucky vagabond's life
among the drifters who live along the waterfront of
Marseilles during the 1920s; his friend, Ray, is
his antithesis (and resembles the author), an
intellectual in search of himself, a man who
articulates McKay's disillusionment with the
Harlem Renaissance.

Reviews: *Afro-American* (Baltimore), 27 April 1929:
James Waldo Ivy; *Bookman*, 69, May 1929, p. 311: R.S.
Bailey; *Chicago Defender*, 13 July 1929: Dennis A.
Bethea; *The Crisis*, 36, July 1929, p. 234: W.E.B.
Du Bois; *The Nation*, 128, 22 May 1929, p. 614: Freda
Kirchwey; *N.Y. Amsterdam News*, 8 May 1929: Aubrey
Bowser; *N.Y.H.T. Books*, 12 May 1929, p. 7: Clifford
McGuinness; *N.Y.T. Book Review*, 12 May 1929, p. 8;
N.Y. World, 9 June 1929, p. 7m: Walter White;
Opportunity, 7, August 1929, p. 287: Gwendolyn B.
Bennett: *Outlook*, 152, 19 June 1929, p. 311: W.R.
Brooks; *Saturday Review of Literature*, 6, 27 July
1929, p. 2: H.W. Odum; *Times* (London) *Literary
Supplement*, 27 June 1929, p. 512.

377a.   *Gingertown*. New York: Harper & Bros., 1932.

          Collection of short stories, set both in New York
          and in the West Indies.

          Reviews: *Bookman*, 75, May 1932, p. v; *Boston
          Transcript*, 30 March 1932, p. 2; *The Nation*, 135,
          10 August 1932, p. 130; *N.Y. Amsterdam News*, 23
          March 1932: N.G.; *N.Y. Herald Tribune*, 25 March
          1932: Lewis Gannett; *N.Y.H.T. Books*, 27 March 1932,
          p. 3: Rudolph Fisher; *N.Y. Post*, 24 March 1932: John
          Cournos; *N.Y.T. Book Review*, 3 April 1932, p. 7;
          Times (London) *Literary Supplement*, 12 May 1932,
          p. 352.

378.   *Home to Harlem*. New York: Harper, 1928.

          Novel about Jake, an ordinary Harlemite home from
          World War I (AWOL from the "white man's war"), who
          moves through this shapeless tale in search of an
          unknown girl to whom he is attracted on his first
          night home.

          Reviews: *Annals of the American Academy of Social
          and Political Science*, 140, November 1928, p. 339:
          D.L. Hunt; *Bookman*, 67, April 1928, p. 183: Burton
          Rascoe; *Boston Transcript*, 24 March 1928, p. 3;
          Chicago Daily Tribune, 9 June 1928, p. 14: R.S.
          Abbott; *Chicago Defender*, 17 March 1928: Dewey R.
          Jones; *The Nation*, 126, 28 March 1928, p. 351: Mark
          Van Doren; *The Nation and Athenaeum*, 43, 23 June 1928,
          p. 397: Raymond Mortimer; *New Republic*, 55, 30 May
          1928, p. 50: T.S. Matthews; *New Statesman*, 31, 18
          August 1928, p. 591: Cyril Connolly; *N.Y. Amsterdam
          News*, 21 March 1928: Aubrey Bowser; *N.Y. Evening Post*,
          21 April 1928, p. 12: R.C. Holliday; *N.Y.H.T. Books*,
          11 March 1928, p. 5: G.B. Bennett; *N.Y. Times*, 24
          June 1928, p. 2: J.R. Chamberlain; *N.Y.T. Book
          Review*, 11 March 1928, p. 5: J.R. Chamberlain; *N.Y.
          World*, 11 March 1928, p. 11m: Abbe Niles; *Norfolk
          Journal and Guide*, 21 April 1928: Thomas W. Young;
          Opportunity, 6, May 1928, pp. 151-52: Herschel
          Brickell; *Outlook*, 148, 18 April 1928, p. 636;
          Philadelphia Tribune, 18 March 1928: Arthur A.
          Schomburg; *Pittsburgh Courier*, 17 March 1928;
          Saturday Review of Literature, 146, 18 April 1928,
          p. 218: L.P. Hartley; *Springfield Republican*, 25
          March 1928, p. 7f; *Survey*, 60, 1 May 1928, p. 178:
          Leon Whipple; *Times* (London) *Literary Supplement*,
          12 July 1928, p. 518.

379.   *Trial By Lynching: Stories About Negro Life in*
        North America. Translated from the Russian by
        Robert Winter. Edited and Introduced by A.L.
        McLeod. N.p., typescript, 1975. (The published
        copy, according to Mr. McLeod, can be obtained by
        writing to the Center for Commonwealth Literature,
        University of Mysore, Mysore, India.)

        Three short stories written by McKay when he was in
        Russia, translated and published in Russian in 1925.
        This edition is the first one to appear in English.
        The stories, awkward in structure and language, are
        entitled: "Trial By Lynching," "The Mulatto Girl,"
        "The Soldier's Return." McKay's concern for justice
        is apparent in the stories, despite the technical
        weaknesses.

                    c. Other Writings

*   Atlanta University. (See item 780.)

*   Howard University. (See item 789.)

*   Indiana University. (See item 790.)

380.   *A Long Way from Home.* New York: Lee Furman, 1937.
        Reprinted, New York: Harcourt Brace & World, 1970.

        Biography that covers his early life, his publications,
        and his travels. Talks about his feud with Alain
        Locke over the poem "The White House" (on pp. 313-14).
        The chapter "On Belonging to a Minority Group"
        expresses the differences he had with native-born
        Afro-American writers and cultural leaders.

*   New York Public Library. (See item 793.)

*   Yale University. (See item 798.)

                    2. Writings About Him

*   Baker, Ruth Taylor. "The Philosophy of the New
        Negro." (See item 806.)

381.   Barksdale, Richard K. "Symbolism and Irony in
        McKay's *Home to Harlem*." *CLA Journal*, 15, No. 3
        (March 1972), 338-44.

        Suggests there is a pattern of exploring the conflict
        between order and disorder and that Jake, the happy-
        go-lucky hero, symbolizes a fusion of the two and
        becomes "a spokesman for social cohesion and racial
        solidarity." Rejects, therefore, the notion that
        Home to Harlem is simply episodic and without design.

382.   Blary, Liliane. "Claude McKay and Black Nationalist
        Ideologies (1934-1948)," in *Myth and Ideology in
        American Culture*, ed. Régis Durand. Lille, France:
        University of Lille, 1976. Pp. 211-31.

        Back from Europe, where he spent his time during the
        whole of the Harlem Renaissance, McKay moves from his
        1920s view of extreme race consciousness to that of
        acknowledging the pluralistic quality of American
        society: this meant, therefore, that Negroes would
        have to work within the framework of existing
        institutions while still maintaining a group spirit.
        The heart of this spirit should be centered on the
        masses, who would be given direction by the
        intellectuals. The end result would be greater
        acknowledgment, also, of the Negro's rightful
        place in society, leading to a period that would
        be "transmuted into the finer sense of belonging
        to the human race."

*   ————. "Claude McKay, 1889-1948." (See item 813.)

*   Brawley, Benjamin. *The Negro Genius*. (See item 33.)

*   Bronz, Stephen. *Roots of Negro Racial Consciousness*.
        (See item 226.)

*   Carty, Wilfred. "Four Shadows of Harlem." (See
        item 292.)

*   Christian, Barbara. "Spirit Bloom in Harlem."
        (See item 822.)

383.   Collier, Eugenia W. "The Four-Way Dilemma of Claude
        McKay." *CLA Journal*, 15, No. 3 (March 1972), 345-53.

        Sees the themes of McKay's poetry as central to
        understanding him, and suggests four that run through

most of his work: living distant from his native
home; the dual self--African and American; the
double-consciousness of being a black in a white
society; and the paradox of living in a society
that expresses a dream that it tries to deny to
black people.

384.   Condit, John Hillyer. "An Urge Toward Wholeness:
         Claude McKay and His Sonnets." *CLA Journal*, 22,
         No. 4 (June 1979), 350-64.

         Argues through the use of McKay's sonnets that he
         transcends the concerns and interests of any
         particular decade and must be assessed in an
         overall sense: he desired unity of self, and this
         was difficult with his alienated feelings; yet,
         throughout, his integrity is evident in his work.
         Notes faulty interpretations of McKay's poetry by
         such critics as Littlejohn (see item 44) and Giles
         (see item 390).

*   Conroy, Sr. M. James. "Claude McKay." (See item 825.)

385.   Conroy, Mary. "The Vagabond Motif in the Writings
         of Claude McKay." *Negro American Literature Forum*,
         5 (1971), 15-23.

         Sees the restlessness of McKay portrayed in his work
         in three aspects of vagabondage: sexual, psychological,
         and religious. And undergirding his novels are
         picaresque features, most noticeably the open-ended
         quality of the conclusions of his books (and the
         irresolute life of his "heroes").

*   Cooper, Wayne. "Claude McKay." (See item 826.)

386.   ————. "Claude McKay and the New Negro of the 1920's."
         Phylon, 25, No. 3 (Third Quarter 1964), 297-306.

         Stresses that the cleavage between McKay and his
         contemporaries was his older age, his absence from
         the United States during the Harlem Renaissance, and
         his rejection of polite, black bourgeois society.
         Indicates, also, the distinction McKay made between
         his prose and poetry, emphasizing the common black
         milieu in prose, writing in a traditional, restrained
         mode in poetry. Believes McKay's poetry, rather than
         his novels, will be his literary legacy.

387.   ————, and Robert C. Reinders. "Claude McKay in
         England, 1920." *New Beacon Reviews*. Edited by John
         La Rose. London: New Beacon Books, 1968.

         Contends that McKay epitomized the disillusioned,
         disaffected colonial who could not find himself even
         among sympathizers and radicals who espoused his
         beliefs. Describes McKay's acquaintances (e.g.,
         E. Pankhurst) and his work in England; in particular,
         discusses the articles he wrote concerning racism,
         labor, and the radical scene during his brief sojourn
         there. Concludes that England helped to mold the
         anti-Western, anti-caucasian value system that
         McKay expresses in his writings.

         First published in *Race*, 9 (1967): Institute of Race
         Relations, London.

388.   Drayton, Arthur D. "McKay's Human Pity: A Note on His
         Protest Poetry." *Black Orpheus*, 17 (June 1965), 39-48.

         Does not see hatred in McKay's protest poetry; instead,
         believes he was writing a defiant call for human
         dignity to be respected. McKay expresses a social
         consciousness that extends beyond racial boundaries.
         Early in his life McKay identified with the common
         people, and this made him sensitive to their sorrows
         as well as their joys. The indignities inflicted
         upon his race represent self-violence by whites;
         therefore, his voice cried out for all mankind to
         respect one another. "His human pity was the
         foundation that made all this possible."

*   [Editorial] "Claude McKay Before the Internationale."
         (See item 595.)

*   [Editorial] "Claude McKay--'If We Must Die.'"
         (See item 596.)

389.   Fabre, Michel. "Aesthetics and Ideology in *Banjo*,"
         in *Myth and Ideology in American Culture*, ed. Régis
         Durand. Lille, France: University of Lille,
         1976. Pp. 195-209.

         McKay was further in his outlook from American writers
         than is usually thought. As he was writing *Banjo*,
         he was careful to balance the black-white situation
         in the book because he was sensitive to white racial
         ideology. By setting the novel in one place, McKay
         maintained his first intention to use the Vieux Port

in Marseilles as the background; moreover, it helped
him to keep a flavor, the atmosphere he wanted for
the book. Finally, in remembering his audience,
McKay made some aesthetic choices in order to
gain and keep this audience.

390.   Giles, James. *Claude McKay*. Boston: Twayne
        Publishers, 1976.

After a biographical overview, McKay's writings are
examined according to genre, first poetry and then
the novels; a later chapter discusses his stories
from *Gingertown*, which are said to be uneven in
quality; finally, the biographical and sociological
books of non-fiction--*A Long Way from Home* and
Harlem: Negro Metropolis--are examined.

Chapter 1 (pp. 15-40)--"The Renaissance, Jamaica,
the Party, and the Church": McKay, who was closer
physically to the "lost generation" group than to
his black peers, never involved himself closely with
either black or white artists because of his complex
views of art and culture. He drew from his African
heritage but did not repudiate the European culture,
since he didn't believe in cultural isolation. In
sum, sees McKay as a Harlem Renaissance poet who
became established with the publication of *Harlem
Shadows* (1922), even though this poetry reveals only
one side of McKay's artistic credo.

*   Graham, James D. "Negro Protest in America."
        (See item 642.)

*   Hansell, William Howard. "Positive Themes in the
        Poetry of Four Negroes." (See item 847.)

*   Jackson, Miles, Jr. "Literary History." (See
        item 362.)

*   Johnson, Ralph Glassgow. "The Poetry of Dunbar and
        McKay." (See item 861.)

391.   Kaye, Jacqueline. "Claude McKay's 'Banjo.'"
        Présence Africaine, N.S. 73, 1st Quarterly (1970),
        165-69.

Explores McKay's "mythology of blackness." Contends
that his efforts to create genuine black characters
in contrast to blacks who had been corrupted by

white culture resulted in caricatures: in championing
the easy-going, simple, good-tempered Negro McKay
"puts black against white while inverting the values
of each" and ends up with another type whites can
denigrate. What McKay failed to do, then, is to go
further in his analysis of character, to go from
self-exploration to self-assertion as was done by
the writers of a later generation.

392.   Kent, George E. "Claude McKay's *Banana Bottom*
        Reappraised." *CLA Journal*, 28, No. 2 (December
        1974), 222-34.

        This last novel (1933) should still be considered as
        having a special place in Harlem Renaissance literature
        because it concerns a quest for identity among blacks
        facing Western ways and civilization.

393.   ————. "The Soulful Way of Claude McKay," in his
        Blackness and the Adventure of Western Culture.
        Chicago: Third World Press, 1972. Pp. 36-52.

        Sees McKay's response to existence as rooted in a
        natural black consciousness; yet agrees with Bronz
        (see item 226) that McKay remained an outsider to any
        group to which he gave allegiance. Shows how his
        writings reflect his complex mind, wherein he
        attempts--especially in his poetry--to speak to
        the needs and group consciousness of blacks, to set
        up "the ideal of the together soul."

394.   Lang, Phyllis Martin. "Claude McKay: Evidence of a
        Magic Pilgrimage." *CLA Journal*, 16, No. 4 (June
        1973), 475-84.

        Relates contents of interviews and articles of McKay
        in Russia during his trip there in 1922-23. McKay
        rails against color prejudice in America, the need
        for black leaders in America, and the absence of
        class consciousness among the black populace. Sees
        this period in McKay's life as one when he received
        adulation rather than rejection.

*   Larson, Charles R. "Three Novels of the Jazz Age."
        (See item 235.)

*   Lederer, Richard. "The Didactic and the Literary."
        (See item 236.)

395.   Lee, Robert A.   "On Claude McKay's 'If We Must Die.'"
        CLA Journal, 28, No. 2 (December 1974), 216-21.

        Believes a narrow, contextual reading of this poem
        should be given rather than reducing it to the universal
        idea of a poem about conflict between the oppressed
        and the oppressor. Should respect the uniqueness of
        the poem in racial terms, even if one then moves on
        to a universal application.

396.   Lewis, Rupert and Maureen.   "Claude McKay's Jamaica."
        Caribbean Quarterly, 23, Nos. 2 and 3 (June-September
        1977), 38-53.

        Although concentrating on McKay's island writings,
        the comments about his racial and class attitudes
        help to illuminate why McKay developed the strong
        social conscience that is evident in such Harlem
        Renaissance works as *Banjo*.

397.   Major, Clarence.   "Dear Jake and Ray."   *American
        Poetry Review*, 4 (1975), 40-42.

        Article not seen. Source states it is a discussion
        of three unpublished McKay manuscripts: "My Green
        Hills of Jamaica," "Romance in Marseilles," and
        "Harlem Glory."

*   Miller, Ruth, and Peter J. Kotopes.   "The Harlem
        Renaissance."   (See item 14.)

*   Morris, Horace Anthony.   "Claude McKay and His
        Native Jamaica."   (See item 877.)

*   Mott, Frank Luther.   "The Harlem Poets."   (See
        item 237.)

398.   Priebe, Richard.   "The Search for Community in the
        Novels of Claude McKay."   *Studies in Black Literature*,
        3, No. 2 (Summer 1972), 22-30.

        A stable life, one in a definite place or setting, is
        desired by McKay characters and pervades his novels.
        Even when one starts over again, such as Jake in
        Home to Harlem, he still represents "an individual
        struggling to assert his ethical sensibility within
        the dualistic world in which he must live." This
        same sort of struggle to belong in a world is seen
        also in *Banjo*, where a disparate group of persons
        is held together by Ray, a cohesive element in a

volatile world, one where there is conflict
between the cultures of the white and black races.

399.   Pyne-Timothy, Helen. "Claude McKay: Individualism
         and Group Consciousness," in *A Celebration of Black
         and African Writing*, ed. Bruce King and Kolawole
         Ogungbesan. Zaria: Ahmadu Bello University Press; and
         London: Oxford University Press, 1975. Pp. 15-29.

         McKay always identified with the poor black, the
         peasant class; and his work possesses propagandistic
         qualities, even in his earliest book of dialect
         poetry. He saw the main problem as the black person's
         trials in trying to live in a Westernized world. He
         remained a radical to the end, and continually sought
         relief for blacks through Socialism. Through group
         consciousness, then, the Negro would come to under-
         stand himself and develop values that would lead
         toward human understanding--all of this necessary
         for the black person's survival.

400.   ————. "Perceptions of the Black Woman in the Work
         of Claude McKay." *CLA Journal*, 19, No. 2 (December
         1975), 152-64.

         Investigates the various black women in McKay's
         fiction and suggests that Bita, in *Banana Bottom*,
         represents the best realized of his females because
         she understands both her environment and her need for
         union with a black male. Believes that McKay women
         generally give sustenance to men--sometimes
         economically as well as psychologically.

*   Redding, J. Saunders. *To Make a Poet Black*. (See
         item 46.)

*   Rosenblatt, Roger. *Black Fiction*. (See item 47.)

*   Singh, Amritjit. *The Novels of the Harlem
         Renaissance*. (See item 160.)

401.   Smith, Robert A. "Claude McKay: An Essay in
         Criticism." *Phylon*, 9, No. 3 (Third Quarter
         1948), 270-73.

         Believes McKay, who did not care to please whites
         and who wrote many protest poems, was successful in
         speaking out against racism and yet did not lose
         his lyricism in this type of poetry.

402.   Stoff, Michael B.   "Claude McKay and the Cult of
        Primitivism," in *The Harlem Renaissance Remembered*,
        ed. Arna Bontemps.   New York: Dodd, Mead & Co.,
        1972.   Pp. 126-46.

        Considers McKay's writing as an "aesthetique retreat
        into primitivism" as his means of artistically por-
        traying the liberated, uncompromised black.   Only in
        this way could the potency and power and true beauty of
        the black race be expressed.   His personal life, though,
        was the opposite of the free life he celebrated.

403.   Tolson, Melvin B.   "Claude McKay's Art."   *Poetry*, 83
        (February 1954), 287-90.

        Review of McKay's *Selected Poems*.   Sees McKay as an
        explorer of the plurality of his existence in a
        multifaceted world--black, white, ideologically
        radical at times, and nostalgic for his original
        homeland, Jamaica.   Represents a black poet who broke
        with the dialect world of Dunbar and became "the
        symbol of the New Negro and the Harlem Renaissance."

*   Turpin, Waters E.   "Four Short Fiction Writers of
        the Harlem Renaissance."   (See item 277.)

*   Van Mol, Kay R.   "Primitivism and Intellect."   (See
        item 498.)

404.   Wagner, Jean.   "Claude McKay," in his *Black Poets of
        the United States from Paul Laurence Dunbar to
        Langston Hughes*.   Urbana: University of Illinois
        Press, 1973.   Pp. 197-257.

        Stresses themes of McKay, and illustrates them with
        generous examples from his poetry.   The themes are:
        loyalty to the earth, the city as the enemy of land
        and the black person as well, racial pride, and
        hatred.   This latter is emphasized: "he, among all
        black poets, is *par excellence* the poet of hate."
        This hatred stems from the adjustment the poet had
        to make in a racially oppressive society.   Still, he
        is not an unabating hater or rebel; his love for
        nature is also dominant in his writings.   Argues
        that McKay looked back to his native Jamaica--not
        to Africa--for inspiration and also asserts he is
        not a Harlem poet because Harlem was not a place
        that could inspire his spiritual life.

405.   Warren, Stanley. "Claude McKay as an Artist."
        Negro History Bulletin, 40, No. 2 (March-April
        1977), 685-87.

        Generous excerpts from McKay letters explain his
        independent views, especially concerning changing
        the title of his poem "The White House" to "White
        Houses." Also letters to Max Eastman that explain
        McKay's resistance to changes in his writings about
        visiting Russia. Sees McKay as a visionary writer.

406.   —————. "A New Poem by Claude McKay." *Crisis*,
        85, No. 1 (January 1978), 33.

        Background information about a poem written in
        praise of B.T. Washington, whose death in 1915
        probably precipitated this outburst (although the
        poem is not dated here).

*   Worblewski, John E. "Claude McKay." (See item 911.)

                M. Richardson, Willis (1889-   )
                   1. His Writings (Selected)
                      a. Plays

407.   "Bootblack Lover." 1-Act Comedy. Typescript,
        Howard University, Moorland Room.

        A Horatio Alger-type ambitious bootblack overcomes a
        father's hostility to him, and he wins his girl.

408.   "The Banjo" (A Prize Play). *Crisis*, 31, No. 4
        (February 1926), 167-71; No. 5 (March 1926), 225-28.

        Some biographical information in the February issue
        (p. 167). A man turns against his friends who, in
        turn, reveal the man's secret (he murdered a man
        in self-defense).

409.   "The Chip Woman's Fortune" (1-Act Play) in *Black
        Theatre U.S.A.*, ed. James V. Hatch and Ted Shine.
        New York: The Free Press, 1974.

        A woman's savings for her son help the family with
        whom she has been living.

410.   "Peacock's Feathers." 1-Act Play. Typescript,
        Howard University, Moorland Room

        Love conquers social-class differences.

*   Howard University. (See item 789.)

*   New York Public Library. (See item 793.)

b. Other Writings

411.   "The Hope of Negro Drama." *Crisis*, 19, No. 1
          (November 1919), 338-39.

          Sees a need for plays that portray the Negro soul,
          not simply for having Negroes performing in plays.
          Compares the Negroes with the Irish and their
          National Theatre, and ends by expressing hope that
          liberal-minded people will demonstrate an interest
          in Negro plays and players.

*   Howard University. (See item 789.)

412.   "The Negro and the Stage." *Opportunity*, 2. No. 22
          (October 1924), 310.

          Laments the lack of plays and a theatre devoted
          exclusively to Negro drama, in comparison to what
          was being done in Jewish or Irish theatre.

413.   "A Negro Audience." *Opportunity*, 3, No. 28
          (April 1925), 123.

          Expresses the belief that the Negro audience is not
          yet ready to accept true Negro drama with an open
          mind, for too many people want idealized blacks on
          stage rather than ones who represent the common
          person. Ends with stating, however, that he expects
          true Negro drama to emerge one day.

*   New York Public Library. (See item 793.)

2. Writings About Him

*   Arata, Esther Spring, and Nicholas J. Rotoli. *Black
          American Playwrights*. (See item 28.)

*   Brawley, Benjamin. *The Negro Genius*. (See item 33.)

*   Hatch, James V., and Abdullah OMANii [sic]. *Black
          Playwrights*. (See item 5.)

*   Hicklin, Fannie Ella Frazier. "The American Negro
        Playwrights." (See item 852.)

414.   Peterson, Bernard L., Jr. "Willis Richardson:
        Pioneer Playwright." *Black World*, 26, No. 6 (April
        1975), 40-48, 86-88.

        Relates the life and work of Richardson, indicating
        which plays were produced and where. Summarizes the
        plots of many of the plays and emphasizes Richardson's
        interest in dramatizing the Negro soul. He tried to
        illuminate contemporary Negro life, but he also
        published many historical dramas about legendary
        people of color. Because of his preoccupation with
        the "soul" of his race, a reevaluation of his work--
        plus publication of it--should take place.

                N. Schuyler, George S. (1895-1977)
                  1. His Writings (Selected)
                     a. Novel

415.   *Black No More*. New York: Macaulay, 1931. Reprinted,
        New York: Macmillan, 1971.

        A satire about the American preoccupation with color,
        wherein Dr. Crookman discovers a whitening process
        for blacks, which confuses black-white issues and
        destroys the original basis for racial prejudice.

        Reviews: *Bookman*, 72, February 1931, p. vii; *Boston
        Transcript*, 21 February 1931, p. 2: D.F.G.; *The
        Nation*, 132, 25 February 1931, p. 218: Dorothy Van
        Doren; *New Republic*, 65, 11 February 1931, p. 362;
        N.Y.H.T. Books, 1 February 1931, p. 5: Rudolph Fisher;
        N.Y.T. Book Review, 1 February 1931, p. 9; *N.Y. World*,
        16 January 1931, p. 14: Harry Hansen; *Opportunity*, 9,
        March 1931, p. 89: Arthur P. Davis; *Saturday Review
        of Literature*, 2 May 1931, p. 799: Leonard Ehrlich;
        Survey, 66, 1 June 1931, p. 290.

                     b. Articles/Archives

416.   "Negro-Art Hokum." *The Nation*, 122 (16 June
        1926), 662-63.

        Expresses the idea that the Afro-American is not very
        different from whites and therefore is unlikely to
        produce a distinct black art. Sees the black person

as a dark-hued white: "Aside from his color, which
ranges from very dark to brown to pink, your
American Negro is just plain American." Views
about racial differences, he declares, are espoused
by racists and should be rejected by intelligent
people.

Schuyler's argument was rejected by Hughes, and was
followed the next week by the poet's philosophical
refutation (see item 289).

*   "Our White Folks." (See item 717.)

*   Syracuse University. (See item 797.)

2. Writings About Him

*   Berzon, Judith R. *Neither Black Nor White*. (See
item 30.)

417.   Long, Richard A. "Renaissance Personality: An
Interview with George Schuyler." *Black World*, 25,
No. 4 (February 1976), 68-78.

The conservative newsman, author of the controversial
1931 novel *Black No More*, talks about a variety of
topics but continues to give little attention to
literature because "[I'm] not an artiste. I'm
still not."

418.   Peplow, Michael W. "George Schuyler, Satirist:
Rhetorical Devices in *Black No More*." *CLA Journal*,
28, No. 2 (December 1974), 242-57.

Often overlooked as a product of the Harlem Renaissance,
Black No More is described as a successful satire,
for Schuyler sets out to ridicule social vices and
follies and succeeds through the use of puns, double
entendres, and rhetorical devices such as *reductio
ad absurdum* and antithesis and anticlimax. He is
particularly good with his parodies of such people
as James Weldon Johnson (Dr. Napoleon Wellington
Jackson) and W.E.B. Du Bois (Dr. Shakespeare
Agamemnon Beard).

419.   Rayson, Ann. "George Schuyler: Paradox Among
        'Assimilationist' Writers." *Black American Literature
        Forum*, 12, No. 3 (Fall 1978), 102-06.

        Concentrates on his autobiography, *Black and Conserva-
        tive*, but also reviews his racial philosophy--which is
        seen as inconsistent and shifting, because he basically
        refused to recognize race as an issue. Therefore,
        he was more of an individualist than an assimilationist.

*   Singh, Amritjit. *The Novels of the Harlem
        Renaissance*. (See item 160.)

*   Columbia Univerity. (See item 784.)

                O. Spencer, Anne (1882-1975)
                  1. Her Writings (Selected)
                See Greene, J. Lee. *Time's Unfading
                Garden*, below, item 421, for bibliography.

                  2. Writings About Her

*   Brown, Sterling A., ed. *The Negro Caravan*.
        (See item 760.)

420.   Greene, J. Lee. "Anne Spencer of Lynchburg." *Virginia
        Cavalcade*, 27, No. 4 (Spring 1978), 178-85.

        Details the poet's life and her personality--retiring
        but not shy, secluded but not isolated. After her
        acquaintance with James Weldon Johnson, her poetry
        was exposed to the world that was in the midst of
        the Renaissance. Her writing habits are described
        (she wrote on "paper bags, in the margins ... of
        books, on envelopes ... on the backs of checks ..."),
        and the importance of her garden is discussed, in
        particular through quotations from her poem "For
        Jim, Easter Eve."

421.   ————. *Time's Unfading Garden: Anne Spencer's Life
        and Poetry*. Baton Rouge: Louisiana State University
        Press, 1977.

        Biography and literary analysis of the poetry of Anne
        Spencer, who remained in Lynchburg, Virginia, throughout
        the Harlem Renaissance but did the bulk of her slender
        production during this period. Friend of many Harlem
        Renaissance writers (McKay, Du Bois, James Weldon
        Johnson), Mrs. Spencer deliberately limited her
        output rather than succumb to the prevailing notion

that black writers should produce racial-protest
poetry. An Appendix of her poems (42) is invaluable,
since her poetry has never been collected.

*   Hull, Gloria T.   "Black Women Poets.   (See item 112.)

*   Perry, Margaret.   *Silence to the Drums.*   (See
         item 153.)

*   Primeau, Ronald.   "Frank Horne and the Second Echelon
         Poets."   (See item 154.)

              P. Thurman, Wallace (1902-1934)
                 1. His Writings (Selected)
                    a. Novels

422.   *The Blacker the Berry.*   New York: The Macaulay Co.,
         1929.   Reprinted, with an introduction by Therman
         B. O'Daniel, New York: Collier Books, 1970.

         Dark-skinned Emma Lou suffers rejection by her family
         and later sexual exploitation by her boyfriend because
         of her sensitivity about her own color.   She
         eventually realizes she must learn to accept her
         color if she is to have freedom and happiness.

         Reviews: *Bookman*, 69, April 1929, p. xxiv; *Boston
         Transcript*, 23 March 1929, p. 6: W.S. [Braithwaite];
         The Crisis, 36, July 1929, p. 249: W.E.B. Du Bois;
         N.Y. Evening Post, 9 March 1929, p. 11m: Vincent
         McHugh; *N.Y.H.T. Books*, 26 May 1929, p. 14: V.F.
         Calverton; *N.Y.T. Book Review*, 17 March 1929, p. 6;
         N.Y. World, 7 April 1929, p. 11m: Shaemas O'Sheel;
         Opportunity, 7, May 1929, p. 162: Eunice Hunton
         Carter; *Springfield Republican*, 1 September 1929,
         p. 7e; *Survey*, 62, 1 June 1929, p. 325: Alain Locke.

423.   *Infants of the Spring.*   New York: The Macaulay
         Co., 1932.

         Bohemians of the Harlem Renaissance--living in a
         house partitioned into rooms and apartments
         (satirically called "Niggerati Manor")--seek meaning
         to their lives but cannot overcome their own self-
         consciousness and artistic weaknesses.   A satire on
         the Harlem Renaissance by one of its most brilliant
         individuals, who could not find himself, either, and
         vents his sense of failure in this hyperbolic novel.

Reviews: *Abbotts Monthly*, April 1932, pp. 51, 63;
The Nation, 134, 10 February 1932, p. 176; *N.Y.H.T.*
Books, 21 February 1932, p. 16: Rudolph Fisher; *N.Y.T.*
Book Review, 28 February 1932, p. 22; *Opportunity*, 10,
March 1932, p. 89: Lois Taylor; *Saturday Review of*
Literature, 8, 12 March 1932, p. 585: Martha Gruening.

424.   with A.L. Furman. *The Interne*. New York: The
        Macaulay Co., 1932.

        Exposé-type novel concerning an ineptly run hospital
        on Welfare Island--a place rife with people without
        morals or a sense of responsibility. Exaggerated
        and melodramtic--and poorly written.

        Reviews: *N.Y.H.T.* *Books*, 15 May 1932, p. 8; *N.Y.T.*
        Book Review, 5 June 1932, p. 17; *Springfield*
        Republican, 15 May 1932, p. 7e.

                        b. Other Writings

425.   "Negro Artists and the Negro." *New Republic*, 52,
        No. 665 (31 August 1927), 37-39.

        Blacks and whites are chided for accepting bourgeois,
        self-serving literature that concentrates on lower-
        class Negroes. His main objection is to literature
        that treats the black "as a sociological problem
        rather than as a human being."

426.   "Negro Life in New York's Harlem: A Lively Picture
        of a Popular and Interesting Section." Girard,
        Kansas: *Haldeman-Julius Little Blue Book* 484, n.d.

        A full "walk-through" tour of Harlem as well as an
        historical guide. Negro journalism is discussed
        briefly, as are the black church, rent parties, the
        numbers game, and strolling down Seventh Avenue on
        Sundays. A portrait as varied as Harlem's population,
        for "There is no typical Harlem Negro as there is no
        typical American Negro." Pen and ink drawings are
        by Richard Bruce.

427.   "Nephews of Uncle Remus." *Independent*, 119 (24
        September 1927), 296-98.

        Sees the Harlem Renaissance as advancing Negroes in
        racial rather than literary matters. Critical
        standards seem not to be applied rigorously to work

produced by Negroes--work still mediocre in many
instances. Praises Toomer and Walrond, dismisses
White and Fauset, and suggests that Hurston has
talent but is "an indifferent craftsman." Also
believes Hughes writes too much and that Cullen
writes not from real experiences and life but from
"vicarious literary experiences which are not intense
enough to be real and vital." Finally, sees the
Negro artist as an American artist, one who must
write and be judged by the same literary canons as
everyone else.

2. Writings About Him

*   Arden, Eugene. "The Early Harlem Novel." (See
        item 52.)

*   Davis, Arthur P. *From the Dark Tower*. (See item 36.)

*   Ford, Nick Aaron. "The Negro Author's Use of
        Propaganda." (See item 841.)

*   Harrison, Paul Carter. *The Drama of Nommo*.
        (See item 41.)

428.   Haslam, Gerald. "Wallace Thurman: A Western Renaissance
        Man." *Western American Literature*, 6, No. 1 (Spring
        1971), 53-59.

        Believes Thurman exhibited Western U.S. traits--
        openness, candor, egalitarianism--so that he felt
        free to write about intraracial problems. Cites him
        also as one of the earliest Negro satirists.

429.   Henderson, Mae Gwendolyn. "Portrait of Wallace
        Thurman," in *The Harlem Renaissance Remembered*, ed.
        Arna Bontemps. New York: Dodd, Mead & Co., 1972,
        Pp. 147-70.

        Biographical account of Thurman's activities and his
        publications--his novels as well as details about the
        periodicals he helped to edit (*Fire!!*; *Harlem*). Pre-
        sents one of the few discussions, if brief, concerning
        Thurman's homosexuality. In sum, sees Thurman as a
        symbol of the Renaissance spirit--restless, searching,
        and controlled always by the reality of his race.

*   Hughes, Langston. *The Big Sea*. (See item 286.)

*   Margolies, Edward. *Native Sons*. (See item 45.)

*   Perkins, Huel D. "Renaissance 'Renegade'?" (See
         item 711.)

*   Singh, Amritjit. *The Novels of the Harlem
         Renaissance*. (See item 160.)

430.   West, Dorothy. "Elephant's Dance: A Memoir of
         Wallace Thurman." *Black World*, 20, No. 1
         (November 1970), 77-85.

         A portrait of perhaps the most bohemian writer of the
         Renaissance, and one who mocked the period in his
         novel *Infants of the Spring*. Thurman is revealed as
         a neurotic and brilliant person who lacked the
         creative talent he desired and sought. Relates the
         story of his brief marriage, but only hints at his
         homosexuality (for more about this, see Henderson's
         article, item 429). Finally, sees Thurman, even in
         his defeat, as a good writer and "perhaps the most
         symbolic figure of the Literary Renaissance in Harlem."

*   Yale University. (See item 798.)

                    Q. Toomer, Jean (1894-1967)
                       1. His Writings
                          a. Fiction

431.   *Cane*. New York: Boni & Liveright, 1923. Reprinted,
         New York: University Place Press, 1951. Reprinted,
         with an introduction by Arna Bontemps, New York:
         Harper & Row, 1969. Reprinted, with an introduction
         by Darwin T. Turner, New York: Liveright, 1975.

         Stories and poems woven together by the common
         elements of the search for self and the Negro soul.
         Isolation, stagnation, fear--all grip the characters:
         the city is beset with materialism, the rural area
         drives people mad with its restrictions or subdues
         them into living highly compromised existences. The
         third section of the book, "Kabnis," portrays a
         young man attempting to come to grips with his racial
         heritage and his own sense of incompleteness.
         Probably the most analyzed of the books produced
         during the Harlem Renaissance.

         Reviews: *Boston Transcript*, 15 December 1923, p. 8;
         New Republic, 37, 26 December 1923, p. 126: Robert

Littell; *N.Y. Tribune*, 14 October 1923, p. 26: J.
Armstrong; *Opportunity*, 1, December 1923, pp. 374-75:
Montgomery Gregory; *Springfield Republican*, 23
December 1923, p. 9a; *Survey*, 51, 1 November 1923,
p. 190 (supplement).

b. Other Writings

432.   "Chapters from *Earth-Being*: An Unpublished Autobiogra-
        phy." *The Black Scholar*, 2, No. 5 (January 1971), 3-13.

        Excerpts from the manuscripts held by Professor
        Michael Krasny, dated as being composed by Toomer
        between 1927 and 1934. The original spelling and
        grammar are retained. Included are sections con-
        cerning Toomer's relationship with his Uncle Bismarck,
        schooling, and the search for a philosophy of life
        ("Towards life in general I have three pairs of main
        attitudes. I see it as comic and tragic, as chemical
        and sacred, as natural and divine.").

433.   *The Wayward and the Seeking: A Collection of Writings
        by Jean Toomer*. Edited with an introduction by
        Darwin T. Turner. Washington, D.C.: Howard
        University Press, 1980.

        The most comprehensive collection of unpublished and
        published writings by Toomer: selections from his
        autobiographical notes, short stories (based on
        Toomer manuscripts, not the published versions),
        poetry (only three among a dozen have been published
        previously), drama, and aphorisms and maxims. Turner
        supplies precise and clarifying notes, revealing a
        careful scholarly approach to editing the material.
        This book represents a "must" for any scholar of
        the Harlem Renaissance.

c. Archives

*   Fisk University. (See item 786.)

2. Writings About Him

434.   Ackley, Donald G.   "Theme and Vision in Jean Toomer's
         Cane." *Studies in Black Literature*, 1, No. 1
         (Spring 1970), 45-65.

         Cane is a book, despite its numerous characters, that
         focuses on "the soul of a people" rather than on any
         particular character. Believes Toomer is less
         interested in race *per se* than he is in contrasting
         the corrupt and bereft Western man (European/White),
         who has become mechanized and materialistic, with the
         free, more humanistic Afro-American. In fact, sees
         the Negro "as the potential spiritual savior for a
         dying nation." Finally, considers that Toomer was a
         writer who rejected abstraction because he wished to
         dramatize his views concretely.

435.   Baker, Houston.   "Journey Toward Black Art: Jean
         Toomer's *Cane*," in his *Singers of Daybreak*. Washington,
         D.C.: Howard University Press, 1974. Pp. 53-80.

         Argues that *Cane* demonstrates the artist's portrait of
         himself as well as a protest against the oppression
         and violence shown to Negroes. Therefore, the book
         reveals the Negro character, portrays self-knowledge,
         and, in writing about the conditions of blacks,
         creates a true black art that is liberating and whole.

435a.   Barthold, Bonnie J.   "Jean Toomer, *Cane*," in her *Black
         Time: Fiction of Africa, the Caribbean, and the
         United States*. New Haven, Conn.: Yale University
         Press, 1981. Pp. 158-63.

         Considers *Cane* a novel that stresses a tension between
         the "folk-spirit" and "the machine." Also believes
         time is suspended so that an ending to the tales is
         not possible. This is related to the "mythic cycle
         of traditional West Africa," and supports the thesis
         of the sort of tension found in *Cane*.

436.   Bell, Bernard [W.].   "Jean Toomer's 'Blue Meridian':
         The Poet as Prophet in a New Order of Man. *Black
         American Literature Forum*, 14, No. 2 (Summer
         1980), 77-80.

         This poem represents Toomer's realization, in writing,
         of the synthesized human being--the American who has
         passed beyond race or sex, the individual who has
         synthesized "contrasting and conflicting forces."

437.   ————. "A Key to the Poems in *Cane*." *CLA Journal*,
         14, No. 3 (March 1971), 251-58.

         Believes the poems in *Cane* have not been explored fully
         by Turner (see item 495) or Lieber (see item 472),
         and that Turner does not realize the functional
         character of the poems: they serve to enlighten the
         reader about meaning in the text, and they act as
         transitions between the stories. Sees the poems
         reflecting Toomer's efforts to synthesize man's
         intellect, emotions, and the body. Divides *Cane* into
         rural thesis (part I), urban antithesis (part II),
         and synthesis (part III), which the poetry reflects.

438.   ————. "Portrait of the Artist as High Priest of
         Soul: Jean Toomer's *Cane*." *Black World*, 23, No. 11
         (September 1974), 4-19, 92-97.

         Explores the textual and philosophical features of
         Cane, section by section, utilizing always the device
         of discovering how Toomer attempted to coalesce
         symbols and action, rhythms, and diction to convey
         the search for identity and wholeness of life among
         his characters. Does not see greater virtue in
         blacks who are close to the soil than in those in the
         city: both types must struggle to reach a higher
         consciousness in order to achieve spiritual truth
         in their lives. After the publication of *Cane*, and
         the subsequent rejection of much of his writing,
         Toomer turned to living his philosophy of wholeness
         as a "Gurdjieffian high priest of soul."

439.   Blackwell, Louise. "Jean Toomer's 'Cane' and
         Biblical Myth." *CLA Journal*, 17, No. 4 (June
         1974), 535-42.

         Contends that to vivify the experiences of blacks
         Toomer made much use of Biblical symbolism, beginning
         with the selection of the title of his book, which
         has a relationship to Canaan--the promised land.
         Other symbols reinforce notions of black dignity
         and beauty.

440.   Blake, Susan L. "The Spectatorial Artist and the
         Structure of 'Cane.'" *CLA Journal*, 17, No. 4
         (June 1974), 516-34.

         Sees the focus of *Cane* as on the author, as artist,
         trying to maintain distance from his work while also
         wanting to be involved in it. The author, then,

becomes a "spectatorial artist." Toomer's characters
have this problem also, because they struggle to
give shape to their experiences.

441.   Bontemps, Arna. "The Negro Renaissance: Jean Toomer
        and the Harlem Writers of the 1920's," in *Anger, and
        Beyond: The Negro Writer in the United States*, ed.
        Herbert Hill. New York: Harper & Row, 1966. Pp. 20-36.

        Cane influenced Negro writers to explore their own
        race's inner life, even though Toomer "turned his
        back on greatness."

442.   Brannan, Tim. "Up From the Dusk: Interpretations of
        Jean Toomer's 'Blood Burning Moon.'" *Pembroke
        Magazine*, 8 (1977), 167-72.

        Suggests the musical sonata form as well as Flemish
        triptychs and allegory reveal Toomer's hope that mind
        and body become healed and whole. "Blood Burning
        Moon" demonstrates what happens when such a synthesis
        does not occur, when humans destroy themselves and
        others because they are ruled by their passions. A
        complicated, poorly organized, and overly burdened
        (with theories) essay.

443.   Cancel, Rafael A. "Male and Female Interrelationship
        in Toomer's *Cane*." *Negro American Literature Forum*,
        5 (1971), 25-31.

        Contends that the female figures in *Cane*, despite
        their victimization or difficulty with finding self,
        are the affirming principle and act as the reconciling
        element between male and female--"through an
        acceptance of the past and the healing contact
        of the soil."

444.   Chase, Patricia. "The Women in *Cane*." *CLA Journal*,
        14 (March 1971), 259-73.

        Describes the female characters as reflecting their
        environment--characters who show the varying aspects
        of womanhood but who also wear masks to cover their
        indifference to their environment and their true
        inner needs. Believes Carrie K. ("Kabnis")
        represents the Toomer desire to present a fully
        synthesized character: "Carrie K. ... is able to
        accept herself and her cultural experience
        totally...."

445.   Christ, Jack M.   "Jean Toomer's 'Bona and Paul':
         The Innocence and Artifice of Words." *Negro
         American Literature Forum*, 9, No. 2 (Summer 1975),
         44-46.

         Relates this story to others in *Cane* by pointing out
         how the need for self-knowledge and redemption by his
         characters is linked to his "multidimensional
         language" that makes use of myths and one's Biblical
         heritage. Also points out puns (e.g., Bona Hale =
         good and hearty) and his use of colors, especially
         purple, symbol of the black people's night.

*   Christian, Barbara. "Spirit Bloom in Harlem."
         (See item 822.)

446.   Clark, J. Michael.   "Frustrated Redemption: Jean
         Toomer's Women in *Cane*, Part One." *CLA Journal*, 22,
         No. 4 (June 1979), 319-34.

         Contends that Toomer and the male characters in *Cane*
         view women only as sex objects. Toomer sees the
         conflicts between men and women and believes the
         failures in male/female relationships hinder wholeness;
         but all of his women are on the brink of the redemption
         that would be possible. The women "at least ... carry
         the seeds of redemption," but they are never given
         the chance to let these seeds ripen.

*   Dillard, Mabel. "Jean Toomer." (See item 832.)

447.   ————. "Jean Toomer--The Veil Replaced." *CLA
         Journal*, 17, No. 4 (June 1974), 468-73.

         Proposes that Toomer saw race as a social rather than
         a racial problem--a matter of public opinion, which
         could be taken care of through science. Saw only the
         American race, not one based on color; and this
         notion is explored in his long poem "Blue Meridian."
         Still, his efforts to suggest racelessness led him
         to lose contact with reality and develop a style that
         "bordered on the psychological and the mystical."

*   Du Bois, W.E.B. "The Younger Literary Movement."
         (See item 185.)

448.   Duncan, Bowie. "Jean Toomer's *Cane*: A Modern Black
        Oracle." *CLA Journal*, 15, No. 3 (March 1972),
        223-33.

        Perceives the design and experience depicted in *Cane*
        in terms of a theme and variation upon an oracular
        message, based on a shifting reality that is akin to
        the concept of space in modern physics. Finds it
        difficult to relate each section to the other: sees
        passion conferring salvation in Part I, an inability
        to communicate physically in Part II, and the story
        of an unredeemed, lost individual in Part III. These
        are all variations on efforts to forge relationships
        and to find a link between the past and the present,
        which are part of the complex message of the oracle.

449.   Durham, Frank. "Jean Toomer's Vision of the Southern
        Negro." *Southern Humanities Review*, 6 (Winter
        1972), 13-22.

        Asserts Toomer presents the Negro soul and demonstrates
        its value and beauty--free, close to the soil, and
        linked with the African past. The Southern Negro is
        an amalgam of pagan Africa and the agrarian South;
        but he is also possessor of a protest spirit--showing
        the effects of injustice and bigotry from Southern
        whites.

450.   Eldridge, Richard. "The Unifying Images in Part One
        of Jean Toomer's *Cane*." *CLA Journal*, 22, No. 3
        (March 1979), 187-214.

        There is a unity in the entire book that is achieved
        through recurrent images, such as dusk and song.
        Closely allied to the dusk is the color purple,
        which is symbolic of the half-hidden world of some
        of the characters. This imagery in the first part
        of the book links with the other sections to form
        a unified artistic production.

451.   Farrison, W. Edward. "Jean Toomer's *Cane* Again."
        CLA Journal, 15, No. 3 (March 1972), 295-302.

        Discusses various critical comments over several
        decades concerning *Cane*--the (sometimes overly)
        enthusiastic response to it initially, and general
        comments that downplay the notion that this book was
        prominent in the development of the Renaissance.
        Sees "Fern" as perhaps the best story in the book.
        "Kabnis" is dismissed rather casually. Appears to

credit Toomer with genius without evincing great
interest in his writing.

452.   Faulkner, Howard. "The Buried Life: Jean Toomer's
         Cane." *Studies in Black Literature*, 7, No. 1
         (Winter 1976), 1-5.

         Believes *Cane* has been misinterpreted by Bone (see
         item 32) and Rosenblatt (see item 47) and that the
         theme of most of the stories and poetry is a need
         for the buried life of the characters to be released
         from the restrictions of their fears in order to give
         way to fulfilling their dreams. Sees the image of a
         rebirth at the end of "Kabnis."

453.   Fischer, William C. "The Aggregate Man in Jean
         Toomer's *Cane*." *Studies in the Novel*, 3, No. 2
         (Summer 1971), 190-215.

         A Jungian interpretation of Toomer characters,
         stressing the shared, communal human experiences
         portrayed in the *Cane* stories and sketches.

454.   Fisher, Alice Poindexter. "The Influence of Ouspensky's
         'Tertium Organum' Upon Jean Toomer's 'Cane.'" *CLA
         Journal*, 17, No. 4 (June 1974), 504-15.

         Toomer's relationships with Hart Crane, Waldo Frank,
         and Gorham Munson suggest that Toomer was influenced
         by Ouspensky's book, which was "a study of conscious-
         ness," a philosophy seeking to see into the nature
         and truth of things.

455.   Fullinwider, S.P. "Jean Toomer: Lost Generation, or
         Negro Renaissance?" *Phylon*, 27, No. 4 (Winter-Fourth
         Quarter 1966), 396-403.

         Searches the question of Toomer's inner identity
         through reciting his family history. Traces development
         of Toomer's personal philosophy and search for self,
         the impact of Georgia upon him, and then cites a
         moment of deep revelation for Toomer, which occurred
         in the summer of 1926. Uses unpublished material
         written by Toomer to suggest "his 1926 conversion
         experience" was what led him to his theory of race-
         lessness and that *Cane*, which appeared in 1923, should
         not be viewed as a former and early attempt of
         Toomer to connect with his race and his times.

456.   Goede, William J.   "Jean Toomer's Ralph Kabnis:
          Portrait of the Negro Artist as a Young Man."
          Phylon, 30 (1969), 73-85.

          Concentrates on the "Kabnis" section of *Cane*,
          examining Toomer's themes and technique--in part, to
          interpret *Cane* and the impact of Toomer's personal
          experiences and philosophy differently from that of
          Fullinwider's view (see item 455).   Sees the themes
          of confinement and the anxiety of modern man
          exemplified through characters like Muriel ("Box
          Seat") and Kabnis.   The latter character, in his
          search for self and his struggle to accept his past,
          ends with the possibility of giving shape to his
          life and finding himself.   Argues that Bone (see
          item 32) is wrong in not interpreting "Kabnis" more
          positively.   Also suggests an interesting parallel
          between "Avey" and Fitzgerald's *The Great Gatsby*.

*   Graham, James D.   "Negro Protest in America."
          (See item 642.)

457.   Grant, Mary Kathryn.   "Images of Celebration in *Cane*."
          Negro American Literature Forum, 5 (1971), 32-34, 36.

          Sees celebration of the natural, instinctive qualities
          of humans and "an underlying spirit of hopeful
          celebration" in symbols (purple dusk, turning to
          the golden glow of dawn = hope) and characterization
          --e.g., descriptions of Karintha as a "cotton
          flower," or Carma as "forest dancing."

*   Gross, Theodore.   "The Negro Awakening."   (See
          item 101.)

458.   Gysin, Fritz.   *The Grotesque in American Negro Fiction:
          Jean Toomer, Richard Wright, and Ralph Ellison*.
          Bern: Francke Verlag, 1975.   Pp. 36-90, 276-79.

          A full analysis of some of the more ambiguous
          portions of *Cane*, approached through examing
          characters, objects, and situations in the book
          in terms of themes and imagery.

459.   Helbling, Mark.   "Sherwood Anderson and Jean Toomer."
          Negro American Literature Forum, 9, No. 2 (Summer
          1975), 35-39.

          Anderson's relationship with the Harlem Renaissance
          is not always acknowledged.   Though he professed

interest in Negroes, and wrote about them, his view
of the race was one of a superior race looking upon
an inferior one; he had an obtuse and condescending
attitude. This can be seen as well in his correspondence
with Toomer, whom he wanted to remain the black writer
even when Toomer was moving beyond some of the racial
concerns that are in *Cane*.

460.   Holmes, Eugene C. "Jean Toomer--Apostle of Beauty."
         Opportunity, 10, No. 8 (August 1932), 252-54, 260.

         Praise for Toomer's poetry and the musical unity of
         Cane (see also Munson, item 479). Believes Toomer
         enters into the lives of his characters and is alive
         to their sorrows. His quest for beauty and truth
         makes him an important poet.

461.   Innes, Catherine L. "The Unity of Jean Toomer's
         Cane." *CLA Journal*, 15, No. 3 (March 1972), 306-22.

         Using P.D. Ouspensky's *Tertium Organum*, examines the
         images and symbols of *Cane* in relation to the theme,
         which is defined as "the striving for racial fusion
         symbolizing spiritual harmony." From Ouspensky
         Toomer drew out the notion of an individual
         attempting to understand the unit of all things.
         (See also item 454.)

462.   Jackson, Blyden. "Jean Toomer's *Cane*: An Issue of
         Genre," in his *The Waiting Years: Essays on American
         Negro Literature*. Baton Rouge: Louisiana State
         University Press, 1976. Pp. 189-97.

         Traces history of critical reactions to *Cane*, most of
         which refuse to see the book as a novel. However,
         the organic unity of the book indicates that it
         probably is a novel, despite the absence of a
         protagonist and a plot. The final definition of
         the book's genre is still to be made.

         Article was first presented before a section of
         the annual meeting of the South Atlantic Modern
         Language Association.

463.   "Jean Toomer," in *Men Seen: Twenty-four Modern
         Authors*, Paul Rosenfeld. New York: The Dial Press,
         1925. Pp. 227-33.

         Evocative, impressionistic appraisal of Toomer as one
         who writes on the levels of both fact and symbolism.

Retells the stories in *Cane* by employing a lyrical
style reminiscent of Toomer's own.

464.   Jung, Udo O.H.   "Jean Toomer: *Fern*," in *The Black
          American Short Story in the Twentieth Century*, ed.
          P. Bruck. Amsterdam: B.R. Grüner, 1977. Pp. 53-69.

          Sees "Fern" as possessing a complicated narrative
          structure that requires the reader to understand the
          story through drawing on "information from outside
          the story." In this way, the reader and narrator
          approach Fern in the same way, on the same level.
          There is mystery in Fern--in her eyes and in her
          name, Fernie May Rosen. She is also able to project
          God through her eyes, and she becomes a virgin and
          unapproachable through something unaccountable within
          her; but this is believable to Southerners, who are
          accustomed to visions.

465.   ————. "'Nora' is 'Calling Jesus': A Nineteenth
          Century European Dilemma in an Afro-American Garb."
          CLA Journal, 21, No. 2 (December 1977), 251-55.

          Asserts that the unnamed woman in "Calling Jesus" is
          Nora, a Nora akin to Ibsen's heroine, restricted and
          denied, alienated from her roots. But there is also
          a split between her body and her soul. Therefore,
          she is empty and unable to find self-fulfillment;
          because she has been separated from her racial past,
          Toomer's Nora is doomed to a loss of her humanity.

466.   Kopf, George. "The Tensions in Jean Toomer's 'Theatre.'"
          CLA Journal, 17, No. 4 (June 1974), 498-503.

          States that much of Toomer's artistic and personal
          vision can be found in this story--a belief in the
          common black experience. In recalling the images
          that make up these experiences, a tension is created
          that holds the story together.

*   Kousaleos, Peter G. "A Study of the Language,
          Structure, and Symbolism in Jean Toomer's *Cane*."
          (See item 865.)

467.   Kraft, James. "Jean Toomer's *Cane*." *Markham
          Review*, 2, No. 4 (October 1970), 61-63.

          Stresses the philosophical influences upon Toomer's
          writing of *Cane* and his drive to seek personal unity;
          therefore, the book is also a spiritual portrait of

Toomer. His characters symbolize the warring elements of blacks in American society as well as the struggle of the artist as an alienated individual. Believes Toomer was suggesting one must go beyond the forms society has erected in order to transform the inner person.

468.   Kramer, Victor A. "'The Mid-Kingdom' of Crane's 'Black Tambourine' and Toomer's 'Cane.'" *CLA Journal*, 17, No. 4 (June 1974), 486-97.

Suggests the Crane poem, which appeared in print two years before *Cane*, might have inspired Toomer in his work on his book; both were concerned about America's worship of the machine and both sought to infuse their work with mythic qualities. They also stressed black alienation from modern society and the black ties to the African past, and the efforts of the black to maintain dignity in a country that rejected him.

469.   Krasny, Michael. "The Aesthetic Structure of Jean Toomer's *Cane*." *Negro American Literature Forum*, 9, No. 2 (Summer 1975), 42.

Sees *Cane* undergirded by the movement of the locale from South, to North and South, to North again, in the manner explained by Toomer himself to his friend Waldo Frank (see item 477).

470.   ————. "Design in Jean Toomer's *Balo*." *Negro American Literature Forum*, 7 (Fall 1973), 103-06.

This dramatic sketch, one of two pieces by Toomer to see dramatic production, reflects Toomer's concern for probing innate spiritual qualities that transcend race but are hampered by society's "forces which inhibit, pervert, and destroy innate spirituality."

471.   ————. "Jean Toomer's Life Prior to *Cane*: A Brief Sketch of the Emergence of a Black Writer." *Negro American Literature Forum*, 9, No. 2 (Summer 1975), 40-41.

Records the facts about Toomer's education and his wanderings. His readings covered a broad range of literature, psychology, yoga, and philosophy as Toomer moved toward writing. He started out exploring the black experience only, but then searched for a means to express "an amalgam of his white and Black responses to life."

472.   Lieber, Todd. "Design and Movement in *Cane*." *CLA Journal*, 13, No. 1 (September 1969), 35-50.

Believes *Cane* has more than a "thematic" unity (see Margolies, item 45), that it has a pattern based on both racial affirmation and linguistic experimentation, which were dominating interests of Harlem Renaissance personalities and writers. Within these patterns Toomer expressed the notion that people needed to get back to their roots and reestablish contact with the environment that had become corrupted by materialism. A spiritual resurrection needs to come after blacks break from white cultural values and accept their own racial heritage: this prevailing notion is present throughout *Cane* and gives it unity.

473.   McCarthy, Daniel P. "'Just Americans': A Note on Jean Toomer's Marriage to Margery Latimer." *CLA Journal*, 17, No. 4 (June 1974), 474-79.

Suggests Toomer's first marriage hurt his career; he was bewildered by the negative reactions to it, and his wife was hurt and defensive. This public reaction and his philosophy were factors in Toomer's downward spiral to literary obscurity.

474.   McKeever, Benjamin F. "*Cane* as Blues." *Negro American Literature Forum*, 4 (1970), 61-63.

Sees *Cane* as an evocation of Toomer's turmoil and search, an autobiographical revelation of his suffering --which is analogous to the sorrow and agony of the blues (and yet also contains celebration and the will to survive). Thus, *Cane* is also oracular (see also item 448) and prophetic in tone and scope.

*   McNeely, Darrell Wayne. "Jean Toomer's *Cane*." (See item 871.)

*   Margolies, Edward. *Native Sons*. (See item 45.)

475.   Martin, Odette C. "*Cane*: Method and Myth." *Obsidian: Black Literature in Review*, 2, No. 1 (Spring 1976), 5-20.

Suggests that *Cane* is cyclical, going from beginnings to endings to movements toward another dimension at the end. The myth of self is central to *Cane*; the method of this quest is fragmentary, involving different levels of searching and belief: for instance, Toomer uses the Christian beliefs of the coming of a Messiah and the Virgin Mary. The fragmentary aspect of the book takes the form of a collage of images--e.g., women as seed bearers for future generations, women as virginal, and the use of symbols for light and dark, male and female, life and death in the unending search for self.

476.   Mason, Clifford. "Jean Toomer's Black Authenticity." *Black World*, 20, No. 1 (November 1970), 70-76.

An urgent, angry, discursive argument against the importance of some Harlem Renaissance writers in order to prove that characters in *Cane* possess true black authenticity because Toomer saw the triumph and tragedy in black life and did not exaggerate either of them, and because he reached down into the subconscious of his characters. Angrily abhors the neglect of Toomer, and feels he should be recognized as a better writer than such others as Wright and Ellison (among the blacks) and Lowell and Bellow (among the whites).

477.   Matthews, George C. "Toomer's 'Cane': The Artist and His World." *CLA Journal*, 17, No. 4 (June 1974), 543-59.

Uses Toomer's letter to Waldo Frank to explore Toomer's suggestion that *Cane* be viewed from "three critical angles"--from the South to the North, to the South again, and back to the North. Toomer suggests a spiritual meaning within these setting moves, and this article explores how Toomer uses symbolism, vignettes, and characterization to search for order and balance and a deep spiritual sense of self.

478.   Mellard, James M. "Solipsism, Symbolism, and Demonism: The Lyrical Mode in Fiction." *Southern Humanities Review*, 7 (Winter 1973), 37-51.

Believes Toomer makes great use of archetypes, and explores this in the story "Blood Burning Moon."

*   Miller, Ruth, and Peter J. Katopes. "The Harlem Renaissance." (See item 14.)

*   Mintz, Stephen. "Jean Toomer." (See item 875.)

479.   Munson, Gorham B.   "The Significance of Jean Toomer."
        Opportunity, 3, No. 33 (September 1925), 262-63.

        There is unity and artistry in *Cane*. Therefore, the
        significance of Toomer lies in his search for the
        answers to the questions of being and the definition
        of self.

480.   Nower, Joyce.   "Foolin' Master." *Satire Newsletter*,
        7, No. 1 (Fall 1969), 5-10.

        Just as for slaves fooling the master was a survival
        technique, Jean Toomer utilizes this same technique,
        where the character separates his mind from his body
        in dealing with whites.

481.   O'Brien, John.   "'Becoming' Heroes in Black Fiction:
        Sex, Iconoclasm, and the Immanence of Salvation."
        Studies in Black Literature, 2, No. 3 (Autumn
        1971), 1-5.

        Conjectures that most black male characters are in a
        state of becoming rather than being Black heroes.
        Suggests this, in one section, by discussing
        Rhobert, Bane ("Carma"), John ("Theater"), Paul,
        and Kabnis from Toomer's *Cane*.

*   Perry, Margaret. *Silence to the Drums*.   (See
        item 153.)

482.   Rankin, William.   "Ineffability in the Fiction of
        Jean Toomer and Katherine Mansfield." *Renaissance
        and Modern: Essays in Honor of Edwin M. Moseley*.
        Saratoga Springs, N.Y.: Skidmore College; Syracuse,
        N.Y.: distributed by Syracuse University Press,
        1976. Pp. 160-71.

        A mystical quality in the writings of both of these
        authors is explored from the angle that each writer
        is attempting to express the inexpressible.

*   Redding, J. Saunders. *To Make a Poet Black*.
        (See item 46.)

*   Reilly, John M. "Jean Toomer: An Annotated Checklist."
        (See item 20.)

483.   ————. "The Search for Black Redemption: Jean
        Toomer's *Cane*." *Studies in the Novel*, 2, No. 3
        (Fall 1970), 312-24.

        Suggests Toomer is showing characters instinctively
        seeking redemption. Toomer wants to show how a
        person with a sterile life, where one retreats from
        natural sensations and represses spontaneity, is cut
        off from redemption (much as the people in Part II
        are separated from the soil and the sources of
        spontaneous life). Thus, in exploring the self, in
        writing about the search for an identity that is
        liberated and spontaneous (even in a repressive
        society), Toomer writes within the tradition "of
        the 20th century black writer's chief theme--the
        redemption of personality."

484.   Riley, Roberta. "Search for Identity and Artistry."
        CLA Journal, 17, No. 4 (June 1974), 480-85.

        Proposes that *Cane* is about the writer's search for
        his black identity and that those characters who seek
        it get their strength from associating themselves
        with the racial heritage and rejecting the
        materialistic, anti-humanistic world about them.

485.   Schultz, Elizabeth. "Jean Toomer's 'Box Seat': The
        Possibility for 'Constructive Crises.'" *Black
        American Literature Forum*, 13, No. 1 (Spring
        1979), 7-12.

        Suggests that in "Box Seat" Toomer demonstrates his
        desire for a synthesis of opposite forces that exist
        in people--good and bad, beauty and ugliness, pain
        and joy--in order to have humankind reach its creative
        potential, to combat a materialistic and mechanistic
        society. Disagrees with Bone's interpretation (see
        item 32) of Dan at the end: believes, instead, that
        he "has attained a maturity of vision." (Even though
        she disagrees with Bone, she indicates that most
        critics ignore the simile of Dan becoming "as cool
        as a green stem that has just shed its flower.")

486.   Scruggs, Charles W. "The Mark of Cain and the
        Redemption of Art: A Study in Theme and Structure
        of Jean Toomer's *Cane*." *American Literature*, 44,
        No. 2 (May 1972), 276-91.

        Primarily sees Toomer employing the myth of Cain
        (the first city dweller, cut off from his roots)

as the theme to explore the inner man, the soul--a
spiritual quest for the true self.

*   Singh, Amritjit. *The Novels of the Harlem
        Renaissance*. (See item 160.)

*   Singh, Raman K. "The Black Novel and its Tradition."
        (See item 161.)

487.   Solard, Alain. "The Impossible Unity: Jean Toomer's
        'Kabnis.'" *Myth and Ideology in American Culture*,
        edited by Régis Durand. Lille, France: Publications
        of the University of Lille, III, 1976. Pp. 175-94.

        Sees the basic theme of "Kabnis" (in *Cane*) to be that
        of the "split" between the character's connection
        with his racial past and his need for self-expression
        as a "poet grappling with his material."

*   ————. "Jean Toomer." (See item 895.)

488.   Spofford, William K. "The Unity of Part One of Jean
        Toomer's *Cane*." *Markham Review*, 3 (May 1972), 58-60.

        Argues Toomer's technique is one of balancing
        opposites in the stories and poems. Also argues
        against Stein (see item 489), whose theory is
        considered narrow and blind to the interrelationships
        Toomer develops.

489.   Stein, Marian L. "The Poet-Observer and Fern in
        Jean Toomer's *Cane*." *Markham Review*, 2 (October
        1970), 64-65.

        Conjectures "Fern" is the pivotal story in *Cane*, for
        it is here that oneness and separateness merge into
        wholeness. Fern is a total person--has all, has
        nothing to give. The "poet-observer [the narrator]
        is one with Fern and separated from her as well."
        Toomer's philosophy of becoming is apparent in this
        story as the mystic and realist meet and communicate
        in a mysterious and poetic manner.

490.   Taylor, Clyde. "The Second Coming of Jean Toomer."
        Obsidian: Black Literature in Review, 1, No. 3
        (Winter 1975), 37-57.

        Cane belongs with the sort of literature that relies
        on folk myth--in this case, the mythic belief in "the
        coming of a delivering and redeeming black messiah."

The symbols used by Toomer to suggest this belief are
references to the Old and New Testaments, the Book of
Revelation, musical motifs (e.g., spirituals),
thematic imagery, such as vegetation (cane, pines)
or harvesting, and the graphic signs (the curves)
used in each section of the book. Sees Father John's
statement to Kabnis, for example, as the mythic curse
of Ham that has been a part of the symbolism of
black literature for ages. By writing symbolically
about the cycle of life--conception, gestation,
birth, etc.--Toomer creates a unifying myth "of a
people's spiritual redemption half-consciously sought
for, carelessly betrayed, violently suppressed,
but never quite totally lost."

491.   Thompson, Larry E. "Jean Toomer: As Modern Man," in
        The Harlem Renaissance Remembered, ed. Arna Bontemps.
        New York: Dodd, Mead & Co., 1972. Pp. 51-62.

        Argues that Toomer does not represent a person with a
        dual nature (see Mason's opposite argument, item 476)
        but was one questing for "singularity"--that is,
        inward and outer freedom from the world's restrictions.
        Describes stories in *Cane*, but does not connect these
        descriptions to this questing notion. Some interpre-
        tations of the material in *Cane* are vulnerable
        because of assessments that do not strike at the
        heart of the work. For example, he states that
        the central theme of *Cane* is that "the essential
        goodness of man [is] being buried by houses, machines
        ... and anything else which represents modern society."

492.   Turner, Darwin T. "--And Another Passing." *Negro
        American Literature Forum*, 1 (1967), 3-4.

        Notes the death of Jean Toomer, and quotes from a
        Toomer letter that ends, "I now doubt that any of
        us will completely find and be found in this life."

493.   ———. "The Failure of a Playwright." *CLA
        Journal*, 10, No. 4 (June 1967), 308-18.

        Discusses history of Jean Toomer's efforts to succeed
        as a dramatist. His lyrical style of writing suited
        him to do flexible, impressionistic work. He did
        not write plotted, "well-made" plays; rather, he
        "anticipated the dramas of Samuel Beckett and
        Ionesco." "Balo," "The Sacred Factory," "The
        Gallonwerps," and "A Drama of the Southwest," his

last drama. Feels later directors would have been interested in these non-representational dramas, which were not accepted for production during the author's lifetime.

494.   ————. "An Intersection of Paths: Correspondence Between Jean Toomer and Sherwood Anderson." *CLA Journal*, 17, No. 4 (June 1974), 455-67.

Discusses the significance of what each writer says to the other: Anderson preferred the lyrical, impressionistic side of Toomer's style to his more realistic writing. For a brief time Toomer expressed the philosophy of a "race man," in reaction to Anderson's attempt to dissect the black soul. But as Toomer moved away from his concentration on blacks to examine "the neuroses of 'the intense white men,'" Anderson was unable to go beyond wanting Toomer to focus on the primitive and passionate side of blacks that he imagined to be unique to the black race.

495.   ————. "Jean Toomer: Exile," in his *In a Minor Chord: Three Afro-American Writers and Their Search for Identity*. Carbondale: Southern Illinois University Press, 1971. Pp. 1-59.

Entering the mind and the work of Toomer enables the author to explore the reasons why Toomer wrote as he did, as well as explicate the limitations of his writing. It is indicated that, from the beginning, Toomer was unable to channel his life into the mold he wished and that this restlessness of soul was reflected in Toomer's inability to shape his art as he wished. A major source for the study of Jean Toomer.

496.   ————. "Jean Toomer's *Cane*: Critical Analysis." *Negro Digest*, 18 (January 1969), 54-61.

Sees Toomer as a lyricist, both in his prose and poetry. Utilizing allegory, for example, in "Kabnis," Toomer nevertheless moves away from lyricism as he emphasizes philosophy and psychology in this section--showing that Jean Toomer the "reformer was coming into being."

*   Turpin, Waters E. "Four Short Fiction Writers of the Harlem Renaissance." (See item 277.)

497.   Twombly, Robert C.   "A Disciple's Odyssey: Jean
        Toomer's Gurdjieffian Career." *Prospects: An Annual
        of American Cultural Studies, Vol. 2.* New York:
        Burt Franklin and Co., 1976. Pp. 437-62.

        Maintains that because Toomer was always searching
        for harmony, for wholeness in his life, he never
        abandoned the philosophy and ways of Gurdjieff--even
        though there was a formal break with the man himself.
        Details the practices of Gurdjieff and describes in
        detail the famous Portage experiment conducted by
        Toomer in 1931. Also believes Toomer's writing
        after *Cane* became weaker because it was too
        philosophical, too vague--all because of his
        interest in Gurdjieff's philosophy.

498.   Van Mol, Kay R.   "Primitivism and Intellect in
        Toomer's *Cane* and McKay's *Banana Bottom*: The Need
        for an Integrated Black Consciousness." *Negro
        American Literature Forum*, 10 (1976), 48-52.

        Suggests that Toomer and McKay, in presenting characters
        seeking black identity, believe the intellectual
        values of whites can be combined with black
        primitivism to create an integrated, whole person.
        Sees the primitivism of both as connected with
        sexuality and agrarianism: McKay, like Toomer,
        "presents his idea of primitivism in terms of
        vegetative and sexual imagery."

499.   Wagner, Jean.   "Jean Toomer," in his *Black Poets of
        the United States from Paul Laurence Dunbar to
        Langston Hughes*. Urbana: University of Illinois
        Press, 1973. Pp. 259-81.

        Declares there is no real line between Toomer's prose
        and poetry: all of Toomer's thinking is that of the
        poet. Also believes that Toomer desired a Whitmanesque
        ideal of living when he made his declarations of
        racelessness. This is why Toomer sought to reconcile
        contradictions in life, and why the quest "for unity
        at the highest level of the spirit" is the most
        important aspect of his art."

500.   Waldron, Edward E.   "The Search for Identity in Jean
        Toomer's 'Esther.'" *CLA Journal*, 14 (March 1971), 277-
        80.

        The link with Africa was a consistent theme during
        the Harlem Renaissance and "Esther" represents a

story that connects with this theme. As Esther rejects Barlo, so too does the American Negro reject Africa.

501.   Watkins, Patricia. "Is There a Unifying Theme in *Cane*?" *CLA Journal*, 15, No. 3 (March 1972), 303-05.

The inability to communicate is the theme that unifies the stories in *Cane*--stories that expose the loneliness and hermetic lives of persons who live both in the city and the country.

502.   Westerfield, Hargis. "Jean Toomer's 'Fern': A Mythical Dimension." *CLA Journal*, 14, No. 3 (March 1971), 274-76.

Believes Toomer emphasizes Fern's last name because he sees her possessing "the mythos of the Jewish Mother of God." See Stein (item 489) for an opposing view.

503.   Withrow, Dolly. "Cutting Through Shade." *CLA Journal*, 21, No. 1 (September 1977), 98-99.

Analysis of Toomer's poem "Reapers," which is seen as projecting a message of "death and destruction," even though the last couplet conveys some hope through the words "*and shade*"--ostensibly a message that blacks can cut through the darkness and find light.

R. Walrond, Eric (1898-1967)
1. His Writings (Selected)
a. Fiction

504.   *Tropic Death*. New York: Boni & Liveright, 1926. Reprinted, New York: Collier Books, 1972.

Stories and sketches of poor blacks in the West Indies and Panama, reflecting the speech, rhythm, and myths that exist among a people faced with starvation, drought, and racial problems.

Reviews: *Boston Transcript*, 6 November 1926, p. 4: C.B.P.; *New Republic*, 48, 10 November 1926, p. 332: Robert Herrick; *N.Y.H.T. Books*, 5 December 1926, p. 9: Langston Hughes; *N.Y.T. Book Review*, 17 October 1926, p. 6; *N.Y. World*, 21 November 1926, p. 10m; *Springfield Republican*, 31 October 1926, p. 7f; *Survey*, 57, 1 November 1926, p. 159: V.F. Calverton.

b. Short Stories

504a.   "The Adventures of Kit Skyhead and Mistah Beauty."
         Vanity Fair, 24, No. 1 (March 1925), 52, 100.

504b.   "A Cholo Romance." *Opportunity*, 2, No. 18 (June
         1924), 177-81.

504c.   "Cynthia Goes to the Prom." *Opportunity*, 1, No. 11
         (November 1923), 342-43.

504d.   "Miss Kenny's Marriage." *Smart Set*, 72, No. 1
         (September 1923), 73-80.

504e.   "On Being a Domestic." *Opportunity*, 1, No. 8
         (August 1923), 234.

504f.   "The Stone Rebounds." *Opportunity*, 1, No. 9
         (September 1923), 277-78.

504g.   "Vignettes of the Dusk." *Opportunity*, 2, No. 13
         (January 1924), 19-20.

504h.   "The Voodoo's Revenge." *Opportunity*, 3 (July 1925),
         209-13.

         Third Prize-Short Story section of *Opportunity* Contest.

c. Other

505.   "The Black City." *The Messenger*, 6 (January 1924),
         13-14.

         An impressionistic, enthusiastic, romantic paean to
         Harlem. Alliterative and metaphoric, one can grasp
         a small part of Harlem's ambiance and tone; but one
         should not read this article for hard facts.

*   Atlanta University. (See item 780.)

2. Writings About Him

*   Bone, Robert. *Down Home*. (See item 31.)

*   Brawley, Benjamin. *The Negro Genius*. See
         item 33.)

*   [Editorial] "Eric Walrond." (See item 606.)

*   Green, Elizabeth Lay. *The Negro in Contemporary*
         American Literature. (See item 40.)

*   Ivy, James W. "Écrits Nègres aux Etats-Unis."
         (See item 116.)

                    S. White, Walter (1893-1955)
                       1. His Writings (Selected)
                          a. Novels

506.   *Fire in the Flint.* New York: Knopf, 1924.

         Propagandistic tale of an idealistic black doctor who
         returns to his home in the South where he thinks he
         can live a normal, uncommitted life. Rape and
         lynching finally convince him to abandon his
         passive and noninvolved attitude.

         Reviews: *Bookman*, 60, November 1924, p. 342: J.F.;
         Boston Transcript, 17 December 1924, p. 5; *Independent*,
         113, 27 September 1924, p. 202; *International Book*
         Review, November 1924, p. 850: H.L. Pangborn; *Literary*
         Review, 1 November 1924, p. 14: Herschel Brickell;
         The Nation, 119, 8 October 1924, p. 386: Konrad
         Bercovici; *N.Y.T. Book Review*, 14 September 1924,
         p. 9; *N.Y. Tribune*, 28 September 1924, p. 5: Freda
         Kirchwey; *Opportunity*, 2, November 1924, p. 344:
         Charles S. Johnson; *Survey*, 53, 1 November 1924, p. 160.

507.   *Flight.* New York: Knopf, 1926.

         The story of Mimi Daquin, a pale Creole, who passes
         through various stages of black bourgeois life in the
         South, goes East and "passes"; she finally returns
         to the black world, because she believes it renews
         her life and she feels personal warmth from the
         black society.

         Reviews.: *Booklist*, 23, November 1926, p. 85; *Boston*
         Transcript, 29 May 1926, p. 4; *Cleveland Open Shelf*,
         November 1926, p. 123; *Independent*, 116, 8 May 1926,
         p 555; *International Book Review*, July 1926, p. 519:
         J.W. Crawford; *Literary Review*, 24 April 1926, p. 4:
         Walter Yust; *The Nation*, 123, 28 July 1926, p. 89:
         Lisle Bell; *New Republic*, 48, 1 September 1926, p. 53;
         N.Y.H.T. Books, 11 April 1926, p. 3: Carl Van Vechten;
         Opportunity, 4, July 1926, p. 227: Frank Horne (Nella

Larsen Imes on Horne review, 4, September 1926, p. 295;
Horne's reply, 4, October 1926, p. 326; Walter White
letter on Horne review, 4, December 1926, p. 397);
Outlook, 143, 4 August 1926, p. 479; *Saturday Review
of Literature*, 2, 10 July 1926, p. 918: Martha
Gruening; *Survey*, 56, 1 September 1926, p. 695;
(London) *Literary Supplement*, 9 December 1926, p. 908;
World Tomorrow, 9, April 1926, p. 133.

b. Other Writing

508.   "The Negro Renaissance." *Palms*, 4, No. 1 (October
         1926), 3-7.

         Traces the African roots of black writers and
         emphasizes the lyric gifts of the young poets who,
         without repudiation of dialect verse, were writing
         in a new and colorful mode.

c. Archive

*   Library of Congress. (See item 791.)

2. Writings About Him

*   Bone, Robert. *The Negro Novel in America*. (See
         item 32.)

*   Brawley, Benjamin. *The Negro Genius*. (See item 33.)

508a.   Cooney, Charles F. "Walter White and Sinclair Lewis:
         The History of a Literary Friendship." *Prospects:
         An Annual Journal of American Cultural Studies*, 1.
         New York: Burt Franklin & Co., 1975. Pp. 63-79.

         Traces the 25-year friendship of these two authors
         through their letters to one another. Lewis aided
         White through his endorsement of White's first
         novel, *Fire in the Flint*. The men met later and
         found themselves compatible because of their view-
         points about the racial woes of the U.S. A list of
         the number of White-Lewis letters in the Library of
         Congress Manuscript Division appears at the end.

508b.   ————. "Walter White and the Harlem Renaissance."
          Journal of Negro History, 57 (July 1972), 321-40.

          Cites White's efforts on behalf of Harlem Renaissance
          writers--e.g., Cullen, Hughes, Fisher, McKay, Larsen
          --to get their work before editors and publishers he
          knew. Although White was more often unsuccessful in
          getting items published, he brought the names of black
          writers to the attention of established literary
          people and organizations.

*   Singh, Amritjit. *The Novels of the Harlem
          Renaissance*. (See item 160.)

509.   Waldron, Edward E. *Walter White and the Harlem
          Renaissance*. Port Washington, N.Y.: Kennikat
          Press, 1978.

          Sees White's role during the Renaissance as neglected.
          Reviews his life and writings; points out that his
          two novels were artistically weak, but they did give
          accurate insight into the psychology of the Negro
          who can "pass" but chooses to remain with the black
          race. Sees White's greatest contribution as helper
          and encourager of other talented writers, such as
          Cullen and McKay. The chapter on this part of his
          life is the subject of an essay by the same author
          (see item 510).

510.   ————. "Walter White and the Harlem Renaissance."
          CLA Journal, 16, No. 4 (June 1973), 438-57.

          Considers that White helped many Harlem Renaissance
          writers get published (which some may dispute) because
          of his contacts with Carl Van Doren. States that
          White's correspondence shows he did not think
          imaginative literature should be sociological, although
          he thought it could improve race relations. Includes
          excerpts from letters received from Claude McKay, where
          comments about other writers are included. Reveals
          White's efforts to get Cullen's first book of poetry
          published, although it is clear that it was not through
          White's influence that Harper finally published this
          work.

          This article is based on letters on file at the Library
          of Congress. There is evidence of White's enthusiasm
          for fellow writers of the Harlem Renaissance, but it
          is not absolutely clear about the extent of his
          influence or role as "one important catalyst who
          helped make the Harlem Renaissance possible."

V. MISCELLANEOUS MATERIALS

Includes articles, parts of books, stories by minor writers, editorials, and film, filmstrip, and record listings.

511. "Aaron Douglas Chats About the Harlem Renaissance," in *The Harlem Renaissance Generation*, ed. L.M. Collins. Nashville: Fisk University, 1972. Pp. 180-203.

   Interview by the editor where Douglas defines the Renaissance as "a cultural experience in a sense, a sort of spiritual experience." Douglas reminisces about such persons as C.S. Johnson, W.E.B. Du Bois, Alain Locke, Wallace Thurman, Langston Hughes, Countee Cullen, Zora Neale Hurston, and Arna Bontemps. Also discusses the short-lived magazine, *Fire!!*, and the aim of the young artists to make it represent the spirit of the new black artists.

512. "Aaron Douglas, Painter, at 79; Founded Fisk Art Department." *New York Times*, 22 February 1979, p. 89.

   Obituary.

513. "The Amy Spingarn Prizes." *Opportunity*, 3, No. 33 (September 1925), 287.

   Announcement of the winners, who included Rudolph Fisher, Langston Hughes, and Countee Cullen.

514. "Arna Bontemps Talks About the Renaissance," in *The Harlem Renaissance Generation*, ed. L.M. Collins. Nashville: Fisk University, 1972. Pp. 207-19.

   Interviewed by the editor, Bontemps reminisces about the *Carolina Magazine*'s special issues devoted to writing by Renaissance authors, the importance of Garvey as an influence on the spirit of the times, and the different phases of the movement itself--from its inchoate beginnings to its more full-fledged, self-conscious flowering in the late 1920s. A vivid recollection by one of the oldest participants and historian of this period.

515.   "The Art of Aaron Douglas." *Crisis*, 38, No. 5
        (May 1931), 159-60.

        Descriptions as well as photographs of Douglas
        murals at Fisk University Library and the Sherman
        Hotel (Chicago).

516.   "Augusta Savage: An Autobiography." *Crisis*, 36,
        No. 8 (August 1929), 269.

        Tells about her life after winning a Rosenwald Fund
        Travelling Fellowship to study sculpture in Paris.
        Photograph of Savage.

517.   "Award of Prizes." *Crisis*, 30, No. 6 (October
        1925), 275-76.

        Announcement of Amy Spingarn Contest in Literature
        and Art winners. "High Yaller," by Rudolph Fisher,
        won the short story prize, for instance, and *The
        Broken Banjo* by Willis Richardson, won the first prize
        for drama. Hughes, Cullen, and Frank Horne were
        other winners.

518.   "Awards." *Opportunity*, 7, No. 7 (July 1929), 227.

        Study abroad for the sculptor Augusta Savage is
        announced.

519.   Baker, Houston, A., Jr. "Arna Bontemps: A Memoir."
        Black World, 22, No. 11 (September 1973), 4-9.

        Primarily a recollection of Bontemps's coming to Yale
        and Baker's encounters with him there and later at
        Fisk. Emphasizes the neglect of Bontemps and
        his work.

520.   Bennett, Gwendolyn [B.]. "The Ebony Flute."
        Opportunity, 4, No. 44 (August 1926), 260-61.

        The first in a series of "literary chit-chat and
        artistic what-not" by one of the minor poets of this
        period. The range extends from announcements about
        new books to such trivia as Rudolph Fisher's calling
        his baby "the new Negro."

521.   ————. "The Ebony Flute." *Opportunity*, 4, No. 45
        (September 1926), 292-93.

        Favorable comments about *Nigger Heaven*, news from
        Countee Cullen in Paris, and information about two
        short stories by Rudolph Fisher.

522.   ————. "The Ebony Flute." *Opportunity*, 4, No. 46
        (October 1926), 322-23.

        Talk about "best lines" written by a Negro, news about
        Dorothy West and Helene Johnson, and another note from
        Countee Cullen in Paris.

523.   ————. "The Ebony Flute." *Opportunity*, 4, No. 47
        (November 1926), 356-58.

        Drama and dancing dominate the topics in this
        month's column.

524.   ————. "The Ebony Flute." *Opportunity*, 4, No. 48
        (December 1926).

        News about Toomer, Cullen, and black artists, such
        as Josephine Baker, who are in Europe.

525.   ————. "The Ebony Flute." *Opportunity*, 5, No. 1
        (January 1927), 28-29.

        A review of literature that appeared in 1926; also,
        forthcoming books are noted, such as Hughes's *Fine
        Clothes to the Jew*.

526.   ————. "The Ebony Flute." *Opportunity*, 5, No. 3
        (March 1927), 90-91.

        A full and wide-ranging array of comments about writers
        and other artists, including comments about Josephine
        Baker in Paris and quotations from a favorable review
        of the short story "Symphonesque," by Arthur Huff
        Fauset.

527.   ————. "The Ebony Flute." *Opportunity*, 5, No. 4
        (April 1927), 122-23.

        A defense of Carl Van Vechten (*Nigger Heaven*), a
        discussion of the play *In Abraham's Bosom*,
        correspondence from Claude McKay (who reported
        the theft of all of his poetry manuscripts, representing
        four years' work), and observations about the possible
        lack that year of a genuine "best Negro novel."

528.   ————. "The Ebony Flute." *Opportunity*, 5, No. 6
          (June 1927), 182-83.

          Praise for J.W. Johnson's *God's Trombones*, quotations
          from a review of a Taylor Gordon recital of spirituals,
          and Arthur Ficke's comments about Hughes's book *Fine
          Clothes to the Jew*.

529.   ————. "The Ebony Flute." *Opportunity*, 5, No. 7
          (July 1927), 212-13.

          Mention of short stories by black writers that were
          cited nationally, and a reprint of a letter to
          Benjamin Brawley from Carl Van Vechten, which is a
          defense of the younger black writers whom Brawley
          criticizes (see item 531).

530.   ————. "The Ebony Flute." *Opportunity*, 5, No. 8
          (August 1927), 242-43.

          A backward glance over the past year's literary news,
          in addition to information about Claude McKay's book
          Harlem Shadows and comments concerning René Maran's
          sequel to *Batoula: Djouma, Chien de Brousse*.

531.   ————. "The Ebony Flute." *Opportunity*, 5, No. 9
          (September 1927), 276-77.

          Favorable comments about Julia Peterkin's work, a
          reply from Brawley (see item 529), once again defending
          his negative assessment of younger black writers,
          and a quotation from H.L. Mencken, who had unkind
          words for black short story writers.

532.   ————. "The Ebony Flute." *Opportunity*, 5, No. 10
          (October 1927), 308-09.

          Rave comments about the show *Rang-Tang*, a note about
          a recent Wallace Thurman article, and favorable
          reaction to Cullen's latest book, *Copper Sun*.

533.   ————. "The Ebony Flute." *Opportunity*, 5, No. 11
          (November 1927), 339-40.

          Excerpts from reviews of the play *Porgy*, and description
          of a visit to the Barnes Foundation in Merion, Pa.,
          are interspersed among literary news such as mention
          of a new novel by W.E.B. Du Bois.

534.   ———. "The Ebony Flute." *Opportunity*, 6, No. 2
        (February 1928), 55-56.

        A broad coverage of book news: forthcoming books,
        discussion of the Harmon Awards for Distinguished
        Achievement Among Negroes for 1926, and brief comments
        about the *Exhibition of Fine Arts by Negro Artists*.

535.   ———. "The Ebony Flute." *Opportunity*, 6, No. 4
        (April 1928), 122.

        Praise for a play by Frank Wilson, news that Van
        Vechten was nominated for *Vanity Fair*'s Hall of Fame,
        and comments from Dr. Nathaniel Dett, the musician
        and composer.

536.   ———. "The Ebony Flute." *Opportunity*, 6, No. 5
        (May 1928), 153.

        Countee Cullen's marriage is announced, books by McKay
        and Nella Larsen are among several new publications
        that are mentioned, and a generous comment about *Porgy*
        from Alexander Woollcott is quoted.

537.   Bledsoe, Jules. "Has the Negro a Place in the
        Theatre?" *Opportunity*, 6, No. 7 (July 1928), 215.

538.   Bontemps, Arna. "A Memoir: Harlem, the 'Beautiful'
        Years." *Negro Digest*, 14, No. 3 (January 1965), 62-69.

        Recalls his early days in Harlem (1920s) and the joy
        he and others felt. Was it because blacks were still
        closer to their primitive origins? Perhaps this notion
        helped to give America something it had lost in its
        struggle for finding valid values for life. But under
        the fun of the 1920s there was the slum in the making;
        and the idea that it might be good to be segregated
        to find one's group spirit turned into alienation
        and frustration after the 1920s.

539.   ———. *100 Years of Negro Freedom*. New York:
        Dodd, Mead & Co., 1961.

        Mentions the Harlem Renaissance and the contributions
        of such persons as Charles S. Johnson, Alain Locke,
        and James Weldon Johnson in promoting black culture.
        Concentrates on publication of collections, although
        Toomer's *Cane* is mentioned briefly in the chapter
        entitled "Home of the Brave."

540.   Broun, Heywood. "It Seems to Heywood Broun." *The Nation*, 125, No. 3250 (19 October 1927), 416-17.

        Criticizes whites who let their racial prejudice cloud their assessment of Negro artists (writers or musicians). Believes blacks are often judged unfairly because of this bias.

541.   Brown, Evelyn S. "The Harmon Awards." *Opportunity*, 11, No. 3 (March 1933), 78-81.

        Background history about these awards for the fine arts and description of a touring art exhibition. Two pages of black and white illustrations follow the article.

542.   ————. "Negro Achievement Revealed by Harmon Awards." *Opportunity*, 5, No. 1 (January 1927), 20-22.

543.   Brown, Sterling A. "Arna Bontemps: Co-Worker, Comrade." *Black World*, 22, No. 11 (September 1973), 11, 91-97.

        A moving, intelligent, tough tribute to one the author says was not of the Harlem Renaissance (Brown gives seven reasons for his opinion). Reviews and assesses *God Sends Sunday* and *Black Thunder* and castigates critics--both white and black--for not appreciating the quality of these novels. Also disdains young blacks (Brown uses the word "Negro" for the race) who do not read or understand Bontemps's poetry, which is described as meditative, and beautiful in its diction, cadences, and tone.

544.   ————. "Concerning Negro Drama." *Opportunity*, 9, No. 9 (September 1931), 284, 288.

        Discusses the connection between the social condition of the Negro and lack of black playwrights. Sees the little theatre movement as a ray of hope for black drama.

545.   ————. "A Literary Parallel." *Opportunity*, 10, No. 5 (May 1932), 152-53.

        The Negro writer needs to refashion the interpretation and presentation of the black race in literature, just as the Irish did in the development of their literature. In drawing a parallel between two "submerged" and despised races, Brown makes a plea for authenticity rather than succumbing to propaganda.

546.   ———. "Our Literary Audience." *Opportunity*, 8,
            No. 2 (February 1930), 42-46, 61.

            Examines the lack of readers among Negroes, the very
            group who should be reading the material that Harlem
            Renaissance writers are producing. Fallacies about
            what "Negro books" should be (in terms of point
            of view as well as of the story) are discussed. The
            major thrust is a reflection on the overall sense of
            values among Negroes who seem to want literature to
            evade the truths about the complete range, good and
            bad, of black life.

547.   Campbell, Barbara. "Harlem Art Fete Hails Poet Countee
            Cullen." *New York Times*, 13 June 1973, p. 51.

            An account of a Cullen festival at the Countee Cullen
            Library in Harlem, which featured an appearance by
            his widow and where there were music series and art
            exhibits as well as poetry readings.

548.   Carrington, Glenn. "The Harlem Renaissance--A
            Personal Memoir." *Freedomways*, 3, No. 3 (1963),
            307-11.

            A bibliographical description of some publications of
            the period, as well as mention of white patrons and
            black writers of the decade. Not "personal" in terms
            of reminiscences related to specific persons; instead,
            a personal overview of the whole period, including
            recollection of such activities as rent parties,
            bootleg liquor buying and selling, and the theatre.

549.   Clarke, John Hendrik. "Remembering Arthur A. Schomburg."
            Encore, 6, No. 18 (26 September 1977), 3.

            An emotional recollection of Clarke's 1934 encounter
            with one of the great supporters of the Harlem
            Renaissance, a man known for his advice that "The
            American Negro must remake his past in order to make
            his future," a suggestion that undergirds the movement
            itself.

550.   Conroy, Jack. "Memories of Arna Bontemps: Friend and
            Collaborator." *American Libraries*, 5, No. 11
            (December 1974), 602-06.

            This reminiscence was reprinted in *Negro American
            Literature Forum*, 10, No. 2 (Summer 1976).

551.   "Contest Awards." *Opportunity*, 3, No. 29 (May
        1925), 142-43.

        Announcement of the "Opportunity Literary Contest"
        winners. It is interesting to note how Hughes and
        Cullen dominated the poetry prizes.

552.   ————. *Opportunity*, 4, No. 41 (May 1926), 156-57.

        The winning manuscripts (out of 1,276 submitted) for
        the "Holstein Prizes" (short stories, poetry, plays,
        essays, personal experiences, musical composition,
        and "The Alexander Pushkin Poetry Prize"), as well
        as "The F.C.W.C. Prizes for Constructive Journalism."
        Arthur Huff Fauset, for example, won the first prize
        for his short story "Symphonesque," and Arna Bontemps
        won the Pushkin Prize for "Golgotha is a Mountain."
        (Since pseudonyms had to be used, some names listed
        are given in that form rather than the author's; e.g.,
        John Henry Lucas = Countee Cullen.)

553.   ————. *Opportunity*, 5, No. 6 (June 1927), 179.

        A listing, by category, of the prize winners for the
        Opportunity contest.

554.   "The Contest Spotlight." *Opportunity*, 5, No. 7
        (July 1927), 204-05, 213.

        Statements by and photographs of *Opportunity*
        contest winners.

555.   "Correspondence." *Opportunity*, 4, No. 48 (December
        1926), 397.

        A letter from Walter White, complaining about the
        opinions of Frank Horne and Nella Larsen (Imes)
        concerning White's novel *Flight*. (See also item
        507, under *Reviews*.)

556.   ————. *Opportunity*, 13, No. 5 (May 1935), 154.

        A letter from Martha Gruening that discusses how
        whites interpret black life. Written in response to
        a controversy started when Sterling Brown panned
        Fannie Hurst's *Imitation of Life*.

557.   Covington, Floyd C. "The Negro Invades Hollywood."
        Opportunity, 7, No. 4 (April 1929), 111-13, 131.

        Discusses the kinds of roles in which Negroes are
        cast in films and their salaries; also asks if there
        will be a black star in the future as blacks move
        from stereotypes to legitimate roles.

558.   "The Creative Art of Negroes." *Opportunity*, 1,
        No. 8 (August 1923), 240-45.

        Sculpture, textiles, masks, and metal work--with
        illustrations.

559.   [Cullen, Countee.] "The Dark Tower." *Opportunity*,
        4, No. 48 (December 1926), 388-90.

        A variety of literary topics is discussed, about white
        as well as Negro writers. Primary purpose appears to
        be informational, although opinions about race and
        literature are expressed editorially.

        The first in a series by Cullen.

560.   ————. "The Dark Tower." *Opportunity*, 5, No. 1
        (January 1927), 24-25.

        Comments on John Vandercook's book, *Tom-Tom*, and
        enthusiastic mention of the appearance of the now-
        famous magazine, *Fire!!*

561.   ————. "The Dark Tower." *Opportunity*, 5, No. 2
        (February 1927), 53-54.

        Reports on Josephine Baker's success in Paris (with
        quoted comments from E.E. Cummings), and also lists
        most popular books in the Harlem branch of the New
        York Public Library. Of the top eight most requested,
        only one is by a black author: *Tropic Death*, by
        Eric Walrond.

562.   ————. "The Dark Tower." *Opportunity*, 5, No. 3
        (March 1927), 86-87.

        Brief but laudatory comments on Hughes's *Fine Clothes
        to the Jew*, comments on a play of interracial interest
        (*Stigma*), and favorable notes about actor Frank
        Wilson, who was appearing in *In Abraham's Bosom*.

563.   ————. "The Dark Tower." *Opportunity*, 5, No. 4
            (April 1927), 118-19.

            Thoughts on the "New Negro" and the "new white man"
            --the need for whites to understand the "spiritual
            renaissance" of blacks. A review of Louis Untermeyer's
            The Forms of Poetry. Ends with a list of the most
            popular books in the Harlem Library (*Nigger
            Heaven* leads the list).

564.   ————. "The Dark Tower." *Opportunity*, 5, No. 5
            (May 1927), 149-50.

            High praise of an eight-year-old writer, Lula
            Lowe Weeden.

565.   ————. "The Dark Tower." *Opportunity*, 5, No. 6
            (June 1927), 180-81.

            Cullen's artistic credo is expressed through his
            observation on articles published by Wallace Thurman
            and Frank Luther Mott in other periodicals of the
            day: in particular, Cullen stresses his belief in
            the artist's being able to use ideas and forms
            that lie outside his heritage.

566.   ————. "The Dark Tower." *Opportunity*, 5, No. 7
            (July 1927), 210-11.

            The caliber of poetry by blacks as judged by white
            critics is the main subject here, although Cullen
            also reflects on racial influences upon black poets
            and concludes that race is no more important
            than talent.

567.   ————. "The Dark Tower." *Opportunity*, 5, No. 8
            (August 1927), 240-41.

            A discussion about Andre Siegfried's book *America
            Comes of Age*.

568.   ————. "The Dark Tower." *Opportunity*, 5, No. 9
            (September 1927), 272-73.

            A review of comments in *Time* magazine concerning
            Josephine Baker and Florence Mills, observations on
            Emil Janning's interpretation of Othello, and
            favorable reaction to the book *Trader Horn*.

* ———. "The Dark Tower." *Opportunity*, 5, No. 10
(October 1927). (See Bruce, Richard, item 181.)

569. ———. "The Dark Tower." *Opportunity*, 5, No. 11
(November 1927), 336-37.

Devoted to discussion of drama, primarily the
Theatre Guild's production of *Porgy*.

570. ———. "The Dark Tower." *Opportunity*, 5, No. 12
(December 1927), 373-74.

A remembrance of two women who died recently--entertainer
Florence Mills and Clarissa Scott Delany, the writer.

571. ———. "The Dark Tower." *Opportunity*, 6, No. 1
(January 1928), 20-21.

Praise for the poetry of E. Merrill Root and criticism
of Ellen Glasgow's patronizing attitude toward
Negroes, and other literary observations.

572. ———. "The Dark Tower." *Opportunity*, 6, No. 2
(February 1928), 52-53.

Devoted mainly to reviews of books--e.g., Amy
Lowell's *Ballads for Sale*--but also a tribute to
Helen Keller, who is praised for her sensitivity
to people.

573. ———. "The Dark Tower." *Opportunity*, 6, No. 3
(March 1928), 90.

A plea to black writers not to present every aspect
of Negro life; rather, the advice given is: "*Put
forward your best foot.*"

574. ———. "The Dark Tower." *Opportunity*, 6, No. 4
(April 1928), 120.

Describes a trip to the South. Comments also on
William Stanley Braithwaite's annual survey of
American poetry.

575. ———. "The Dark Tower." *Opportunity*, 6, No. 5
(May 1928), 146-47.

Cullen translates from French an article by André
Maurois entitled "Negro Poetry in the United States,"
which is a brief overview of the nature and themes
of poetry being written by black writers of the 1920s.

Maurois illustrates his explication with selections
of poetry. The poetry quoted remains in French,
however.

576.   ————. "The Dark Tower." *Opportunity*, 6, No. 6
         (June 1928), 178-79.

         Quotations from the letter of a liberal Texas white
         woman do not lessen the poet's notion that this state
         may still be an "earthly gehenna." Praise is given
         to a long dramatic narrative by Leslie Pinckney Hill,
         Toussaint L'Ouverture, and a critical observation
         about the *Blackbirds of 1928* concludes these
         monthly comments.

577.   ————. "The Dark Tower." *Opportunity*, 6, No. 7
         (July 1928), 210.

         News notes about the Karamu Theatre (Cleveland)
         production of *In Abraham's Bosom*, and a synopsis,
         mildly evaluative, of the novel *Toucoutou*, by
         Edward Larocque Tinker.

578.   ————. "The Dark Tower." *Opportunity*, 6, No. 9
         (September 1928), 271-73.

         After a gentle rebuke of Wallace Thurman's tendency
         to criticize his own race (its "severest critic"),
         the bitter and the sweet experiences of Cullen's
         trip to France and Algiers are described in
         impressionistic, romantic terms.

579.   ————. "Elizabeth Prophet: Sculptress."
         Opportunity, 8, No. 7 (July 1930), 204-05.

         Discusses her life and work.

580.   ————. "What Love Meant for Isadora Duncan."
         Translated from the French notebook of Cullen by
         Michael Fabre. *New Letters*, 41, No. 3 (March
         1975), 3-14.

         A story, a dream, an impression, a wish--all describe
         this prose-piece that Cullen wrote in French,
         although the editor speculates about its authorship.
         The style and tone, in any case, capture the
         essence of Isadora Duncan. And Cullen's own
         admiration of Duncan can be sensed as he writes
         about love and the body's transcendence of age through
         love and the evocation of beauty.

581. Dancy, John. *Sand Against the Wind*. Detroit: Wayne State University Press, 1966. Pp. 124-27.

     Surprising background information concerning Countee Cullen, which has not been verified. Dancy (who is dead) says Cullen appeared as an offender in Juvenile Court where the author, then a social worker, was also present.

582. Davis, Allison. "Our Negro 'Intellectuals.'" *Crisis*, 35, No. 8 (August 1928), 268-69, 285-86.

     A regular, harsh critic of Harlem Renaissance literary artists writes a tirade against them and their subject matter, accusing the writers of exploiting the low life of Negroes and of extolling primitivism. Angry and basically hostile to any new forms, Davis's scant praise here and there is overshadowed by the article's violent denunciation of "Menckenites" and "Van Vechtenites." (See also item 647.)

583. Davis, R.H. ["Letter to Charles S. Johnson"], in *The Harlem Renaissance Generation*, ed. L.M. Collins. Nashville: Fisk University, 1972. Pp. 415-17.

     Comments concerning the fiction manuscripts entered in the *Opportunity* Awards Contest for 1924. Comments on stories by Hurston and Matheus.

584. "Debut of the Younger School of Negro Writers." *Opportunity*, 2, No. 17 (May 1924), 143-44.

     Report of a gathering of black writers and white publishers at the Civic Club on 21 March to attend a "coming out party" for Jessie Fauset, whose book *There Is Confusion* had just appeared. Alain Locke and Charles S. Johnson were there, as was Du Bois, who spoke about the problems older black writers had faced in getting work published. List of attendees as well as a copy of one poem that was read--"To Usward," by Gwendolyn Bennett.

585. Deutsch, Helen, and Stella Hanau. "The Provincetown Theatre and the Negro." *Crisis*, 38, No. 11 (November 1931), 373-74, 396.

     Traces history (and problems) of producing plays with black characters during the 1920s--plays presented in the belief that experimenting with new themes and settings was important. Tells of production (1923-24) of *All God's Chillun Got Wings*, with Paul Robeson, as an example.

586.   Diggs, Arthur. "Unknown Artists and Their Art."
        Abbott's Monthly, [2] (May 1931), 49-54, 85.

        Noting increased interest in the use of the black man
        as a subject in art, describes current work being
        done by black artists (who were few). Artists
        discussed briefly, and descriptively rather than
        critically, are: Meta Warrick Fuller, Archibald J.
        Motley, Jr., and Aaron Douglas.

587.   "'Dramatis Personae': Florence Mills." *Crisis*, 34,
        No. 7 (September 1927), 229, 248.

        Photograph and human interest story about the best-
        known and greatly admired star of black musical
        shows, such as *The Blackbirds*. Story taken from the
        London *Daily Express*.

588.   Du Bois, W.E.B. "The Black Man Brings His Gifts."
        Survey Graphic, 53 (1 March 1925), 655-709.

        A satiric story about race prejudice--white ignorance
        about writers and leaders who are black. Characters,
        such as they are, preach about who's who among Negroes.

589.   ————. "So The Girl Marries." *Crisis*, 35, No. 6
        (June 1928), 192-93, 207-09.

        A self-indulgent, sentimental reminiscence about
        being a father. His daughter, Yolande, married
        Countee Cullen, and there are photographs of the
        wedding party. Interesting, inasmuch as Langston
        Hughes and Arna Bontemps are among the attendants.

590.   [Editorial] "Abbott's Monthly Magazine." *Opportunity*,
        8, No. 12 (December 1930), 358-59.

        Announcement about a new Negro magazine, "designed
        frankly to appeal to popular taste."

591.   [Editorial] "American Negro Art." *Opportunity*, 4,
        No. 44 (August 1926), 238-39.

        Discusses the what-is-Negro-art? argument between
        George Schuyler and Langston Hughes that appeared in
        two 1926 issues of *The Nation* magazine. (Hughes's
        article was the now-famous "The Negro Artist and the
        Racial Mountain.") See also items 289 and 416.

592.   Item deleted.

593.   Item deleted.

594.   [Editorial] "The Best Short Stories of 1932."
         Opportunity, 10, No. 10 (October 1932), 303.

         Announces the names of black writers and their
         stories which were mentioned in Edward O'Brien's
         Best Short Stories of 1932 collection.

595.   [Editorial] "Claude McKay Before the Internationale."
         Opportunity, 1, No. 9 (September 1923), 258-59.

         Criticism of McKay's statements made in Russia about
         Negroes and their status in the United States.

596.   [Editorial] "Claude McKay--'If We Must Die.'"
         Opportunity, 26, No. 4 (October-December 1948), 127.

         A memorial concerning McKay's death, written by
         Philip Butcher.

597.   [Editorial] "The Contest." *Opportunity*, 3, No.
         29 (May 1925), 130-31.

         Comments from the judges of "Opportunity's
         Literary Contest."

598.   [Editorial] "The Contest." *Opportunity*, 3, No. 34
         (October 1925), 291-92.

         Positive comments about the "Opportunity Literary
         Contest" and the announcement of the next contest.

599.   [Editorial] "The Contest." *Opportunity*, 4, No. 41
         (May 1926), 143-44.

         Comments on the caliber of works submitted to
         "Opportunity's Second Literary Contest."

600.   [Editorial] "The Contest." *Opportunity*, 5, No. 6
         (June 1927), 159.

         Brief discussion about the 1927 *"Opportunity* Contest"
         (awards were made on 7 May).

601.   [Editorial] "Countee Cullen." *Opportunity*, 4, No.
         47 (November 1926), 337.

         A note about Cullen's new editorial job with
         Opportunity.

602.   [Editorial]   [Du Bois, W.E.B.]   "Mencken."   *Crisis*,
         34, No. 8 (October 1927), 276.

         Answers persons who are upset with Mencken's views
         (see item 609) by citing artistic achievements among
         blacks--such as Roland Hayes, the singer, the poets
         Cullen, Hughes, and McKay, and other writers and
         artists, concluding that "we Negroes are quite well
         satisfied with our Renaissance."

603.   [Editorial]   [Du Bois, W.E.B.]   "The Negro and
         Radical Thought." *Crisis*, 22, No. 3 (July 1921),
         102-04.

         Replies to Claude McKay's charge that *The Crisis*
         sneered at the Russian Revolution and does not support
         the needs of poor blacks.

604.   [Editorial]   [Du Bois, W.E.B.]   "Negro Writers."
         Crisis, 19, No. 6 (April 1920), 298-99.

         Denies black editors "defer to white editors'
         opinions" in accepting manuscripts from black
         writers. Is an answer to a charge made by McKay
         (not made directly to Du Bois, however).

605.   [Editorial] [Du Bois, W.E.B.]   "Our Monthly Sermon."
         Crisis, 36, No. 5 (May 1929), 161.

         Encourages readers to let publishers know what black
         readers want, in the hope that new editions of work
         by good black writers (such as Toomer) and new
         writers can be published.

606.   [Editorial]   "Eric Walrond."   *Opportunity*, 5, No. 3
         (March 1927), 67.

         Mentions Walrond's resignation as Business Manager of
         Opportunity; praises his writing ability, and credits
         him as "one of the first to sense the new public
         spirit on Negro aspirations and work."

607.   [Editorial]   "Garvey and the 'Garvey Movement.'"
         Opportunity, 6, No. 1 (January 1928), 4-5.

         Reflections on the true meanings of Garvey's black
         pride philosophy at the time of his release from
         federal prison.

608.   [Editorial] "The Judges and the Entries."
         Opportunity, 4, No. 42 (June 1926), 174

         Comments concerning winners of *Opportunity*'s Second
         Literary Contest, including Robert Frost's favorable
         words about Arna Bontemps.

609.   [Editorial] [Mencken, H.L.] "Hiring a Hall." *New
         York World* (editorial section), 17 July 1927, [p. 1].

         Sees Negroes as being accepted socially at last, for
         they lend charm to life in New York City. However,
         does not think the artistic achievement of Negroes is
         great, despite attention it receives. Even music by
         blacks is deemed second rate ("The best jazz of today
         is not composed by black men, but by Jews--and I mean
         best in every sense"). Prose and poetry by blacks are
         characterized as poor, especially their short stories,
         which do not rise above the level of those by white
         hacks. Sees hope in the black business class, which
         could lead blacks away from the black preacher, whom
         Mencken castigates for keeping the race "ignorant
         and ridiculous." (See Du Bois's editorial, item 602.)

610.   [Editorial] "More About the Opportunity Contest."
         Opportunity, 12, No. 8 (August 1934), 231.

         Comments of a critic who notes some of the stylistic
         weaknesses of the writers who submitted writings
         to the contest, with added editorial remarks that
         remind readers about the tendency--especially
         during the Renaissance--of praising nearly everything
         written by Negroes.

611.   [Editorial] "Negro Poetry." *Opportunity*, 4, No.
         44 (August 1926), 240.

         Discusses the subjects that interest black poets.

612.   [Editorial] "A New Ideology." *Opportunity*, 7, No.
         4 (April 1929), 108.

         Expresses the belief of the National Urban League
         that black problems in the United States were social
         rather than racial, that color had been an excuse
         rather than a reason for inequality.

613.   [Editorial]   "The New Opportunity Awards."
         Opportunity, 9, No. 11 (November 1931), 331.

         Disappointment with the caliber of short stories
         submitted for the 1931 contest is the subject of
         this editorial.

614.   [Editorial]   "The 1932 Opportunity Literary Contest."
         Opportunity, 10, No. 10 (October 1932), 303.

         Announcement concerning manuscripts submitted
         this year.

615.   [Editorial]   "On the Meaning of Names."   *Opportunity*,
         4, No. 45 (September 1926), 270-71.

         Discussion about the nuances of words "nigger,"
         "Negro," "colored," and others.   Carl Van Vechten's
         controversial novel *Nigger Heaven* had just been
         published.

615a.   [Editorial]   "An Opportunity Award."   *Opportunity*,
         9, No. 10 (October 1931), 298.

         One hundred dollars is offered for the best story or
         essay "of Negro life."   Other observations are about
         racial attitudes of whites who clamor to see Negro
         productions but are unwilling to be associated with
         the Negro in a social sense.

616.   [Editorial]   "The *Opportunity* Contest."   *Opportunity*,
         5, No. 9 (September 1927), 254.

         Announcement of a one-year suspension of the
         literary contest.

616a.   [Editorial]   "An Opportunity for Negro Writers."
         Opportunity, 2, No. 21 (September 1924), 258.

         The influence of this magazine was great during the
         1920s and reflected the bourgeois aims of most writers;
         certainly, there is a contrast in aims between *The
         Crisis* editor, Du Bois, and this editorial that
         exhorts writers to create a literature "free of
         deliberate propaganda and protest."

617.   [Editorial]   "The *Opportunity* Literary Award."
         Opportunity, 13, No. 1 (January 1935), 7.

         College student awards program announced.

618. [Editorial] *"Opportunity* Literary Award 1933."
Opportunity, 11, No. 10 (October 1933), 294-95.

Announcement about the upcoming contest.

619. [Editorial] *"Opportunity* Literary Contest."
Opportunity, 11, No. 12 (December 1933), 361.

Contest of 1933 is extended. Comments about the
story qualities desired are presented, in order
to alert potential writers about such matters as
style and vocabulary.

620. [Editorial] *"Opportunity* Short Stories." *Opportunity,*
13, No. 5 (May 1935), 135.

Notes "distinction" awards that black short story
writers who appeared in *Opportunity* received from
Edward O'Brien's *The Best Short Stories.*

621. [Editorial] *"Opportunity's* Literary Record for 1925."
Opportunity, 4, No. 37 (January 1926), 38.

A "roll of honor" concerning black short story writers.

622. [Editorial] "Out of the Shadow." *Opportunity,* 3,
No. 29 (May 1925), 131.

A defense of the magazine's insistence that submissions
to "Opportunity's Literary Contest" pertain "directly
or indirectly to the Negro." The magazine saw itself
as a champion of the "New Negro."

623. [Editorial] [Ovington, Mary White.] "A Word for the
New Year." *Crisis,* 27, No. 3 (January 1924), 103-04.

Stresses opinion that literary artists such as
Cullen should avoid propaganda and concentrate on
beauty, which is truth.

624. [Editorial] "The Passing of Garvey." *Opportunity,*
3, No. 27 (March 1925), 66.

With Garvey arrested for fraud, there remained the
question of who would help the people who were
caught up in his movement.

625. [Editorial] "Rudolph Fisher and Wallace Thurman."
Opportunity, 13, No. 3 (February 1935), 38-39.

Tributes to these recently dead writers.

626.   [Editorial] "Some Perils of the 'Renaissance.'"
        Opportunity, 5, No. 3 (March 1927), 68.

        Warns about indiscriminate praise of nearly all
        literary work written by blacks.

627.   [Editorial] "The Third Opportunity Contest."
        Opportunity, 4, No. 46 (October 1926), 304-05.

        Urges that material sumbitted deal with Negro life.

628.   [Editorial] "Welcoming the New Negro." *Opportunity*,
        4, No. 40 (April 1926), 113.

        Concerns the famous anthology edited by Alain Locke.
        See also item 772.

629.   "Eighth Street Market, New York City." *Opportunity*,
        13, No. 1 (January 1935), 22.

        Sketches by Romare Bearden.

630.   Elmes, A.F. "Garvey and Garveyism--An Estimate."
        Opportunity, 3, No. 29 (May 1925), 139-41.

        A more sympathetic view of Garvey than was usually
        found in the black bourgeois press, ending with the
        observation that "Many an outsider like myself may
        be brought sooner or later to admit: after all there
        was something to it!"

631.   "Faces from a Legendary Era." *Black World*, 20,
        No. 1 (November 1970), 98-105.

        Photographs of Harlem Renaissance personalities, such
        as Langston Hughes, Arna Bontemps, Countee Cullen,
        Frank Horne, and Arthur Schomburg.

632.   "Facts on Gotham Fascinators." *New York Amsterdam
        News*, 25 March 1939, p. 9.

        Biographical sketch of Jessie Fauset.

633.   Fauset, Arthur Huff. "Symphonesque." *Opportunity*,
        4 (June 1926), 178-80, 198-200.

        Cudjo, a kind, natural country boy, is beset with
        desire for his long-time friend, Amber Lee. Set at
        a pace to parallel musical movements, the story ends
        with Cudjo overcoming his temptation and passion.

This short story received the first prize in the 1926
Opportunity contest and was included later in O'Brien's
Best Short Stories of the Year.

634.   Fax, Mark. "The Lost Zoo." Symphonic Suite for
        Orchestra. M.M. thesis, Eastman School of Music,
        1945. (Based on poetry by Countee Cullen.)

635.   Fisher, Rudolph. "The Caucasian Storms Harlem."
        The American Mercury, 11 (1927), 393-98.

        After a five years' absence from Harlem, Fisher finds
        the cabarets there full of whites--whites who copy
        black dances and who frequent the cabarets nightly.
        Is amazed at this phenomenon.

636.   Frazier, E. Franklin. "The Garvey Movement.
        Opportunity, 4, No. 47 (November 1926), 346-48.

        Examines the appeal of Garvey at a time when his
        movement was eclipsed by his imprisonment.

637.   "From the Harmon Foundation Art Exhibit, 1934."
        Opportunity, 12, No. 6 (June 1934), 186.

        Black and white illustrations of two paintings by
        Charles H. Alston and one by Aaron Douglas.

638.   Gale, Zona. ["Letter to Charles S. Johnson,"] in
        The Harlem Renaissance Generation, ed. L.M. Collins.
        Nashville: Fisk University, 1972. Pp. 415-17.

        Comments about the eleven stories submitted to the
        Opportunity Awards Contest for 1924 that did not win
        prizes but which she deemed worthy of comment.

639.   Gordon, Eugene. "Outstanding Negro Newspapers, 1927."
        Opportunity, 5, No. 12 (December 1927), 358-62.

        Insight into the interests and concerns of blacks
        during the late 1920s.

640.   ------. "A Survey of the Negro Press." *Opportunity*,
        5, No. 1 (January 1927), 7-11, 32.

        Characterizes the Negro press as vigorously race
        conscious and then assesses a number of newspapers as
        to news coverage, editorials, features, and makeup.

641.   Gordon, Taylor. *Born to Be.* Introduction by Muriel
         Draper, a Foreword by Carl Van Vechten, and
         Illustrations by Covarrubias. New Introduction by
         Robert Hemenway. Seattle: University of Washington
         Press, c1975, c1929.

         Hemenway, in an enlightening and penetrating essay,
         fills in the life of Gordon and explores the signifi-
         cance of this autobiogaphy (which covers the first
         36 of his 78 years), especially in relation to the
         Harlem Renaissance. Gordon, "a born raconteur,"
         wrote an absorbing, rather innocent **history** of his
         life, which included being a singer of spirituals,
         and a man of many trades with Ringling Brothers.
         During the 1920s Gordon flourished as a singer and
         "personality," and was susceptible to the praise of
         whites and blacks whc touted the more exotic
         elements of this period.

642.   Graham, James D. "Negro Protest in America, 1900–
         1955: A Bibliographical Guide." *South Atlantic
         Quarterly*, 67, No. 1 (Winter 1968), 94–107.

         Works by James Weldon Johnson, Claude McKay, and Jean
         Toomer are briefly commented upon in this guide.

643.   Harrington, Donald Szantho. *Langston Hughes, Soul
         Singer*. New York: The Community Pulpit, The Community
         Church of New York (40 East 35th Street), 1967.

         Reminiscences of Hughes, presented by the author at
         a memorial service he conducted at the Community
         Church on 4 June 1967. A photograph of the young
         Langston Hughes (by James L. Allen) is on the cover
         of the booklet. Selections from Hughes's poetry
         are also included.

644.   Hartt, Roland Lynde. "The New Negro." *The Independent*,
         105 (15 January 1921), 59–60, 76.

         Indicates that the new spirit of blacks means they
         will no longer be docile to injustice, that there is
         audacity and fighting spirit in the people which is
         further reflected in the Negro press.

645.   Haynes, George Edmund. "The Harmon Awards in 1926."
         Crisis, 33, No. 3 (January 1927), 156–57.

         Winners and judges are listed.

646.   Hubert, James H. "Harlem Faces Unemployment."
         Opportunity, 9, No. 2 (February 1931), 42-45.

647.   Hughes, Langston. [Letter to the Editor.] *Crisis*,
         35, No. 9 (September 1928), 302.

         Answers Allison Davis's charge that Hughes's poetry
         was influenced by Carl Van Vechten: "I do not resent
         Mr. Davis' criticism of my work.... To such people
         my poems are as the proverbial red rag to the bull....
         I have never pretended to be keeping a literary
         grazing pasture with food to suit all breeds of
         cattle." See also Davis's article, item 582.

648.   ————. "When I Worked for Dr. Woodson." *Negro
         History Bulletin*, 13, No. 8 (May 1950), 188.

         Reminiscences about how Hughes learned to be methodical
         and accurate in work because of Woodson's devotion
         and labor in the cause of Negro history. Stresses
         importance of responsibilities to the "race," learned
         from one of the prime "Race Men" of the 1920s.

649.   Ikonne, Chidi. "*Opportunity* and Black Literature,
         1923-1933." *Phylon*, 40, No. 1 (March 1979), 86-93.

650.   "In the News Columns." *Opportunity*, 15, No. 2
         (February 1937), 38.

         A tribute to Charles S. Johnson on his election as
         Vice President of the American Sociological Society.
         (Johnson was a great help to the writers of the
         Harlem Renaissance.)

651.   Jacobs, George W. "Negro Authors Must Eat." *The
         Nation*, 128, No. 3336 (12 June 1929), 710-11.

         Deplores the cult of the primitive and the more
         sensational novels by Negroes. Wonders why Africa
         should be important to the writers. Praises the
         work of Fauset and Larsen and ends with a wish that
         stereotypical work will cease to be written.

652.   Jelliffe, Rowena Woodham. "The Negro in the Field of
         Drama." *Opportunity*, 6, No. 7 (July 1928), 214.

         Declaring the black musical comedy nearly dead, the
         author urges black writers to produce fewer race-
         conscious dramas, although she professes a belief
         in folk drama and does not think the black dramatist
         should succumb to propaganda by writing plays that
         put the "best racial foot foremost."

653.   "Jessie Fauset Portrays People She Knows, She Tells
        Group." *The Afro-American* (Baltimore), 27
        February 1932.

        Speech to the Co-Operative Women's League in which
        Fauset emphasizes her need to be familiar with the
        characters about whom she writes.

654.   Johnson, Campbell. "Our Opportunity to Literature."
        The Stylus (June 1916), 8-9.

        An early encouragement for black writers to move from
        protest and controversial writing to another sort
        of race literature that is founded on philosophy
        and portrays how blacks attempt to solve life's
        problems in their racially distinct ways. Urges
        new writers to have pride in their own heritage in
        order to find their own identity.

655.   Johnson, Charles S. "After Garvey--What?"
        Opportunity, 1, No. 8 (August 1923), 231-33.

        If one would know the Harlem Renaissance, one must
        understand Garvey and the attitude of those who lived
        at his time. As Johnson says in this article,
        "Garvey is a symbol--a symptom." Even though he is
        critical of Garvey, Johnson understood the meaning
        of his movement to the burgeoning black self-
        identity efforts.

656.   ————. "Countee Cullen Was My Friend," in *The
        Harlem Renaissance Generation*, ed. L.M. Collins.
        Nashville: Fisk University, 1972. Pp. 270-74.

        A restrained but warm reminiscence about the poet,
        whom he saw as witty, charming, well disciplined in
        his writing, and absolutely dedicated to expression
        that portrayed the beauty Cullen sought in life.
        States that Cullen "will symbolize the eternal
        freshness of the literature and art for which this
        building [Countee Cullen Branch of the New York
        Public Library] is the custodian." Delivered at
        the dedication of the building on 12 September 1951.

657.   ————. "Literature and the Practice of Living," in
        The Harlem Renaissance Generation, ed. L.M. Collins.
        Nashville: Fisk University, 1972. Pp. 4-12.

        An address made on 7 January 1950, at Yale University,
        for the opening of the James Weldon Johnson Memorial

Collection of Negro Arts and Letters. Cites relationship
between J.W. Johnson and Carl Van Vechten, and also
concentrates on the symbolism of Johnson as both an
exemplar of culture and as precursor to the writers
of the Renaissance. Sees Johnson as laying the
groundwork for these writers.

658.   ————. "The New Frontage on American Life," in *The
New Negro: An Interpretation*, ed. Alain Locke. New
York: Albert and Charles Boni, 1925. Pp. 278-98.

Traces sociological changes--population shifts, creation
of the urban Negro, unionization--as well as noting
cultural changes, such as interest of Negroes in
their folklore and musical heritage. In sum, there
is a spirit of progressivism in the moves the Negro
is making as he enters gradually into the mainstream
of a society that, in the past, rejected him.

659.   Johnson, Edwin D. "The Jewel in Ethiope's Ear."
Opportunity, 6, No. 6 (June 1928), 166-68.

Criticism of drama by black writers is presented
through a castigation of the critics who, the author
suggests, pay more attention to their personal
feelings than to the canons of good literary criticism.
The major need suggested is for writers who are
"artistic and not propagandic."

660.   Johnson, Fenton. "Harlem by Day and Night." *The
Favorite Magazine,* 4 (July 1920), 363-64.

Sees Harlem as the "soul of a progressive America,"
a place that has every aspect of life represented--
the church, social services organizations like the
Urban League and, drawing great praise, the U.N.I.A.
of Marcus Garvey. A "one-man's opinion" that
presents a positive and optimistic picture of
Harlem right at the beginning of the 1920s.

661.   Johnson, James Weldon. "Negro Authors and White
Publishers." *Crisis*, 36, No. 7 (July 1929), 228-29.

Examining the complaint of black writers who claimed
white publishers wanted only work about the "lower
elements of Negro life, attempts to refute this idea
through listing the various books already published
by black writers. Optimistically states that no good
book has been refused publication solely on the
basis of the color of its author.

662.   Jones, Eugene Kinckle. "The Negro's Opportunity
         Today." *Opportunity*, 6, No. 1 (January 1928), 10-12.

         An overview of progress made by Negroes in areas such
         as health conditions, occupations, home ownership,
         and literature, concluding with the belief that the
         black race would join other ethnics in receiving the
         full benefits of living in the United States.

663.   Kallen, Horace M. "Alain Locke and Cultural
         Pluralism." *The Journal of Philosophy*, 54
         (1957), 119-27.

         Locke's philosophy presented itself in a practical
         manner in his encouragement of persons (blacks) whom
         he felt were different but equal to the dominant
         race. He made it his goal to let the young Negroes
         know they were not the cause of prejudice against
         them: the new Negro had to change his concept about
         himself, accept his différence; the next phase is
         co-existence with those who are different. This is
         his basic philosophy, then, about race and the
         relationships among persons of differing colors
         and races.

664.   Kellner, Bruce. *Carl Van Vechten and the irreverent
         Decades*. Norman: University of Oklahoma Press, 1968.

         Presents a brief, superficial recounting of Van
         Vechten's relationships with and interest in blacks
         during the 1920s. Concentrates in detail chiefly
         upon Von Vechten's novel *Nigger Heaven*, how it was
         examined carefully by black readers and a lawyer
         before publication, and the reactions of different
         people whose letters are quoted.

665.   Kinneman, John A. "The Negro Renaissance." *Negro
         History Bulletin*, 25 (1962), 200, 197-99 [sic].

         Discusses the interest Robert Kerlin had in Negro
         writers during the Renaissance (see item 43, for
         instance), and his contributions toward advancing
         knowledge of writers (see item 193). Also describes
         the *Survey Graphic* special Negro issue. Sees the
         Renaissance as a period of cultural emancipation
         for the Negro--a period that achieved impressive
         artistic attainments.

666.   Knox, George. "The Harlem Renaissance Today (The
        1920's 'New Negro Movement' Reviewed)--Notes on a
        Neglected Theme." *California English Journal*, 7
        (December 1971), 29-33.

        Description of a course--giving a rationale and
        bibliography of works assigned--taught by the author
        at the University of California (Riverside) at a
        time when he felt this period was being overlooked
        by teachers of American literature. Covers all of
        the major as well as many of the minor writers.

667.   "Krigwa: *Crisis* Prizes in Literature and Art, 1926."
        Crisis, 33, No. 2 (December 1926), 70-71.

        List of winners in this contest, with a photograph
        of them in a group setting.

668.   "Krigwa 1926." *Crisis*, 31, No. 2 (December 1925),
        67-68.

        Announcement of the categories and the deadline for
        entries to the Spingarn writing and drawing awards.

669.   "Krigwa, 1927." *Crisis*, 33, No. 4 (February 1927),
        191-93.

        Announcement of categories and prizes for works
        of literature and art.

670.   "Krigwa Players Little Negro Theater." *The Crisis*,
        32, No. 3 (July 1926), 134-36.

        Relates the aims of a new theater movement in Harlem,
        aimed at dramas about blacks, written by blacks for
        a black audience.

671.   Leuders, Edward. *Carl Van Vechten and the Twenties*.
        Albuquerque: University of New Mexico Press, 1955.

        Suggests that Van Vechten's role in relation to the
        black writers of the Harlem Renaissance was to call
        attention to an already-existing, distinct culture.
        Therefore, the publication of his novel, *Nigger
        Heaven*, helped to expose the active and burgeoning
        artistic movement.

671a.   Levine, Lawrence W. "The Concept of the New Negro
          and the Realities of Black Culture," in *Key Issues
          in the Afro-American Experience*, ed. Martin Kilson,
          Daniel M. Fox, and Nathan I. Huggins. Vol. 2. New
          York: Harcourt Brace Jovanovich, 1971. Pp. 125-47.

          Uses black music and folk songs of the early 20th
          century to demonstrate the essential elements of
          black culture--elements too often overlooked by
          writers who probe the meaning of the "New Negro"
          (a term that was used most frequently to describe
          the race during the Harlem Renaissance, but also
          before that time as well). Suggests the words of
          the songs are more important than the music, and the
          words reflect the true tenor of Negro life and
          thought (e.g., reflect pride in one's color).

672.   [Literary Information.] *Opportunity*, 3, No. 35
          (November 1925), 345-46.

          Notes about Cullen and Walrond, as well as some
          comments about Negro folklore.

673.   [Literary Information.] *Opportunity*, 4, No. 37
          (January 1926), 28.

          News about Hughes and Cullen.

674.   [Literary Information.] *Opportunity*, 4, No. 47
          (November 1926), 362.

          Winners of *The Crisis* literary and art contest are
          announced, and mention is made of the upcoming issue
          of the magazine *Fire!!*

675.   Item deleted.

676.   Locke, Alain. "Beauty Instead of Ashes." *The
          Nation*, 126, No. 3276 (18 April 1928), 432-34.

          Calls for a maturing of black artistic expression,
          utilizing the folk temperament to create original
          work of genuine realism and beauty. By using the
          artistic heritage of blacks the new Negroes will
          "move with full power and freedom in the domain of
          the novel and the drama ... poetry and music."

677.   ————. "The High Cost of Prejudice." *Forum*, 78,
          No. 4 (October 1927), 500-10.

          A debate with Lothrop Stoddard (see item 720) on the
          subject "Should the Negro Be Encouraged to Cultural
          Equality?" Locke writes his answer as yes, for he
          points out the genuineness of Negro expression and
          the force with which the young artists present works
          that are enjoyed by whites. Complete equality should
          follow the acceptance of the Negroe's contributions.

678.   ————. "Max Rheinhardt [sic] Reads the Negro's
          Dramatic Horoscope." *Opportunity*, 2, No. 17
          (May 1924), 145-46.

          A conflict between Locke's vision of the Negro's need
          to produce "serious Negro drama" and Reinhardt's
          interest in the more exotic, rhythmic drama that
          was in vogue during the 1920s.

679.   ————. "Negro Youth Speaks," in his *The New Negro:
          An Interpretation*. New York: Albert and Charles Boni,
          1925. Pp. 47-53.

          Praises racial expression in the work of young
          writers like Toomer, Hughes, Cullen, Fisher, and
          Hurston. A brief introduction to the anthology of
          literary pieces by numerous writers of this period.

680.   ————. "Our Little Renaissance," in *Ebony and
          Topaz: A Collectanea*, ed. Charles S. Johnson. New
          York: National Urban League, 1927. Pp. 117-18.

          Sees the Renaissance as becoming an integral part of
          American life. Points out the use of sources from
          the roots of the black American's past.

681.   ————. "The Technical Study of Spirituals——A Review."
          Opportunity, 3, No. 35 (November 1925), 331-32.

682.   ————. "To Certain of Our Phillistines [sic]."
          Opportunity, 3, No. 29 (May 1925), 155-56.

          Locke's artistic theories are a key to understanding
          this period. Here he argues for representative Negro
          art, but for art that is not tainted by distortions
          of propaganda. He exhorts black artists to develop
          art that expresses the uniqueness of black culture
          without yielding to exoticism.

683.   ————. "Toward a Critique of Negro Music."
            Opportunity, 12, No. 11 (November 1934), 328-31;
            12, No. 12 (December 1934), 365-67, 385.

            Exhorts Negro musicians to produce a music closer to
            the black idiom. Claims blacks are a victim of
            either too much praise or "calculated disparagement"
            (p. 328). Sees musicians as slaves to commercialism
            as well as being unable to create a musical tradition.
            Duke Ellington is praised, however (through a quotation
            from another article), as one who "'has emancipated
            American popular music from text for the first time
            since Colonial days.'"

684.   Long, Richard A. "The Genesis of Locke's *The New
            Negro*." *Black World*, 25, No. 4 (February 1976), 14-20.

            A recounting of the behind-the-scenes efforts to produce
            first the *Survey Graphic* issue and then the now-
            famous anthology of poetry, prose, music, and art,
            The New Negro, which burst upon the cultural scene
            in 1925.

685.   *Louis Armstrong--A Self Portrait*. Interview by Richard
            Meryman. New York: Eakins Press, 1971.

            Reminiscences of the famous trumpeter, with a brief
            portion devoted to vivid encounters during the 1920s
            with such persons as Joe Oliver and Bix Beiderbecke.

686.   Lyman, John. "A Negro Theatre." *Opportunity*, 12,
            No. 1 (January 1934), 14-17.

            Outline of goals and background of the Repertory
            Playhouse Associates, which was devoted to training
            and providing opportunities to "the colored actor,
            playwright, director, technician and worker ...
            of the theatre."

687.   "Masterpieces of Crisis Poetry, 1910-1931." *Crisis*,
            38, No. 11 (November 1931), 380-81.

            Reprint of "Lament," by Countee Cullen, "Cross," by
            Langston Hughes, "Song of the Son," by Jean Toomer,
            and "Nocturne at Bethesda," by Arna Bontemps.

688.   Matheus, John F. "Anthropoi." *Opportunity*, 6
            (August 1928), 229-32.

            A short story. Two different families--one black,
            one Greek-American--see how race makes a difference

in attaining the American dream of success: once
friends, the families grow away from one another as
the Greek family reaps the benefits belonging to the
"white" race. It is only after World War I, when
the sons are grown and both intolerant of injustice,
that the fathers of each family understand the value
of respecting human dignity, no matter the skin color.
There is, then, reconciliation at the end--reconciliation
and understanding.

689.   ————. "Fog." *Opportunity*, 3 (May 1925), 144-47.

A short story. People of different races are on a
bus that has a near-fatal mishap on a bridge, during
a heavy fog. This common experience helps all of
the people realize, if only for a short time, that
there can be oneness among divergent peoples.

690.   ————. "Swamp Moccasin." *Crisis*, 33, No. 2
(December 1926), 67-69.

Short story.

691.   Matthews, Mark D. "His Philosophy and Opinions:
Perspective on Marcus Garvey." *Black World*, 25,
No. 4 (February 1976), 36-48.

Examination of Garvey's major ideas with an emphasis
on the materialistic elements.

692.   Miller, Kelly. "Where is the Negro's Heaven?"
Opportunity, 4, No. 48 (December 1926), 370-73.

Spurred by the novel *Nigger Heaven* by Carl Van
Vechten, a sociologist rates Washington, D.C., as a
better place for Negroes to live because of such
factors as better housing and the presence of the
most famous Negro institution of higher education,
Howard University.

693.   "Miss Augusta Savage." *Opportunity*, 1, No. 6
(June 1923), 25.

Tells of the artist's rejection by the American
committee for an application to study in Fountain-
bleau--a story fictionally recounted in the novel
Plum Bun, by Jessie Fauset (see item 250).

694.   Mitchell, Lofton. "Harlem My Harlem." *Black World*,
        20, No. 1 (November 1970), 91-97.

        A second-hand review of people and places during the
        Harlem Renaissance, because the author, in his
        pre-teens during the 1920s, was aware not so much of
        the artistic movement as of an air of vitality and
        joie de vivre that existed. What he related about
        the period is easily available in any review of
        the period.

695.   ————. "The Negro Theatre and the Harlem Community."
        Freedomways, 3, No. 3 (Summer 1963), 384-94.

        Only very brief mention of some musicals produced
        during the 1920s.

696.   ————. *Voices of the Black Theatre*. Clifton,
        N.J.: James T. White & Co., 1975.

        Introductory remarks and then interviews of persons
        who participated in drama activities among blacks
        during the 1920s and early 1930s: Eddie Hunter,
        Regina M. Andrews, and Dick Campbell. These
        reminiscences give the ambiance of the times as
        well as discuss the role of *The Crisis* magazine's
        support of drama writing.

697.   Moore, William H.A. "Richmond Barthé--Sculptor."
        Opportunity, 6, No. 11 (November 1928), 334.

        An impressionistic description of this artist's work,
        with four photographic illustrations.

698.   Morris, Lloyd. "The Negro 'Renaissance.'" *The
        Southern Workman*, 59, No. 2 (February 1930), 82-86.

        States the Renaissance can be attributed to white
        interest in Negroes rather than to what blacks are
        producing. Thinks past contributions written by
        Negroes (e.g., Phillis Wheatley) should be remembered.
        Nothing about Harlem Renaissance writers or their
        writings; rather, an overview of 18th-19th-century
        black writers, even though names of Renaissance
        writers are listed in one paragraph.

699.   Moryck, Brenda Ray. "I, Too, Have Lived in Washington."
        Opportunity, 5, No. 8 (August 1927), 228-31, 243.

        A defense of Washington, D.C., by a woman who felt
        the city was unjustly criticized by Langston Hughes.

This pretentious, unsubstantial "defense" demonstrates
the problem many bourgeois blacks had in adjusting
to the more inventive Renaissance writers.

700.   "Most Popular Books at the 135th Street Branch
        (Harlem), New York Public Library." *Opportunity*,
        7, No. 2 (January 1929), 58.

        Bad Girl by Delmar and *Scarlet Sister Mary* by Julia
        Peterkin lead the list; *Orlando* by Woolf is a distant
        fourth in number of reserves.

701.   Mulder, Arnold. *"Wanted*: A Negro Novelist." *The
        Independent*, 112, No. 3871 (21 June 1924), 341-42.

        Sees the need for the horrors of racism and the
        inner life of blacks to be revealed, not through
        facts but in fiction. Does believe this may be
        starting, as evidenced by Fauset's recently published
        There Is Confusion.

702.   Nance, Ethel Ray. "The New York Arts Renaissance,
        1924-1926." *Negro History Bulletin*, 31, No. 4 (April
        1968), 15-19.

        Describes the dinner of the New York Writers Guild
        held at the Civic Club on 21 March 1924, when black
        writers and white editors declared the "'debut' of
        young Negro writers." (See also item 584.) Goes
        on to describe events afterwards--the manuscripts
        received at *Opportunity* magazine, the *Survey Graphic*
        special issue of Negro writing, as part of a review
        of literary happenings during the 1920s. Mrs. Nance
        was an assistant to Charles S. Johnson when he was
        Editor of *Opportunity*.

703.   "The Negro in Art: How Shall He Be Portrayed?" *Crisis*,
        31, No. 4 (February 1926), 165; 31, No. 5 (March
        1926), 219-20; 31, No. 6 (April 1926), 278-80; 32,
        No. 1 (May 1926), 35-36; 32, No. 2 (June 1926), 71-73;
        32, No. 4 (August 1926), 193-94; 32, No. 5 (September
        1926), 238-39; 33, No. 1 (November 1926), 28-29.

        A symposium by mail, asking six questions of each
        correspondent--white and black authors and editors--
        concerning what sort of material should be used in
        black literature, what sort of characters should be
        used, whether blacks should write only on racial
        subjects, etc. Many prominent persons sent in their
        answers--blacks such as Cullen, whites such as
        Van Vechten.

704.   "A Note on the New Literary Movement." *Opportunity*,
         4, No. 39 (March 1926), 80-81.

         Cautions black writers to adjust to the standards of
         good writing, and not to succumb to thinking that
         anything written will be accepted on the strength
         alone of its having been written by a Negro.

705.   "Notes." *Palms*, 3, No. 6 (March 1926), 189.

         Announcement about a special edition with writings by
         black writers of the then-called "Negro Renaissance."

706.   Osofsky, Gilbert. "Symbols of the Jazz Age: The New
         Negro and Harlem Discovered." *American Quarterly*, 17,
         No. 2, Pt. 1 (Summer 1965), 229-38.

         The Harlem Renaissance grew out of "broader changes
         in American society," and was undergoing complex
         changes (the increase in the number of urban Negroes,
         for instance). But the view promulgated by the
         writers and other artists--both black and white--was
         the exotic side, the mythological Harlem, symbol
         of the jazz age

707.   "Our Prize Winners and What They Say of Themselves."
         Opportunity, 4, No. 42 (June 1926), 188-89.

         Photographs and statements from winners of
         Opportunity's Second Literary Contest.

708.   *Palms*, 4, No. 1 (October 1926).

         A special issue devoted to literature by Negro writers.
         Contains a brief article by Walter White about this
         period (see item 508). Poetry is by Bontemps, Cuney,
         Spencer, Cullen, Fauset, and Hughes, among others.
         Locke also reviews Hughes's *The Weary Blues*.

709.   Pawa, J.M. "Black Radicals and White Spies: Harlem,
         1919." *Negro History Bulletin*, 35, No. 6 (October
         1972), 129-33.

         The work performed by Lusk agents (i.e., people on a ·
         New York State legislative committee that investigated
         "seditious activities"), in reaction to a series of
         meetings in Harlem, is explored to demonstrate the
         fear the government had of Socialists organizing
         among black and white radicals during the early
         part of the 20th century.

710.   Pearson, Ralph I.   "Combatting Racism with Art:
       Charles S. Johnson and the Harlem Renaissance."
       American Studies, 18, No. 1 (1977), 123-34.

       Article not seen.

711.   Perkins, Huel D.   "Renaissance 'Renegade'?: Wallace
       Thurman."   *Black World*, 25, No. 4 (February 1976),
       29-35.

       Concludes that this unhappy, caustic writer was more
       critic than renegade--a critic who provided a leveling
       element during a time of too much indiscriminate
       praise to black writers.

712.   "Pot-Pourri: A Negro Renaissance'."   *Opportunity*, 3,
       No. 30 (June 1925), 187.

       A reprint from the *New York Herald Tribune* commenting
       on the literary and other artistic talents of
       American Negroes.

713.   "The Prize Winners."   *Opportunity*, 3, No. 30 (June
       1925), 186.

       Photographs of the "Opportunity Literary Contest"
       winners.

714.   Richardson, Harry V.   "The New Negro and Religion."
       Opportunity, 11, No. 2 (February 1933), 41-44.

715.   Rose, Al.   *Eubie Blake*.   New York: Schirmer Books
       (Macmillan), 1979.

       A "breezy," informal portrait of the musician whose
       all-black musical *Shuffle Along* (1921), provided a
       unique portion of the ambiance of the Harlem
       Renaissance, and also helped to define the special
       quality of the period the author calls the "golden
       years for ... Blake."   This biography is enhanced
       greatly by Blake's own descriptions of his life and
       times.   Of particular usefulness is a "Selected List
       of Compositions"; further, there is a listing of
       recordings by Blake ("Discography"), "Piano
       Rollography" (list of player piano rolls issued
       by Blake), and films about and with Blake.   Indeed,
       the Harlem Renaissance cannot be understood fully
       without being exposed to the music as well as the
       commentary of Eubie Blake.

716.   "The Schomburg Library Opened to Students."
        Opportunity, 4, No. 42 (June 1926), 187.

717.   Schuyler, George. "Our White Folks." *American
        Mercury*, 12, No. 48 (December 1927), 385-92.

        Mordant comments on black people's greater knowledge
        of whites than of the latter's knowledge of blacks
        (although, as he points out, they continue to write
        stereotypical stories and articles about them).
        Black survival techniques have made the black person
        develop a high degree of intelligence, and there is
        a greater variety of types among Negroes than among
        whites. In summary, the Negro also sees America as
        black and white, not as a purely white civilization.

718.   Sheffey, Ruthe T. "Zora Neale Hurston: The Morgan
        Connection." *Morgan Magazine* (Winter 1976), 4-6.

        Hurston was once a student of Morgan Academy (high
        school for Morgan College) and spent two happy years
        there before going to Washington, D.C., where she
        studied at Howard University. Sees the Morgan
        Academy atmosphere as having a positive and warm
        effect on her life.

719.   "The Speech of the American Negro Folk." *Opportunity*,
        5, No. 7 (July 1927), 195-97.

720.   Stoddard, Lothrop. "The Impasse at the Color Line."
        Forum, 78, No. 4 (October 1927), 510-19.

        Reply to Alain Locke (see item 677) concerning their
        written debate on "Should the Negro Be Encouraged
        to Cultural Equality?" His answer is no, because
        the tradition of White America must be maintained.
        He does not mean to imply inferiority but differentness
        --the sort that should encourage a biracial system
        where Negroes meet their needs among their own race.

721.   "Survey of the Month." *Opportunity*, 6, No. 8
        (August 1928), 249.

        News about Arthur Schomburg's gift of an oriental
        classic to the New York Public Library, and a note
        about Countee Cullen's trip to Europe.

722.   "Survey of the Month." *Opportunity*, 8, No. 8
         (August 1930), 250.

         Brief news section announces publications by
         Langston Hughes and James Weldon Johnson, accompanied
         by a photograph of each man.

723.   "Survey of the Month." *Opportunity*, 8, No. 11
         (November 1930), 345.

         News about a mural designed and painted by
         Aaron Douglas.

724.   "Survey of the Month." *Opportunity*, 10, No. 3
         (March 1932), 92.

         Announcement of the production of Zora Neale
         Hurston's dramatic presentation *Great Day*.

725.   "Survey of the Month." *Opportunity*, 10, No. 4
         (April 1932), 124.

         Announcement of novels by Wallace Thurman, Jessie
         Fauset, and Countee Cullen. Photographs of the
         three authors.

726.   "Survey of the Month." *Opportunity*, 12, No. 7
         (July 1934), 221.

         News of Countee Cullen's appointment at Dillard
         University to a post he ultimately did not accept.

727.   "Survey of the Month." *Opportunity*, 14, No. 7
         (July 1936), 219-20.

         News about Augusta Savage, followed by a photograph.

728.   "Survey of the Month." *Opportunity*, 14, No. 12
         (December 1936), 384.

         News about Langston Hughes's play *Troubled Island*,
         under the section entitled "Drama."

729.   "Survey of the Month." *Opportunity*, 15, No. 4
         (April 1937), 120.

         News about a $2,500 fellowship that Zora Neale
         Hurston received.

730.   Thornhill, Gertrude C.   "The Negro Becomes a Literary
        Contributor." *Poet Lore*, 39 (1928), 431-35.

        Acknowledges literary movement, especially the
        poetry, and suggests the strongest feature of black
        poetry is its race consciousness. Despite stressing
        the primitive, rhythmic qualities, suggests
        "Apostles of Keats are they all." Projects the
        mind of one who finds Negroes simple and enchanting
        primitives.

731.   Tignor, Eleanor Q.   "Rudolph Fisher: 'This is Harlem'
        --1920's." Unpublished Speech, Delivered at the
        New York College English Association meeting, 22
        March 1980.

        "Fisher's writings seem to say, 'This is Harlem'--
        1920's. Harlem is his setting, and his characteriza-
        tions are woven from his knowledge and observations
        of Harlemites, the naive Southern migrant, the strong
        grandmother, and the preacher being his favorite
        delineations. A realist, the author also alludes to
        the NAACP and the Garvey Movement and takes the reader
        inside of the 1920's places of pleasure. No (Black)
        Van Vechten, however, Fisher shows Negro Harlem as
        it was, without exaggeration." (Annotation supplied
        by Tignor, who is on the faculty of LaGuardia
        Community College, Long Island City, N.Y.)

732.   Van Doren, Carl.   "The Roving Critic: Negro
        Renaissance." *The Century Magazine*, 111, No. 5
        (March 1926), 635-37.

        This article congratulates the Negro for demonstrating
        he had achieved "the unmistakable signs of an advanced
        civilization" by producing the sort of literature
        found in Alain Locke's *The New Negro*. It is stated
        that, by comparison with the achievement of whites
        by 1826, Negro writers had produced creditable if
        not outstanding work. One interesting observation:
        "the negro [sic] is better as analyst than as artist,"
        indicating the writer's greater praise for articles
        than for stories or poems (with the exceptions of
        works by Cullen and Toomer).

733.   ————.   "The Younger Generation of Negro Writers."
        Opportunity, 2, No. 17 (May 1924), 144-45.

        Expresses an optimistic view about the contribution
        that black writers had to make, especially in terms

of the natural propaganda that could result from
simply exposing authentic black experiences in
America.

734.   Van Vechten, Carl. *"Keep A-Inchin' Along": Selected
         Writings of Carl Van Vechten About Black Art and
         Letters.* Edited by Bruce Kellner. Westport, Conn.:
         Greenwood Press, 1979.

         Includes articles on James Weldon Johnson, Van
         Vechten's answers to *The Crisis* survey on "The
         Negro in Art: How Shall He Be Portrayed?," and
         photographs of Negroes (e.g., Hughes, Cullen,
         and Hurston).

735.   Walrond, Eric. "The New Negro Faces America."
         Current History, 17, No. 5 (February 1923), 786-88.

         Contends that there is no real leader for blacks in
         the U.S. to follow: each leader (Du Bois, Garvey,
         Moton) lacks something that the masses need.
         Nevertheless, the Negro has made progress and hopes
         to participate fully in American culture (points
         out that most blacks do not want to go to Africa).

736.   Weaver, Savilla E. "Randolph's *Messenger* (1917-1922)."
         Negro History Bulletin, 34, No. 8 (December 1971),
         182-84.

         Describes history of *The Messenger* and cites, as
         well, contents of specific articles that stress
         social and political (rather than literary) concerns.

737.   Webb, George A. "The Profanation of Negro Spirituals."
         Opportunity, 6, No. 6 (June 1928), 182.

         Protests white appropriation of Negro spirituals,
         not only because of the style of singing but also
         because of the condescending dramatization routinely
         used with the singing.

737a.   West, Dorothy. "Hannah Byde." *The Messenger*, 8
         (July 1926), 197-99.

         A short story about a woman who is carrying a child
         she does not want but is resigned to her pregnancy
         after botching a suicide attempt.

737b.   ————. "Prologue to a Life." *The Saturday
             Evening Quill* (Boston) (April 1929), 5-10.

             A neurotic woman can only relate to her children
             in this short story that probes an upper middle-
             class marriage among Boston blacks.

737c.   ————. "The Typewriter." *Opportunity*, 4 (July
             1926), 220-22, 233-34.

             Second prize short story in the 1926 *Opportunity*
             Contest. An unachieving black man aids his daughter
             in her quest to better herself and becomes so
             wrapped up in an imaginary world she has created
             for learning to type that he is emotionally maimed
             when reality once more is established in their
             household

737d.   ————. "An Unimportant Man." *The Saturday Evening
             Quill* (Boston) (June 1928), 21-32.

             A short story about a man who finally passes his bar
             examination at "barely forty" and then is faced with
             having to retake it because of a technicality. He
             knows he cannot pass again, so he will continue to
             be "an unimportant man."

738.   Wilkins, Roy. "The Negro Press." *Opportunity*, 6,
             No. 12 (December 1928), 362-63, 385.

             The special qualities of black newspapers are explained
             (e.g., racial uplift articles, propaganda); in par-
             ticular, criticisms of the black press are examined
             in reference to these unique qualities and concerns,
             such as concentrating on crime, sensationalism, and
             trivia. Believes, however, that the larger papers
             are improving, and that most Negro newspapers still
             provide news--social; sports, educational, etc.--
             about Negroes that blacks cannot find in the white
             press.

739.   Williams, Blanche Colson, ed. "Comments on Eleven
             Stories of Which No Copies Had Been Made," in *The
             Harlem Renaissance Generation*, ed. L.M. Collins,
             Nashville: Fisk University, 1972. Pp. 411-12.

             Further comments (see item 740) about stories submitted
             to *Opportunity* Awards Contest (year not indicated).
             Most in this group did not get stories published, but
             they demonstrate the interest in major Renaissance
             themes.

740.   ————. "Second Group of Stories Submitted," in
         The Harlem Renaissance Generation, ed. L.M. Collins.
         Nashville: Fisk University, 1972. Pp. 407-10.

         Comments on 23 stories submitted to the *Opportunity*
         Awards Contest (year not indicated). Interesting
         insight into critical assessments of the literature
         being produced during the Harlem Renaissance, some
         of which was not published. Comments here on "Spunk"
         and "John Redding Goes to Sea," by Hurston; and
         appraisals of "Fog," by John Matheus (a contest winner).

741.   "Words of the Judges." *Crisis*, 30, No. 6 (October
         1925), 276-78.

         Comments by some of the judges about the literature
         submitted for the Amy Spingarn Contest (see item 517).

742.   Young, P. Bernard, Jr. "News Content of Negro News-
         papers." *Opportunity*, 7, No. 12 (December 1929),
         370-72, 387.

                          FILMSTRIPS

743.   "The Harlem Renaissance and Beyond." (Guidance
         Associates, Pleasantville, N.J.) No. 6210-1320.
         2 filmstrips, 2 tape cassettes, 2 LP records.

744.   "The History of Black America." (Universal Education
         and Visual Arts.)

745.   "Quest for Equality, 1910 to Present." (Encyclopedia
         Britannica Educational Corporation.) Not in their
         catalogue.

745a.   "Harlem in the Twenties." (Encyclopedia Britannica
         Educational Corporation.) No. 3073. 10 minutes.

         Teachers College Films (New York City):

746.   "Black Renaissance" (Lecturer: St. Clair Drake).
         30 minutes. LC 74-704078.

747.   "The Problems of the Twenties" (Lecturer: St. Clair
         Drake). 30 minutes. LC 70-704077.

748.   "Writers and Artists of the New Era" (Lecturer:
        Edgar Toppin). 30 minutes. LC 70-704074.

749.   "Garvey and His Predecessors" (Lecturer: Essien-Udom).
        30 minutes. LC 78-704079.

750.   "Harlem: The Making of a Community" (Lecturer: John
        H. Clark). 30 minutes. [no LC no.]

751.   "The Creative Twenties" (Lecturer: Julian Mayfield).
        30 minutes. LC 73-704083.

752.   "Me and My Song" (Lecturer: Barbara A. Teer).
        30 minutes. LC 77-704084.

753.   "Harlem Shadows" (Lecturer: Jessie Devore & the
        Voices). 30 minutes. LC 70-704085.

RECORDS & AUDIOTAPES

754.   "The Life of W.E.B. Du Bois: 'Back to Africa' and
        Harlem in the 20's." (Pacifica Tape Library,
        Berkeley, Calif.)

755.   "The History of the Black Man in the United States.
        Part V: 'Black Renaissance.'" (Educational
        Audiovisual, Pleasantville, N.J.)

756.   "Anthology of Negro Poets in the U.S.A.--200 Years."
        (Folkways.)

757.   "Anthology of Negro Poets." (Folkways.)

758.   "Poems." By Langston Hughes. (Spoken Arts.)

VI. ANTHOLOGIES

A selected list of anthologies where material written
during the Harlem Renaissance can be found.

759.   Barnet, Sylvan, Morton Berman, and William Burto, eds.
        Nine Modern Classics: An Anthology of Short Novels.
        Boston: Little, Brown, 1973.

        Includes excerpts from *Cane* on pp. 351, 445-49, with
        notes that provide comments on Gertrude Stein's
        influence upon Toomer.

760.   Brown, Sterling A., Arthur P. Davis, and Ulysses Lee,
        eds. *The Negro Caravan.* New York: The Dryden
        Press, 1941.

        Extensive commentary about the different genres of
        literature, followed by selections from all of the
        major and many of the minor Harlem Renaissance
        authors: Hughes, Cullen, Fisher, J.W. Johnson, J.
        Fauset, Schuyler, Thurman, McKay, Toomer, Bontemps,
        Walter White, Georgia D. Johnson, Angelina Grimké,
        Hurston, and Sterling Brown. The discussion preceding
        the short story section is one of the earliest to be
        printed about this genre as written by Afro-Americans.
        A chronology at the end covers events and publications
        from earliest U.S. history to 1941.

760a.   Collins, L.M., comp. *The Harlem Renaissance
        Generation.* Nashville: Fisk University, 1972.
        (Bound Typescript.)

        In the brief introduction (pp. i-iv), presents an
        overview of the period and the major writers. Sees
        the magazine *Fire!!* as a reflection of the true spirit
        of the Harlem Renaissance--heralding a new awakening
        of the artists' sense of blackness and projecting a
        new assertiveness among blacks.

        The selections are vast, and many items do not appear
        in any other anthology concerned with this period--

e.g., see items 511, 514, 638, 739, 740. Concentrates
on articles about the people and period rather than on
the literature written by the artists themselves.

761.   Cromwell, Otelia, et al. *Readings from Negro Authors
        for Schools and Colleges with A Bibliography of Negro
        Literature.* New York: Harcourt, Brace and Co., 1931.

        A wide range of writings by Harlem Renaissance writers
        here--poetry by Cullen, Hughes, and Waring Cuney, one-
        act plays by Willis Richardson and John Matheus, as
        well as stories by Rudolph Fisher, Zora Neale Hurston,
        and John Matheus. The bibliography is one of the
        earliest to include writings by the major and minor
        Harlem Renaissance writers. However, there is a
        middle-class bias, for Toomer and the less conventional
        writings of Claude McKay and Hughes are omitted.

762.   Cullen, Countee, ed. *Caroling Dusk.* New York:
        Harper & Brothers, 1927.

        An anthology "of verse by Negro poets rather than an
        anthology of Negro verse" (p. xi), including poetry
        by writers who eschew dialect and do not noticeably
        betray their color, except in choice of theme.
        Biographical sketches of the contributors, some of
        whom predate the Harlem Renaissance.

763.   Cunard, Nancy, ed. *Negro: An Anthology.* London:
        Wishart, 1934. Reprinted, New York: Frederick
        Ungar Publishing Co., 1970.

        A huge anthology of articles, poetry, and prose
        covering every aspect of black life, from Africa to
        the United States and the West Indies--politics,
        sociology, literature, art, the stage, with photo-
        graphs of the contributors, street scenes, farm
        scenes, jail settings--every conceivable topic related
        to the black race. The reprinted edition also has
        an introduction about the fascinating woman who
        conceived this book.

        Some articles are annotated separately (see items
        70, 79, 325).

764.   Davis, Arthur P., and Michael W. Peplow, eds. *The
        New Negro Renaissance: An Anthology.* New York:
        Holt, Rinehart and Winston, 1975.

        Using a wide definition of time (1910-1940) for the
        Harlem Renaissance, presents a brief historical

introduction to black writing, followed by selections
--poetry and prose--under eight topical headings:
Protest Literature--The Genteel School; "We Are
Like You ..."; Nigger Heaven: Variations on a Theme;
The African Heritage; About the Folk; Race Pride; The
Stirrings of Black Nationalism; and The Critical
Debate (i.e., what is black art?).

A chronology of events and biographical information
about the authors are included.

765.   Emanuel, James A., and Theodore L. Gross, eds. *Dark
        Symphony: Negro Literature in America*. New York:
        The Free Press, 1968.

        Part II, "The Negro Awakening," contains a capsule
        history of the 1920s, starting with comments about
        Locke's anthology, *The New Negro*. Mentions the
        sociological and historical changes that influenced
        the cultural atmosphere. Selections are not
        extensive, but the major authors are represented:
        Cullen, Hughes, Toomer, McKay, J.W. Johnson, Locke,
        Fisher, S. Brown, and Eric Walrond.

766.   *Four Negro Poets: Claude McKay, Jean Toomer, Countee
        Cullen, Langston Hughes*. Introduction by Alain
        Locke. New York: Simon and Schuster, 1927.

        Anthology of poetry, selected and with some comments
        about the above-named poets.

767.   Henderson, Stephen. *Understanding the New Black
        Poetry: Black Speech and Black Music as Poetic
        References*. New York: William Morrow, 1973.

        Sees Harlem Renaissance as the first time black life
        was systematically explored through poetry. Thematic
        concerns centering on blackness, racial pride,
        protest, and a wider treatment of the masses emerged
        during the 1920s. Poetry by Renaissance writers is
        also included (Toomer, Cullen, Hughes, Brown,
        and McKay).

768.   Huggins, Nathan Irvin. *Voices from the Harlem
        Renaissance*. New York: Oxford University Press, 1976.

        A wide range of literature and art from the 1920s and
        early 1930s. Stories, poetry, parts of novels, jour-
        nalism, by representative participants of the period
        such as Langston Hughes, Countee Cullen, Claude McKay,

Arna Bontemps, Alain Locke, and George S. Schuyler.
Black and white photographs of the art work.

769.   Hughes, Langston, and Arna Bontemps, eds. *The Poetry
        of the Negro 1746-1970*. New York: Doubleday &
        Co., 1970.

        Beyond the poetry itself are brief biographical
        sketches at the end. Major Harlem Renaissance
        writings appear--that is, poems by Langston Hughes,
        Countee Cullen, Claude McKay, Anne Spencer, etc.,
        written during the 1920s.

770.   Johnson, Charles S., ed. *Ebony and Topaz: A
        Collectanea*. New York: National Urban League, 1927.

        An anthology of articles, stories, poems, and drawings
        about Negro life--folk life, artistic life, an ex-
        ploration of racial problems and attitudes and
        appraisals of Negro life and habits. Many of the
        Harlem Renaissance writers contribute stories or
        poems: Hughes, Cullen, Hurston, Locke, and Bontemps.

771.   Johnson, James Weldon. *The Book of American Negro
        Poetry*. New York: Harcourt, Brace and Co., 1922.

        Cites cultural contributions Negroes have made to
        America, such as music (blues, ragtime), dances (e.g.,
        the "eagle rock"), and literature. The introduction
        presents the reader with a history of Afro-American
        writers and their works--from the beginnings to
        Claude McKay. A generous sampling of several Harlem
        Renaissance poets is presented here in the earliest
        significant collection of poetry and literary history
        in the twentieth century. Included is poetry by
        Georgia Douglas Johnson, Claude McKay, Jessie Fauset,
        and Anne Spencer. Biographical information about
        each author is at the end of the anthology.

772.   Locke, Alain, ed. *The New Negro: An Interpretation*.
        New York: Albert and Charles Boni, 1925.

        The book that gave the term "New Negro" meaning by
        presenting poetry, stories, and essays by the newer
        writers and their older mentors. The optimism was
        based on a belief that Negroes would be applauded
        for their contribution to American culture. This
        is expressed by Locke (see item 679) as well as by
        James Weldon Johnson (see item 130). Most of these

are reprints from the 1 March 1925 edition of
Survey Graphic.

Reviews: *The Nation*, 121, 30 December 1925, p. 761:
V.F. Calverton; *N.Y.T. Book Review*, 20 December 1925,
p. 5: Dorothy Scarborough; *N.Y. Tribune*, 20 December
1925, p. 5: Carl Van Vechten; *N.Y. World*, 10 January
1926, p. 6m: Janet Ramsay; *Opportunity*, 3, August
1925, ɔ. 251: Robert W. Bagnall.

773.   ————, and Montgomery Gregory,, eds. *Plays of Negro
Life*. New York: Harper, 1927.

Locke sees the interest in drama by and about Negroes
as a national rather than racial phenomenon. Although
the problem play was dominant, Locke predicted the
future of drama in this genre to be the Negro folk
play. An anthology, basically, of plays by black
and white dramatists.

774.   Miller, Ruth, ed. *Blackamerican Literature, 1760-
Present*. Beverly Hills, Calif.: Glencoe Press, 1971.

Part Four, covering the years 1915-1939, opens with
a brief chronology followed by Alain Locke's essay--
"The New Negro"--from the anthology of the same title.
The choice of the year 1915 remains unclear; but each
selection in this anthology is preceded by an introduction to the author and the work. Renaissance
authors represented here are J.W. Johnson, McKay,
Cullen, Brown, Matheus, Toomer, Schuyler, and Hughes.

775.   Ouchi, Glichi, and Mikio Suzuki, eds. *Harlem Story*,
by Rudolph Fisher and Ann Petry. Tokyo: Kaibunsha,
Ltd., c1974, 1972.

A reprint of "Miss Cynthie," by Fisher. Explanatory
notes are in Japanese.

776.   Richardson, Willis, and May Miller. *Negro History in
Thirteen Plays*. Washington, D.C.: The Associated
Publishers, 1935.

Plays primarily stressing the African background of
American Negroes, but also indicating black contributions
to Europe and America. Included are five plays by
Richardson: *Antonio Maceo*, *Attucks, the Martyr*,
The Elder Dumas, *Near Calvary*, and *In Menelek's Court*.
Two plays by Georgia Douglas Johnson also appear:
Frederick Douglass and *William and Ellen Craft*. A

tendency to romanticize the past through these plays
about brave and virtuous persons appears to be an
effort to glorify the African race in its various
non-African as well as African settings.

777.   Turner, Darwin T., ed. *Black American Literature—
          Poetry*. Columbus, Ohio: Charles E. Merrill Publishing
          Co., 1969.

          After a brief introduction, in which the Harlem
          Renaissance is characterized as "an era of poetic
          wealth," poems by the following Harlem Renaissance
          authors appear: James Weldon Johnson, Georgia Douglas
          Johnson, Claude McKay, Jean Toomer, Countee Cullen,
          Langston Hughes, Arna Bontemps, and Sterling Brown.

778.   Watkins, Sylvestre C., ed. *Anthology of American Negro
          Literature*. New York: The Modern Library, 1944.

          States this anthology contains works by "the true
          American of Negro parentage speaking his mind about
          his problem." Concentrates on essays, but also
          includes short stories and selections from auto-
          biographies and biographies. Excludes poetry and
          selections from novels. Harlem Renaissance authors
          include Fisher, Hurston, Bontemps, Du Bois, C.S.
          Johnson, Schomburg, and J.W. Johnson.

779.   White, Newman Ivey, and Walter C. Jackson, eds. *An
          Anthology of Verse by American Negroes*. Durham, N.C.:
          Trinity College Press, 1924.

          A sympathetic pair of professors present a mildly
          critical introduction and then selections of poetry
          from and biographical data on Negro writers, including
          the following Harlem Renaissance poets—Jessie Fauset,
          Claude McKay, Georgia Douglas Johnson, and Countee
          Cullen. This was one of the first anthologies
          published with Harlem Renaissance authors (see also
          Johnson, item 771), and contains just one poem by
          Cullen, the little-known "The Touch." Bibliographical
          and critical notes about many of the poets appear at
          the end of the book.

VII. LIBRARY AND OTHER
SPECIAL COLLECTIONS

The following institutions hold collections of material--
manuscripts, correspondence, etc.--concerning Harlem Renaissance
figures. The listings that follow do not intend to be all-
inclusive but do suggest the scope of materials available
at different places.

The listing is alphabetical by principal name of
institution.

780.   Atlanta University. Trevor Arnett Library: Negro
         Collection.

         The Cullen-Jackman Memorial Collection contains
         archival/manuscript materials relating to the Harlem
         Renaissance. Harold Jackman, friend of many of the
         writers, and close friend of Countee Cullen, was the
         guiding spirit and collector of materials here. In
         addition to manuscripts, there are photographs, sheet
         music, tapes, and broadsides.

         Countee Cullen Papers: Manuscripts include: typescript
         of *The Medea* in his adaptation called "Byword for
         Evil" (see also: Fisk University, Cullen papers),
         with incidental music by Virgil Thomson; proof sheets
         for *On These I Stand*; proof sheets for *The Lost Zoo*,
         with corrections written in by Cullen; signed
         manuscript of poem "Christus Natus Est"; galley of
         "The Ballad of the Brown Girl"; handwritten copy
         (perhaps a gift?) of "The Ballad of the Brown Girl,"
         noted "for Harold, Sincerely, Countee, Christmas 1923."
              Sheet music: "Dear Friends and Gentle Hearts,"
         signed (©1943); "Mary Mother of Christ": (©1925).
              Correspondence: To Harold and Ivie Jackman,
         1930s-1940s.
              Miscellaneous: Clippings of reviews; clipping
         from *Pittsburgh Courier*, 5 April 1930, concerning his
         divorce from Yolande Du Bois; obituary clippings;
         photographs (snapshots and portraits also by Van
         Vechten), including formal ones of his wedding (with
         Yolande Du Bois).

Claude McKay Papers: Consists of his correspondence to Ivie Jackman (sister of Harold Jackman) from the years 1934 to 1948. Fifty-four handwritten and typed letters. Valuable for an insight into the McKay character, which was fairly consistent if difficult and demanding.

James Weldon Johnson Papers: Correspondence, between 1937 and 1938, to Claude McKay in connection with a proposal of McKay's to start a black writers' guild. Six letters and some postcards.

Langston Hughes Papers: Much of the material concerns the 1940s-50s. There are clippings, announcements, copies of book reviews, and correspondence.
  Correspondence: Postcards of travels, sent to Harold Jackman during 1924 and 1930s.
  Manuscripts: Handwritten copy of his "Dream Variation." Handwritten copy of his "Caribbean Sunset," April 1925. Typed copy of "Three Poems of Harlem." Copy of a manuscript, "Three Students Look at Lincoln in 1929," a paper for a sociology class while at the university.
  Miscellaneous: Playbill for *Mulatto*, October 1935. Copy of a wood-cut of his high school. Photograph of Hughes and Wallace Thurman (1934).

W.E.B. Du Bois Papers: Two letters related to the Renaissance period.
  Letter written in 1926 to Robert B. Eleazer concerning Du Bois's opinion of certain people whom he calls "White Folks' Niggers."
  Letter, dated 31 January 1928, to Countee Cullen concerning his upcoming wedding to Yolande Du Bois.
  Manuscript: "The Passing of Alain Locke," typed manuscript (1954).

Georgia Douglas Johnson Papers: Correspondence and manuscripts of poems, both typescript and handwritten.
  Correspondence: From the period of 1938-50. Her letter to Arna Bontemps, 19 July 1941, speaks of her poetic philosophy, which was a consistent vision throughout her lengthy career.

Dorothy West Papers: One letter; one manuscript.
  Correspondence: Letter to Claude McKay, n.d. (but ca. 1937) concerning why she can't join in the group he wishes to form (black writers' guild; see also J.W. Johnson papers above).
  Manuscript: Short story, "The House Across the Way,": undated; typed.

Elmer A. Carter Papers: Of interest is the typed manuscript "In Memoriam of Charles Spurgeon Johnson." Discusses Johnson's aims and role in connection with *Opportunity*. Said his interest was in imaginative as well as in scholarly writing; and that he was also interested in African culture because he believed that "Negro life in itself offers possibilities of the highest spiritual expression."

There are also less significant items in the files of Eric Walrond, Arna Bontemps, Wallace Thurman, Harold Jackman, George Schuyler, and Carl Van Vechten.

Biographical File: This is essentially a vertical file of clippings, book jackets, copies of printed articles, and other miscellaneous items. Because most of the material is in the form of printed publications, the names of persons who have a file and are pertinent to the Harlem Renaissance will be listed here, but no specific material will be cited: Arna Bontemps; Aaron Douglas; W.E.B. Du Bois; Jessie Fauset; Rudolph Fisher; Langston Hughes; Zora Neale Hurston; J.W. Johnson; Claude McKay; George Schuyler.

Picture File: A good file of some interesting photographs of some of the Harlem Renaissance figures.

Arna Bontemps: One photograph ca.1931; others of a later time.

Countee Cullen: An early, undated photograph; Cullen with Christopher Cat; Van Vechten photograph of Cullen in Central Park; an undated, close-up, half-profile of Cullen when young; undated portrait photograph of the young Cullen. (See also: Cullen papers.)

Jessie Fauset: Undated, early adult photograph (very lovely); magazine page with a copy of a painting of Fauset in later life, by Laura Wheeler Waring.

Langston Hughes: Many photographs, mostly of him in his mid- or later life; a 1924 photograph, on a postcard from the "Harlem on My Mind" show--group photo of Hughes, C.S. Johnson, E. Franklin Frazier, Rudolph Fisher, and Hubert Delany at the home of Regina M. Andrews and Ethel Ray Nance; several photographs with students during his tours; a 1949 photograph by Carl Van Vechten, Hughes with Nicolas Guillén; a 1927 photograph; two other Carl Van Vechten photographs (1937 and 1943).

Zora Neale Hurston: A Carl Van Vechten photograph of her before a patterned background; a 1937 magazine reproduction of the young Hurston.

Charles S. Johnson: Three 1947 and 1948 Carl Van
Vechten photographs.
Jean Toomer: Undated photograph to Harold
Jackman (very good).
Wallace Thurman: With Langston Hughes on some
steps, with glasses of ice and a gin bottle; an
undated photograph of Thurman alone (very good).
Carl Van Vechten: Simply lots of him, many self-
photographs. Most on postcards sent to Harold
Jackman.
Dorothy West: A Carl Van Vechten photograph on a
postcard; three poses of large photographs, done by
Van Vechten in 1948; photograph of her during a
radio interview.
Eric Walrond: Two snapshots of him outside a
café in Toulon (France) in 1931.

Tape Collection: A small number from this collection
may have interest for scholars of the Harlem
Renaissance. Tapes were not heard, and there is
no close description of the contents.
Ivie Jackman interviewed by James Hatch.
Conversation with Ivie Jackman, Pearl Fisher
(sister of Rudolph Fisher), and Wayne Cooper.
Owen Dodson on Paul Robeson; Alain Locke (other
side of this tape).
Owen Dodson on Countee Cullen; Langston Hughes
(other side of this tape).
Interview with Eubie Blake.
Richmond Barthe interviewed by Ivie Jackman,
4 December 1975.
Margaret Bonds (musician who set many Renaissance
poems to music) interviewed by James Hatch.

Miscellaneous: Undated letter to Harold Jackman from
Yolande Du Bois, telling of her meeting Countee
Cullen. The original of this letter is in the
vault, but copies of it are available to see; it is
not in any particular file.
Broadsides illustrating Langston Hughes poems,
with illustrations by Aaron Douglas. "Bound No'th
Blues," "Feet O'Jesus," "Misery," "Lonesome Places,"
and "Hard Luck." These are stunning prints.

781.   Boston University. Mugar Memorial Library: Special
         Collections.

         There are signed letters from Sterling Brown, Arna
         Bontemps, W.E.B. Du Bois, and Langston Hughes post-
         1950 in the collection. Other Hughes holdings are
         described below.

         Hughes, Langston: Much of the material postdates the
         Harlem Renaissance period. Items close to or related
         to that period include: photograph (1928) of Hughes
         on the cover of *Langston Hughes, Poet of the People*
         (1967) by Milton Meltzer; Hughes correspondence to
         Bruce Nugent (from the 1950s); Hughes letters to Arthur
         Spingarn, 1931-64 (one concerning his collaboration
         with Hurston on the play *Mule Bone*); agreement with
         the American Play Company concerning his play *Mulatto*;
         Hughes letter to T.M. Campbell asking about "our
         song" (3 January 1928).

         West, Dorothy: Correspondence to West, photographs,
         and a manuscript of Countee Cullen's "Sonnet in
         Absence," Paris (1933)--a signed typescript.
             Correspondence to West from: Bontemps; Cullen
         (thirteen letters and postcards); Hughes (three from
         the 1930s); Hurston; McKay (two from 1930s, one from
         1940); Schomburg; Thurman; and Van Vechten (eight
         letters and postcards).
             Photographs: two snapshots of Hurston; W.C. Handy
         with Langston Hughes (signed by Handy).

         Collections not seen by author.

782.   Brown University Library: Archives.

         There are unpublished short stories by Rudolph Fisher
         here. He was a student at Brown, where he received
         both his undergraduate degree and a masters degree.

         Short Stories: "Across the Airshaft"; "The Lindy Hop";
         "Lost Love Blues"; "Passing for Black" or "False Face"
         [or "Incident in Harlem"?]. Typewritten manuscripts,
         with handwritten corrections and markings. The
         stories are undated. The last story listed has all
         of its titles crossed out, including one in pencil
         which appears to be "Incident in Harlem." There
         are three versions of "The Lindy Hop."

783.   Chicago Public Library. Carter G. Woodson Regional
         Library: The Vivian G. Harsh Collection of Afro-
         American History and Literature.

         There are three typewritten drafts of *The Big Sea*,
         Langston Hughes's autobiography wherein he describes
         the Harlem Renaissance.

         Collection not seen by this author.

784.   Columbia University: Oral History Collection.

         A guide to this collection has been edited by Elizabeth
         B. Mason and Louis M. Starr, and should be available
         at any university library. This guide indicates
         availability of access to individual interviews.
         Contact: Oral History Research Office, Box 20, Butler
         Library, Columbia University, New York, N.Y. 10027.
         Tel. no. (212) 280-2273.

         Abdul, Raoul: Private secretary to Langston Hughes,
         1957-67. Date of interview: 1975. 65 pp. "Permission
         required to cite or quote."

         Hutson, Jean B.: Curator, Schomburg Center for Research
         in Black Culture. Date of interview: 1978. 65 pp.
         "Permission required to cite or quote."

         Schuyler, George S.: Journalist, author of *Black No
         More*. Date of interview: 1960. 723 pp. "Permission
         required to cite or quote."

         Van Vechten, Carl: Author and friend of Harlem
         Renaissance authors. Author of *Nigger Heaven* (1926).
         Date of interview: 1960. 355 pp. "Open."

785.   Dillard University (New Orleans, La.): The Amistad
         Research Center.

         Countee Cullen Papers, 1921-69: Correspondence,
         manuscripts, clippings, galleys, research papers
         written at Harvard, French notebooks, legal papers,
         and other memorabilia.
             Correspondence: from Gwendolyn Bennett; Witter
         Bynner; W.E.B. Du Bois; Jessie Fauset; Langston Hughes;
         Harold Jackman; Charles S. Johnson; Alain Locke; Claude
         McKay; Carl Van Vechten; Eric Walrond; Dorothy West;
         and Walter White. The Du Bois letters are frank
         concerning the marital problems between Cullen and
         Yolande Du Bois Cullen. Jackman's letters are long
         and give comments on many of the people in their
         literary set. He also offers literary opinions.

Carl Van Vechten mentions his disagreement with Cullen concerning the latter's review of Langston Hughes's book *The Weary Blues*. The letters of Dorothy West are affectionate and filled with ideas about literature and life. Some of her letters are from the time she travelled in Russia.

Manuscripts: Many poems in typescript, with revisions noted in handwriting. Handwritten "Sonnet to Yolande," dated 7 September 1923. Play manuscripts include "Heaven's My Home" (1935), done in collaboration with Harry Hamilton; an untitled play, also in collaboration with Hamilton; "Byword for Evil"--an adaptation of *The Medea*. A typed copy of "St. Louis Woman" (dated 1 December 1945), written in collaboration with Arna Bontemps. Galleys of juvenile manuscripts.

Miscellaneous: Correspondence from persons doing work on Cullen; diplomas of Cullen; a paper on Walter Pater, written in 1926 for Prof. Irving Babbitt at Harvard; lesson plans and workbooks for Cullen's teaching at his New York school; scrapbooks, 1925-45; obituary clippings concerning Cullen.

Collection seen on microfilm.

786.   Fisk University (Nashville, Tenn.) Library: Special Collections.

This library had at one time Arna Bontemps as its Director of Library (1943-64). Charles S. Johnson was the first black president of Fisk University (in 1928), and all of his papers--a clear contribution to Harlem Renaissance scholars--are in the library. The jewel of the collection--the Jean Toomer Papers-- may be transferred to Yale in the next few years. Fisk is also strong in oral history, and these holdings will be described below.

Negro Collection (Special Collections)

Charles S. Johnson Papers: This is a large collection that covers much more than items connected with the Harlem Renaissance. Of the latter, the following are noted.

Manuscripts: Copies of his working papers with revisions in handwriting for such essays as "The Negro Renaissance and Its Significance," "Can There Be a Separate Negro Culture in America?" "The New Negro" (an address), and "The Negro's Contribution to American Civilization."

Typescript of a talk given on radio station WEVD (place not known), 24 August 1928, concerning the reason for and scope of *Opportunity*.

Manuscripts submitted to *Opportunity* by Hurston, Bontemps, McKay, Frank Horne, John Matheus, Thurman, Cullen, Helene Johnson, Arthur Huff Fauset, and Dorothy West. Some of these submissions contain critical comments of an editor or critic (a collection of comments made about contest submissions appear separately in this bibliography: see Williams, items 739 and 740).

Jean Toomer Papers: The description that follows was gathered during a visit to Fisk University, during which time I was informed that the complete collection would be sent to Yale at the request of Mrs. Toomer, widow of the writer. This is the major Toomer collection for scholars.

Manuscripts, notes, etc.: There are notes and the first draft of his autobiography, *Earth-Being* (see also item 432), articles concerning race, drafts of stories and poems, untitled notes of his writings, notes about Gurdjieff and his institute, Gurdjieff lectures, some of his boyhood schoolwork, and photographs. Among the typescripts of poetry is one of "The Blue Meridian." One of his undated articles, "Life's Centre," concerns his search for true freedom for the self. His college scrapbook has body-building cut-outs. There is also a collection of other persons' writings that Toomer collected.

Correspondence: Letters to Waldo Frank where he explains the symbolism of the curves that are printed in *Cane*. He also discusses his views on race (undated letter). In another undated letter to Frank he gives his opinion of Sherwood Anderson, and he laments Anderson's simple categorization of him as a Negro without trying to understand his nature in relation to the wider world.

Toomer letter to Gurdjieff where he describes Mabel Dodge Luhan (undated).

Georgia O'Keeffe letters to Toomer, which are beautifully written, sometimes in an impressionistic style. She also expresses great affection for Toomer.

Margery Latimore (Toomer) letter dated June 1931 where she expresses enthusiasm for Toomer. Several other letters by her in the collection, but none of a deeply personal nature.

There are, in addition to the above-mentioned items, materials relating to his later years as a Quaker, as well as his encounters with L. Ron Hubbard and Toomer's study of dianetics with Hubbard.

W.E.B. Du Bois Papers: There is a typed manuscript copy, with handwritten revisions, of *Dark Princess* (1928), his novel. Other manuscripts are of stories --"The Comet" and "Jesus Christ in Texas"--which were printed in *Darkwater*. Financial papers of *The Crisis* from 1910 to 1925 are also here.

Langston Hughes Papers: Fourth draft (final revisions) of *The Big Sea*, completed 5 February 1940 (revisions are in Hughes's handwriting); broadsides written in 1931 (four).

Countee Cullen Papers: Copies of correspondence to Cullen from Sterling Brown (1935); Pearl Busk (1933), wherein she praises him for his poetry; Langston Hughes correspondence between 1921 and 1925; and other minor correspondence from Locke, Augusta Savage, and Padraic Colum.
     Manuscript of "Byword for Evil," an adaptation of *The Medea*, which he later published.

Aaron Douglas Papers: This is the major repository for his papers, many of which deal with his work as an art professor at Fisk. His interview (see below in Oral History section) is of major value to Renaissance scholars.

Black Oral History Collection

The following persons who were interviewed made significant remarks concerning the Harlem Renaissance.

Bontemps, Arna: Gives his insiders insight into the period and the people, with vivid descriptions of Langston Hughes, Countee Cullen, Claude McKay, James Weldon Johnson, and Zora Neale Hurston. He also discusses the interest persons at the University of North Carolina had in the Renaissance. Date of interview: 14 July 1972. 177 minutes.

Cooper, Ida Mae Cullen: Widow of the poet gives a portrait of Cullen at the height of his career and discusses his work. Date of interview: 15 July 1970. 90 minutes.

Douglas, Aaron: Discusses his work as well as giving
insightful profiles of such persons as Langston Hughes,
Wallace Thurman, James Weldon Johnson, Charles S.
Johnson, W.E.B. Du Bois, Countee Cullen, Alain Locke,
and Carl Van Vechten. Comments on reactions to their
work and philosophy. Date of interview: 16 July
1971. 90 minutes.

Gayle, Addison: A current critic and writer gives his
views on the literature of the Harlem Renaissance.
Date of interview: 5 November 1972. 60 minutes.

Hutson, Jean Blackwell: Noted Director of the
Schomburg Collection narrates a history of the
collection as well as giving insight into the Harlem
community from the 1930s. Describes Arthur A.
Schomburg, Langston Hughes, and Countee Cullen. Date
of interview: 20 October 1973. 79 minutes.

Nance, Ethel Ray: As Assistant to Charles S. Johnson,
when he was Editor of *Opportunity*, Nance describes the
social life and climate of the Harlem Renaissance,
narrating her impressions of such personalities as
Aaron Douglas, Langston Hughes, Countee Cullen, Du
Bois, J.W. Johnson, Van Vechten, Charles S. Johnson,
Jessie Fauset, Eric Walrond, Gwendolyn Bennett, and
Zora Neale Hurston. Nance believes she may be Olive
in Van Vechten's *Nigger Heaven* (but she says she
never warmed up to Van Vechten). Dates of interview:
18 November 1970 and 23 December 1970. 117 minutes.

Redding, J. Saunders: As the author of one of the
earliest criticisms and history of Afro-American
literature, Redding's comments are valuable and, of
course, parallel his views expressed in *To Make a
Poet Black*. Date of interview: 4 November 1972.
61 minutes.

Turner, Darwin T.: "He talks of his early attraction
to black literary figures, draws parallels between the
Harlem Renaissance and the black cultural explosion of
the 1960's." (From the bibliographic guide to Black
Oral History Collection). Date of interview: 3
November 1972. 58 minutes.

Picture File

Special Collection has photographs of the following
Harlem Renaissance personalities: Arna Bontemps;
Sterling A. Brown; Countee Cullen; Aaron Douglas;
W.E.B. Du Bois; Jessie Redmon Fauset; Frank Horne;

Langston Hughes; Zora Neale Hurston; Charles S.
Johnson; James Weldon Johnson; Augusta Savage.

Miscellaneous

The following anthology, which is listed in the
Anthologies section (selections from it are also
included in this bibliography), may be available only
at Fisk because it is not a printed work: Collins,
L.M., comp. *The Harlem Renaissance Generation: An
Anthology*. Nashville: Fisk University, 1972 (bound
typescript). (See item 760a.)

787.   University of Florida Libraries (Gainesville): Rare
        Books & Manuscripts.

        Hurston, Zora Neale: Correspondence and manuscripts,
        including the incomplete typescript of her unpublished
        novel, *Herod the Great*, and the typescript of "Seraph
        on the Suwanee." The correspondence contains about
        forty letters written by Hurston (some concerning
        racial problems). Correspondence to her is from
        friends and relatives (e.g., Dorothy Owen, Margritt
        Sabloniere, LeRoy Campbell, Everette Hurston, and
        Frank and George Smathers).
            A forty-page index to the collection is available
        to researchers who visit the collection.

        Collection not seen by this writer.

788.   Hemenway, Robert. Department of English, University
        of Kentucky, Lexington, Ky. 40506.

        Professor Hemenway has a collection of Zora Neale
        Hurston materials, some of which are cited in his
        book about her (see item 331).

        Collection not seen by this author.

789.   Howard University (Washington, D.C.): Moorland-
        Spingarn Research Center.

        The Moorland Room contains reference materials and
        the stacks with first editions, theses, and some
        manuscripts in typescript. The Manuscript Division
        contains archival materials--manuscripts, correspondence,
        notebooks, etc., of individuals.

Moorland Room

Two Harlem Renaissance authors for whom there is
scant material available have items here that should
be noted.

Fauset, Jessie Redmon: There is a complete typescript
of all of Fauset's publications, prepared by Janet L.
Sims, a librarian at the Research Center. She has
annotated reviews of Fauset's books and has collected
printed articles concerning her. There is also a
collection of theses relating to Fauset. Ms. Sims
is an authority on Fauset and can be contacted for
further information concerning her.

See manuscript section below for more information
about Fauset.

Richardson, Willis: There are typescripts of the
following plays by this author--"Bootblack Lover," a
one-act comedy (in Richardson's handwriting, "This
play won 1st Prize in the Crisis Literary Contest of
1926."); "Peacock's Feathers," a one-act play.

Other plays in typescript, listed in the card
catalog, were not available at the time of my visit.

Manuscript Division

The following persons related to the Harlem Renaissance
have materials in this collection--Alain Locke, Angelina
W. Grimké, Claude McKay, Jessie Fauset, Eric Walrond,
Countee Cullen, Jean Toomer, Wallace Thurman, Langston
Hughes, Charles S. Johnson, Zora Neale Hurston, and
Carl Van Vechten. Most of the material about these
persons is in the Alain Locke papers, which will be
opened for researchers by the time this book is
published.

(Note: The Rosey E. Pool papers are not relevant
to the Harlem Renaissance.)

Locke, Alain: This collection is a treasure trove of
correspondence in particular; clippings, photographs;
and papers concerning the special *Survey Graphic*
issue (1 March 1925). There is a collection of Zora
Neale Hurston/Mrs. Rufus Osgood Mason (her "Godmother,"
or patron) correspondence written between 1930 and
1932. Below, in greater detail, are some of the
holdings.

McKay correspondence (Box 151): There are letters
from the period of 1920 to 1938. Some correspondence
is not dated. Anyone doing serious work on McKay should
see these letters, for he talks about his work, his
literary views, attitudes, and gives the reader a
barometer of the Locke-McKay relationship, which was
often stormy. The controversy about the title of
his poem "The White House" (which Locke changed to
"White Houses") is discussed, 10-7-24.

Fauset correspondence (Box 149): Letters from
1922-25 and 1933. The letters are, for the most part,
friendly and charming; but there is one spectacular
exception in the letter dated 1/9/33. In this letter
she gives an incisive, angry criticism of Locke's
views concerning her work. This is a Fauset of fire!

Toomer correspondence (Box 151): A few notes and
letters written between 1919 and 1923. The most
significant items were written on 1/26/21 where he
speaks of his philosophy of trying to find a common
basis of existence, and on 11/8/21 from Sparta, Georgia,
where he talks about using Negroes as subjects in
imaginative literature.

Hurston correspondence (Box 150): Letters from
1927 to 1943, plus some undated ones. Two letters
reveal her feelings about Mrs. Mason (her "Godmother"/
patron), which were positive and warm (letters dated
10/29/34 and 3/20/33). Her letter of 5/10/28 is useful
for her comments on Negro folk songs.

Hughes correspondence (Box 150): A few letters
written between 1923 and 1933, plus undated. "I,
Too, Sing America" written in hand on back of a letter
from 1924. Talks also of Cullen's wedding and makes
corrections in some poems. Comments on his reaction
to McKay's *Home to Harlem* in an undated letter. He
also mentions "Godmother" Mason frequently (she was
his patron as well as Hurston's).

Johnson (Charles S.) correspondence (Box 150):
Letters from the years 1923 to 1951. Writes a good
deal about publication matters (for *Opportunity*).
Writes comments about Cullen's review of *The Weary
Blues*.

Peterson (Dorothy) correspondence (Box 151): Two
letters written in 1929, comment on Wallace Thurman.

Grimké, Angelina Weld: This collection of materials
related to the author of *Rachel* and of poetry contains
correspondence to Grimké, manuscripts of her play and
poetry; in particular, poetry manuscripts show various
revisions she made of her poems.

Hughes correspondence (Box 38-1): A letter dated 1927 where he thanks her for her comments on *Fine Clothes to the Jew* and offers his own point of view on his book.

Rachel (Box 38-13): Numerous copies of reviews of the book publication of this play (1920).

790.   Indiana University.   The Lilly Library: Manuscripts Department.

Claude McKay Papers: Correspondence from between 1919 and 1948 to Max Eastman, author.   Letters are from Petrograd, Moscow, Avignon, Berlin, Barcelona, and from Tangier, Morocco, where McKay spent four years. Letters after his return to the United States discuss his publishing problems, ill health, and money problems.   Other items include receipts for money forwarded to McKay by Eastman and snapshots of McKay's tombstone.   103 items.

Collection not seen by this author.

791.   Library of Congress: Manuscript Division.

National Association for the Advancement of Colored People (NAACP) Papers: Includes correspondence by Walter White concerning his efforts on behalf of Harlem Renaissance writers.   (See Waldron, items 509 and 510.)

Carl Van Vechten Photographs: 1930-60s.

Harmon Foundation: Etchings, lithographs, etc.   These last two collections are a part of the pictorial collection.

Collection not seen by the author.

792.   University of Massachusetts (Amherst).   University Library: Archives.

W.E.B. Du Bois Papers: Extensive correspondence, manuscripts, and papers concerning his professional activities, such as the editorship of *The Crisis*. The collection is in the process of being filmed--89 reels--and a guide to the microfilm edition of the papers was in process at the time this book was being written.

Collection not seen by the author.

793.   New York Public Library: Schomburg Center for Research
        in Black Culture.

        The materials in this library will be noted within the
        following categories: Archives; Vertical Files;
        Photographs.

        Archives

        Archival material is now on microfilm.

        Hughes, Langston: Consists of bibliographies,
        correspondence (to/from); articles; reviews of
        books; books; poems (printed copies of single poems);
        short stories; songs; radio broadcast scripts; drafts
        for "The Strollin' Twenties"; and newspaper clippings.
        Much of the material consists of copies of material
        sent to Yale (Beinecke Library).
            First drafts of and signed copy of major books.
        Galley of *Not Without Laughter*. Second and fourth
        draft of this book.
            Programs of personal appearances from 1926.
            Music manuscripts for poems set to music:
        "Midnight Nan," "Jazz Boys," and "Mother to Son."
            Poetry in typescript (no early work, however).
            Copies of material at Worcester Public Library
        (insignificant); SUNY-Buffalo (insignificant);
        University of Kansas (insignificant); and the
        National Institute of Arts and Letters (some
        librettos: "Negro Speaks of Rivers"--two different
        versions, one by Margaret Bonds and one by Howard
        Swanson; "Six Shades of Blue"--music by Heywood).
            Correspondence from: Arna Bontemps; Nancy Cunard;
        Zora Neale Hurston; Charles S. Johnson; Georgia
        Douglas Johnson; Anne Spencer; Gwendolyn Bennett;
        George Schuyler; Nella Larsen; Countee Cullen; Dorothy
        West; A.D. Nelson; Mary White Ovington; Jessie Fauset;
        Alain Locke. It appears that these are copies of
        letters sent to Yale.
            Material from the old vertical file of Schomburg
        (clippings, etc.).

        McKay, Claude: Typescripts; correspondence (to); copy
        of notebook; agreements with publisher: all originals
        have been sent back to his Executor (contact Carl
        Cowl, 84 Remsen St., Brooklyn, N.Y. 11201). Microfilm
        copies at Schomburg.
            Writings: Copy of typescript, with handwritten
        correction, of *Banana Bottom* (323 pages); copy of
        typescript, with handwritten corrections, of *Banjo*

(chapters 1–23, 380 pages); copy of typescript, with
some corrections, of *Harlem Glory*, an unfinished novel
(156 pages); copy of music manuscript of "If We Must
Die," for A minor baritone. Music by Jack Flodin;
copy of a typescript of a plan for a Negro magazine
to encourage art and literature.

Correspondence: From Louise Bryant, 14 February
(no year) with comments on his stories (e.g., "High
Ball"); from Max Eastman, 4/27/37, concerning McKay's
autobiography. For letters written by McKay, see
Schomburg archive, which follows.

Schomburg, Arthur A.: Correspondence (to). Letters
are from Langston Hughes, Claude McKay, W.E.B. Du
Bois (all business, and none of apparent significance),
Charles S. Johnson (concerning *Opportunity* and young
Negro writers), Georgia Douglas Johnson, James Weldon
Johnson, and Alain Locke.

Hughes correspondence: 2/5/33 concerning his trip
to Soviet Asia. 8/17/33 concerning sending something
for the Pushkin collection. Suggests it would be
good for a Negro scholar to spend a summer in Leningrad
and Moscow to work on Pushkin research. 1/4/34 with
information about receiving a manuscript from McKay
concerning Scotsboro (a sale, presumably, to raise
money for this matter); indicates he does not know
McKay but would like to become acquainted with him.

McKay correspondence: Many letters from the years
1920 to 1937. McKay complains frequently about neglect,
his need for money, Schomburg's failure to answer
his letters, and freely gives his opinions about
such persons as Locke, Mencken, and Du Bois. Also
describes his feelings as an artist. For serious
work on McKay, these letters are essential.

Locke correspondence: 3/9/37 concerning his
opinion of McKay (not complimentary).

Johnson, J.W., correspondence: 4/21/37 concerning
McKay's *A Long Way from Home*, especially noting McKay's
misunderstanding of Locke.

Johnson, G.D., correspondence: 2 letters, 5/15/31
and 10/5/34--the letter of the latter date indicates
she is looking for a job. In the letter of the former
date she asks him (rather coyly, it appears) what
made him lose interest in her career.

Hurston, Zora Neale: Penciled copy of *Jonah's Gourd
Vine*.

Vertical Files

Vertical file material is now on microfiche.
Most of the vertical files consist of book review
clippings, personal life clippings (obituaries, e.g.),
programs, and magazine articles. The following
authors are represented in the files: Arna Bontemps;
Sterling A. Brown; Countee Cullen; W.E.B. Du Bois;
Arthur Huff Fauset; Jessie Redmon Fauset; Rudolph
Fisher; Zora Neale Hurston; Georgia Douglas Johnson;
James Weldon Johnson; Nella Larsen; Claude McKay;
Wallace Thurman; Walter White.

Photographs

In the Archives section of the library.

There are numerous photographs of Harlem during the
1920s-30s. The following writers have individual
photographs: Countee Cullen; W.E.B. Du Bois; Jessie
Fauset; Rudolph Fisher; Langston Hughes; Zora Neale
Hurston; Nella Larsen; Claude McKay; Arthur A.
Schomburg; George Schuyler; Jean Toomer.

794.   Radcliffe College (Cambridge, Ma.). The Arthur and
        Elizabeth Schlesinger Library on the History of Women
        in America: Black Women Oral History Project.

        West, Dorothy: Taped interview by Genii Guinier with
        the short story writer of the Harlem Renaissance who
        later edited *Challenge* and *New Challenge*. As of the
        date of this publication, the interviewee is editing
        the interview.

795.   Rollins College (Winter Park, Fla.): Archives.

        A modest amount of news service releases, newspaper
        articles, and private correspondence about Zora Neale
        Hurston, written for the most part by acquaintances
        in Florida. One signed letter by Hurston (8 October
        1934) to Hamilton Holt, President of Rollins College.

796.   Anne Spencer Memorial Foundation: 1313 Pierce Street,
        Lynchburg, Va. 25401.

        A museum and research center devoted to the work and
        interests of the poet Anne Spencer. Many of her papers
        and notes are still being uncovered and organized.
        Persons interested in visiting and working here should
        contact her son, Mr. Chauncey Edward Spencer, at the
        above address.

797.   Syracuse University (New York). Bird Library: The
        George Arents Research Library.

        Bontemps, Arna: Fifty boxes of biographical information,
        literary and personal correspondence, original galley
        proofs concerning Bontemps, for the years 1939-67.
        Correspondence is from a wide range of persons--from
        William Rose Benet, Countee Cullen, Carl Van Vechten,
        to Pearl Bailey. W.E.B. Du Bois correspondence to
        Bontemps covers the years from 1941 to 1955.
        Manuscripts and galleys of such Bontemps work as:
        Black Thunder, *Anyplace But Here*, *The Old South*, and
        The Harlem Renaissance Remembered. Manuscripts by
        others are Langston Hughes's "Greetings to Carl Van
        Vechten" and L.D. Jones's "Arna Bontemps."
            Other material includes: Notes and ideas; musical
        manuscripts; radio broadcasts and interviews; and a
        play outline entitled *Les Cenelles*.
            Restricted material: Correspondence from Max
        Lieber; correspondence from John Turner.

        Schuyler, George: Nine boxes of material, including
        correspondence (fifteen folders) between 1915 and 1917,
        scrapbooks from 1921 through 1961, and copies of
        his writings.
            Material not seen by this writer. In the inventory
        there is no mention of any materials relating to
        Black No More, his Renaissance novel.

798.   Yale University: The Beinecke Rare Book and Manuscript
        Library.

        This is the institution that houses the James Weldon
        Johnson Memorial Collection of Negro Arts and Letters,
        spearheaded by Carl Van Vechten and encouraged through
        his gifts and those of others (including writers like
        Hughes) in order to gather the largest collection of
        its kind. The Collection was officially dedicated on
        7 January 1950 and has the richest holdings in
        manuscripts and correspondence concerning writers of
        the Harlem Renaissance. There are miscellaneous
        materials as well: phonograph records, sheet music,
        photographs, and paintings. Some highlights of the
        collection follow.

        Johnson (James Weldon) Papers (3 series, 560 items):
        The value of this collection is in the letters he
        received from the numerous Renaissance writers, some
        of whom are listed below.

Spencer (Anne) correspondence: This gentle poet
remained in her native Virginia during the Harlem
Renaissance, but she kept up with her peer-poets in
great part through her correspondence with Johnson.
Letters from 1919 to 1930--nine from Spencer, thirty
from Johnson to Spencer. He gives advice on where she
should submit her poetry, and he puts her in touch
with H.L. Mencken. In her letter of 1/1/20 she
discusses her poem "The Feast of Shushan." Johnson
counsels her in a letter of 9/14/21 to use form,
but not to worry too much about conventional form
since her strong point is being out of the ordinary.
These persons admire each other; but the useful thing
about their correspondence is their literary comments.

Larsen (Nella) correspondence: Larsen material is
scarce, so these few letters and cards are useful:
nine from Larsen and one from Mrs. J.W. Johnson
between 1931 and 1933. The most useful item concerns
a remark about her marriage (or end of it), in a
letter dated 9/6/33.

West (Dorothy) correspondence: Letters dating
from 1931 to 1934, plus an undated letter: seven from
West, five from Johnson to West. The most important
is dated 10/23/33 wherein she laments the wasted
chances of writers during the Harlem Renaissance and
asks him to write an introductory editorial for a
new magazine (*Challenge*) she wishes to edit.

Hughes (Langston) Papers (3,902 items): Material not
seen at time of this author's visit. Material is
restricted in that one must obtain permission from
Professor Arnold Rampersad of Stanford University to
see the collection. (There is no indication that
bona fide scholars would have trouble in this matter.)

According to information on microfilm at the
Schomburg Center, Hughes sent about 1,000 letters
dated between 1920 and 1940 to Yale--letters from such
persons as Bontemps, Locke, Carl Van Vechten, Waring
Cuney, Dorothy West, Mary White Ovington, Jessie
Fauset (in particular about his publications in
The Crisis), Charles S. Johnson, and Zora Neale
Hurston. In these papers are letters about the "Mule
Bone" controversy between Hughes and Hurston. Hughes
faithfully added to this collection; therefore, this
must be seen as the major Hughes archive.

Van Vechten (Carl) Papers: There is no exaggeration in saying that Van Vechten knew every Negro writer of the 1920s and beyond, as well as their friends (like Dorothy Peterson, from whom he has an enormous correspondence). Some of the contents of his collection follow.

Manuscripts and notes: Original typescript of notes for the album (1959) of *God's Trombones* wherein he describes Johnson's personality and his positive effect on people.

Manuscript (2 pages) of "Countee Cullen," which appeared in *Vanity Fair* (June 1925).

First, second, and final drafts of his Foreword to Taylor Gordon's *Born to Be*. Final draft dated 23 August 1929.

First, second, and final drafts of a blurb for a Paul Robeson concert at the Greenwich Village Theatre in 1925. Final draft dated 20 April 1925.

Typescript (carbon), signed, of "Introducing Langston Hughes to the Reader," introduction to *The Weary Blues*. Dated 3 August 1925.

Notes and suggestions made by Fisher, J.W. Johnson, and J. Rosamund Johnson concerning *Nigger Heaven*.

Correspondence: The largest number of letters to Van Vechten seem to be from Dorothy Peterson, written between 1926 and 1970. There are over 700 letters, plus notes, postcards, and telegrams. Many concern Langston Hughes.

Hughes correspondence: Over 100 letters, 169 autographed postcards, notes, between the years 1925 and 1966.

Imes (Nella Larsen) correspondence: Includes sixty-four letters, typed letters, telegrams from the years 1925-41.

Cullen correspondence: For 1925-44 there are nineteen letters, seventeen typed letters, and some postcards

Hurston correspondence: Besides some scattered correspondence of about thirty letters, both typed and handwritten, and postcards for 1925-49, there are 109 signed letters and sixty-eight notes concerning Langston Hughes to Van Vechten.

McKay correspondence: There are four signed letters and eight typed letters to Van Vechten from 1928 to 1941.

Fisher correspondence: Nine signed letters from 1925 to 1929.

Cullen (Countee) Papers (4 boxes): Correspondence and manuscripts. Letters to Cullen from Yolande Du Bois, 1923-29, are restricted.

Manuscripts: Original handwritten version of *The Black Christ*; galleys of *Copper Sun*; typed carbon of the script for *The Medea*; typed manuscript with revision of *One Way to Heaven*; and poems--titled and untitled--handwritten as well as typescript with handwritten revisions. Indicates where some poems were sent, other places considered, and where some poems were accepted. His French notebook in his own handwriting contains his essay in French concerning Isadora Duncan (see item 580, which is a printed translation).

Correspondence: From Langston Hughes (concerning Cullen's upcoming marriage), and from Rex Littleboy.

Cullen letters to Harold Jackman, Carl Van Vechten, and Edward Atkinson. Cullen's personality emerges clearly in these letters. Some of them describe his travels abroad.

Hurston (Zora Neale) Papers (2 boxes): Manuscripts and correspondence.

Manuscripts: Handwritten, in pencil, copy of *Their Eyes Were Watching God*. 152 pages (up to episode where Jody Starks dies). "Mule Bone" manuscript by Hurston and Hughes (Act 1). Restricted.

Correspondence: From Langston Hughes to Carl Van Vechten concerning the "Mule Bone" controversy. To Carl Van Vechten from Hurston about the same matter.

Thurman (Wallace) Papers (3 boxes): Typescripts of articles, versions of the play *Harlem* and correspondence.

Manuscripts: Articles about life in Harlem, in collaboration with W.J. Rapp, are handwritten as well as typed, with revisions. Different versions of *Harlem*--early untitled versions, version under the name of "City of Refuge," and assorted revised pages of *Harlem*.

Correspondence: Six letters from Langston Hughes. One discusses a new edition of *Fire!!* which never did appear. In one other he jokes about signing and dating his correspondence so future scholars will benefit from such accuracy.

Correspondence to William Jourdan Rapp, his collaborator, sixteen letters from 1928 to 1929. Restricted. Ten other undated letters to Rapp are not restricted.

Letters from Thurman to Harold Jackman; four
letters from between 1928 and 1934. One letter, dated
May 1928, concerns his reading (Nietzsche, Matthew
Arnold, St-Beuve) and also describes his working day.
Does not reveal where he is but hints at some possibly
"unacceptable" behavior. In a letter of March 1934
(the year he died) he mentions he read 10 books in
the past week. This fits the description given of
him by Hughes in *The Big Sea*.

McKay (Claude) Papers: Manuscripts and correspondence.
Manuscripts: Typescripts of *My Green Hills of
Jamaica*; three notebooks, written in pencil. No date.
Notes about Garvey, but also mentions Westbrook
Pegler. Rants about white racism. Some appear to
be notes for his autobiography.

Correspondence: There are not many early letters
or ones dealing specifically with the Renaissance.
There is a letter dated 24 August 1926 to Jessie Hyde
concerning *Home to Harlem*. Family letters from his
sister, Rachel McKay Cooper.

Peterson (Dorothy) Papers (74 folders): Correspondence
from writers. There are restrictions on the use of
this collection, and some letters are sealed (Fisher
and Toomer letters from Peterson).

Correspondence is from the following authors:
Countee Cullen, seven letters, from 1927 to 1945;
Langston Hughes, sixteen letters, from 1926 to 1941 and
other years; Harold Jackman, four letters, from 1929
to 1933 and undated; Nella Larsen, six letters, from
1927 to 1933 and undated; Alain Locke, three letters,
1928-29; Carl Van Vechten, from 1925 to 1959.

Peterson correspondence to Rudolph Fisher,
fourteen letters, from 1919 to 1928; to Jean Toomer,
eighteen letters from 1925 to 1928 and nineteen
letters from 1928 to 1934.

There are other files that contain useful information
to the scholar interested in the Harlem Renaissance.
The richness of this collection has only been hinted
at in the descriptions of some of the major holdings.
Certainly the Beinecke Library is the first stop
for the scholar who wishes to do serious research
on the Harlem Renaissance.

VIII. DISSERTATIONS

This section contains notation of doctoral, masters, and one research paper. Theses in French are interfiled with those in English: an * after the date of a French thesis indicates it has not been completed. The name of the advisor for each person doing a thesis at a French university is included. For further information concerning these theses, contact: Fichier Central des Thèses, Université de Paris X, Nanterre, 92001 Nanterre, France.

799.   Abramson, Doris Elizabeth. "A Study of Plays by Negro Playwrights: From 'Appearances' to 'A Raisin in the Sun' (1925-1959)." Ph.D. dissertation, Columbia University, 1967.

800.   Adams, Bruce Payton. "The White Negro: The Image of the Passable Mulatto Character in Black Novels, 1853-1954." Ph.D. dissertation, University of Kansas, 1975.

801.   Akinkoye, Ajibike. "La Voix des exiles--Langston Hughes et Aimé Césaire." Ph.D. dissertation, Bordeaux (III), 1975. (Robert Escarpit.)

802.   Alexander, Sandra Carlton. "The Achievement of Arna Bontemps." Ph.D. dissertation, University of Pittsburgh, 1976.

803.   Anderson, Jeanette H. "A Study of Social Protest of Contemporary Negro Poets." M.A. thesis, Virginia State College, 1943.

804.   Armstead, T.J. "The Social Realism of Langston Hughes and Sterling Brown." M.A. thesis, Boston University, 1946.

805.   Ashe, Betty Taylor. "Arna W. Bontemps, Man of Letters." M.A. thesis, Howard University, 1972.

806.   Baker, Ruth Taylor. "The Philosophy of the New
        Negro as Reflected in the Writings of James Weldon
        Johnson, Claude McKay, Langston Hughes, and Countee
        Cullen." M.A. thesis, Virginia State College, 1941.

807.   Barisonzi, Judith Anne. "Black Identity in the Poetry
        of Langston Hughes." Ph.D. dissertation, University
        of Wisconsin (Madison), 1971.

808.   Barksdale, Howard Reed. "James Weldon Johnson as a
        Man of Letters." M.A. thesis, Fisk University, 1936.

809.   Bayliss, John Francis. "Novels of Black Americans
        Passing as Whites." Ph.D. dissertation, Indiana
        University, 1976.

810.   Bell, Bennie Venetta. "Short Stories by Negro Authors:
        A Study of Subject Matter." M.A. thesis, Fisk
        University, 1934.

811.   Berriam, Brenda. "L'Influence des poètes Afro-
        Americains de la Harlem Renaissance sur la poésie
        Africaine et des Caraibes." Ph.D. dissertation,
        Paris (III), 1976. (Michael Fabre.)

812.   Berzon, Judith Rae. "Neither White Nor Black: The
        Mulatto Character in American Fiction." Ph.D.
        dissertation, New York University, 1974.

813.   Blary, Liliane. "Claude McKay, 1889-1948." Ph.D.
        dissertation, Grenoble (III), 1977.* (Jean Wagner.)

814.   Blue, Ila Jacuith. "A Study of Literary Criticism
        by Some Negro Writers, 1900-1955." Ed.D. dissertation,
        University of Michigan, 1960.

815.   ————. "A Study of the Poetry of Langston Hughes."
        M.A. thesis, North Carolina Central University, 1945.

816.   Bouachrine, Assila. "Le Noir Americain dans l'oeuvre
        de Langston Hughes." Ph.D. dissertation, Toulouse
        (II), 1979.* (Maurice Levy.)

817.   Brown, Martha Hursey. "Images of Black Women: Family
        Roles in Harlem Renaissance Literature." Ph.D.
        dissertation, Carnegie-Mellon University, 1976.

818.   Brown, Michael Robert. "Five Afro-American Poets: A
         History of the Major Poets and Their Poetry in the
         Harlem Renaissance." Ph.D. dissertation, University
         of Michigan, 1971.

819.   Burke, Marianne Turpin. "The Negro as Hero in the
         Twentieth Century American Novel." M.A. thesis,
         University of Tennessee, 1944.

820.   Burns, Loretta S. "The Black Metropolis in the Poetry
         of Langston Hughes." M.A. thesis, Ohio State
         University, 1967.

821.   Byrd, James Wilburn. "The Portrayal of White
         Character by Negro Novelists, 1900-1950." Ph.D.
         dissertation, George Peabody College for Teachers,
         1955.

822.   Christian, Barbara. "Spirit Bloom in Harlem. The
         Search for a Black Aesthetic During the Harlem
         Renaissance: The Poetry of Claude McKay, Countee
         Cullen, and Jean Toomer." Ph.D. dissertation,
         Columbia University, 1970.

823.   Clark, Peter W. "A Study of the Poetry of James
         Weldon Johnson." M.A. thesis, Xavier University at
         New Orleans, 1942.

824.   Coleman, Leon Duncan. "The Contribution of Carl Van
         Vechten to the Negro Renaissance: 1920-1930." Ph.D.
         dissertation, University of Minnesota, 1968.

825.   Conroy, Sr. M. James. "Claude McKay: Negro Poet
         and Novelist." Ph.D. dissertation, University of
         Notre Dame, 1968.

826.   Cooper, Wayne. "Claude McKay: The Evolution of a
         Negro Radical, 1899-1923." M.A. thesis, Tulane
         University, 1965.

827.   Copeland, George Edward. "James Weldon Johnson:
         Bibliography." M.A. thesis, Pratt Institute
         Library School, 1951.

828.   Crane, Clare Bloodgood. "Alain Locke and the Negro
         Renaissance." Ph.D. dissertation, University of
         California (San Diego), 1971.

829.   Crawford, Lucille Hayes. "Musical Activities of James
        Weldon Johnson." M.A. thesis, Fisk University, 1941.

830.   Dailly, Iroko Christ. "Le Mouvement 'Nouveau Nègre'
        et les intellectuals Africains, 1920-1970." Ph.D.
        dissertation, Paris, 1978.* (Michael Fabre.)

831.   Dance, Daryl Cumber. "Wit and Humor in Black American
        Literature." Ph.D. dissertation, University of
        Virginia, 1971.

832.   Dillard, Mabel. "Jean Toomer: Herald of the Negro
        Renaissance." Ph.D. dissertation, Ohio University,
        1967.

833.   Drake, Mary Mean. "W.E. Burghardt Du Bois as a Man
        of Letters." M.A. thesis, Fisk University, 1934.

834.   Durden, Frances Collier. "Negro Women in Poetry from
        Phillis Wheatley to Margaret Walker." M.A. thesis,
        Atlanta University, 1947.

835.   Ega, Jean Luc. "Harlem, Renaissance et Négritude,
        esthétique et ideologie (années 1920-1940)." Ph.D.
        dissertation, Paris (III), 1976.* (Michael Fabre.)

836.   Ellington, Mary Davis. "Plays by Negro Authors with
        Special Emphasis Upon the Period from 1916 to 1934."
        M.A. thesis, Fisk University, 1934.

837.   Ellison, Curtis William. "Black Adam: The Adamic
        Assertion and the Afro-American Novelist." Ph.D.
        dissertation, University of Minnesota, 1970.

838.   Engel, Trudie. "The Harlem Renaissance." M.A. thesis,
        University of Wisconsin (Madison), 1959.

839.   Etonde-Ekoto, Grace. "Langston Hughes et l'esthétique
        de la simplicité." Ph.D. dissertation, Pau, 1975.
        (Robert Mane.)

840.   Fennell, Robert E. "The Death Figure in Countee Cullen's
        Poetry." M.A. thesis, Howard University, 1970.

841.   Ford, Nick Aaron. "The Negro Author's Use of Propaganda
        in Imaginative Literature." Ph.D. dissertation,
        State University of Iowa, 1945.

842.   Gear, Alice J.   "Career and Writing of James Weldon
        Johnson." M.A. thesis, University of Kansas, 1936.

843.   Gipson, Carolyn R.   "Intellectual Dilemmas in the
        Novels of W.E.B. Du Bois." Ph.D. dissertation,
        University of Michigan, 1971.

844.   Goede, William J.   "Tradition in the American Negro
        Novel." Ph.D. dissertation, University of California
        (Riverside), 1967.

845.   Grissom, Ruby M.   "Contribution of the Negro to
        American Literature (Richard Wright, Arna Bontemps,
        James Weldon Johnson, Booker T. Washington)." M.A.
        thesis, Southwest Texas State University, 1940.

846.   Hall, Rubye M.   "Realism in the Poetry of Langston
        Hughes." M.A. thesis, University of Oklahoma, 1959.

847.   Hansell, William Howard.   "Positive Themes in the
        Poetry of Four Negroes: Claude McKay, Countee Cullen,
        Langston Hughes, and Gwendolyn Brooks." Ph.D.
        dissertation, University of Wisconsin (Madison), 1972.

848.   Harper, Clifford Doyl.   "A Study of the Disunity Theme
        in the Afro-American Experience: An Examination of
        Five Representative Novels." Ph.D. dissertation, St.
        Louis University, 1972.

849.   Harris, Carol Ann.   "Black Women in Langston Hughes'
        Poetry and Short Fiction." M.A. thesis, Atlanta
        University, 1972.

850.   Hayashi, Susanna Campbell.   "Dark Odyssey: Descent
        into the Underworld in Black American Fiction."
        Ph.D. dissertation, Indiana University, 1971.

851.   Helbling, Mark Irving.   "Primitivism and the Harlem
        Renaissance." Ph.D. dissertation, University of
        Minnesota, 1972.

852.   Hicklin, Fannie Ella Frazier.   "The American Negro
        Playwright." Ph.D. dissertation, University of
        Wisconsin, 1965.

853.   Hill, Eloise H.   "Langston Hughes: Versatile Spokesman
        for His Race." M.A. thesis, Northeast Missouri
        State College, 1957.

854.   Howard, Lillie Pearl. "Zora Neale Hurston: A
         Non-Revolutionary Black Artist." Ph.D. dissertation,
         University of New Mexico, 1975.

855.   Hudson, Theodore, R. "An Analysis of the Poetry of
         Langston Hughes." M.A. thesis, Howard University,
         1967.

856.   Ives, Chauncey B. "Development in the Fictional
         Themes of Negro Authors." Ph.D. dissertation, University
         of North Carolina, 1957.

857.   Jackson, Augusta V. "The Renascence of Negro
         Literature, 1922-1929." M.A. thesis, Atlanta
         University, 1936.

858.   Jackson, (George) Blyden. "Of Irony in Negro Fiction:
         A Critical Study." Ph.D. dissertation, University of
         Michigan, 1953.

859.   Johnson, Beulah Vivian. "The Treatment of the Negro
         Woman As a Major Character in American Novels, 1900-
         1950." Ph.D. dissertation, New York University, 1955.

860.   Johnson, Gloria J. "Hurston's Folk: The Critical
         Significance of Afro-American Folk Tradition in
         Three Novels and the Autobiography." Ph.D. disserta-
         tion, University of California at Irvine, 1978.

861.   Johnson, Ralph Glassgow. "The Poetry of Dunbar and
         McKay: A Study." M.A. thesis, University of
         Pittsburgh, 1950.

862.   Jones, Norma Ramsay. "The Image of the 'White
         Liberal' in Black American Fiction and Drama." Ph.D.
         dissertation, Bowling Green State University, 1973.

863.   Julien, Claude. "L'Infance et l'adolescence chez les
         romanciers Afro-Americains, 1920-1970." Ph.D.
         dissertation, Paris (VIII), 1978.* (Mme. Monique
         Frazee.)

864.   Kitamura, Takao. "Langston Hughes: American Negro
         Poet." M.A. thesis, Howard University, 1966.

865.   Kousaleos, Peter G. "A Study of the Language, Structure
         and Symbolism in Jean Toomer's *Cane* and N. Scott
         Momaday's *House Made of Dawn*." Ph.D. dissertation,
         Ohio University, 1973.

866. Krasny, Michael Jay. "Jean Toomer and the Quest for Consciousness." Ph.D. dissertation, University of Wisconsin at Madison, 1972.

867. Laurent, Dominique. "'Black is Beaufitul' ou Genèse de la notion de négritude dans la littérature Afro-Americaine." Ph.D. dissertation, Paris (IV), 1978.* (Roger Asselineau.)

868. Lawrence, Katie Elizabeth Campbell. "Black Versus Bourgeois During the Harlem Renaissance: The Study of a Literary Conflict." Ph.D. dissertation, University of Illinois (Urbana-Champaign), 1974.

869. Lewis, Adelene E. "The Concept of Freedom in the Negro American Novel, 1865-1941." M.A. thesis, Fisk University, 1943.

870. Lucas, Portia Marguerite. "Ethno-Centrism in the Poetry and Fiction of Contemporary Negro Authors: A Critical Analysis." M.A. thesis, Fisk University, 1939.

871. McNeely, Darrell Wayne. "Jean Toomer's 'Cane' and Sherwood Anderson's 'Winesburg, Ohio': A Black Reaction to the Literary Conventions of the Twenties." Ph.D. dissertation, University of Nebraska (Lincoln), 1974.

872. Matthews, George Christopher. "Subjects and Shadows: Images of Black Primitives in Fiction of the 1920's." Ph.D. dissertation, University of Iowa, 1977.

873. Milandou, David. "L'Afrique et l'âme Africaine dans l'oeuvre de Richard Wright et dans celle de W.E.B. Du Bois." Ph.D. dissertation, Bordeaux (III), 1975.* (Jean Beranger.)

874. Millican, Arthenia Bates. "James Weldon Johnson: In Quest of an Afrocentric Tradition of Black American Literature." Louisiana State University, 1972.

875. Mintz, Stephen. "Jean Toomer." Unpublished under-graduate research paper, Oberlin College, 1972.

876. Mootry, Maria Katella. "Studies in Black Pastoral: Five Afro-American Writers." Ph.D. dissertation, Northwestern University, 1974.

877.   Morris, Horace Anthony. "Claude McKay and His Native
        Jamaica." M.A. thesis, Howard University, 1975.

878.   Myers, Randolph Louis. "Development of the Negro
        Novelist." M.A. thesis, Atlanta University, 1941.

879.   Ndu, Pol Nnamuzikam. "The Mythology of Ancestry:
        Character in Black American Literature (1789-1974)."
        Ph.D. dissertation, State University of New York
        at Buffalo, 1974.

880.   Newman, Anne E. "Contemporary Southern Literature
        (... James Weldon Johnson ...)." M.A. thesis,
        University of Alabama, 1926.

881.   Newsome, Elaine M. "W.E.B. Du Bois's 'Figure in the
        Carpet': A Cyclical Pattern in the Belletristic Prose."
        Ph.D. dissertation, University of North Carolina, 1971.

882.   Peronnin, Genevieve. "W.E.B. Du Bois et la prise de
        conscience noire aux États-Unis." Ph.D. dissertation,
        Paris (IV), 1976.* (Claude Perotin.)

883.   Pinkston, Annette Earline. "The Literary Career of
        Lnagston Hughes." M.A. thesis, Atlanta University,
        1943.

884.   Queen, Eleanor Claudine. "A Study of Rudolph Fisher's
        Prose Fiction." M.A. thesis, Howard University, 1961.

885.   Ramsey, Priscilla Barbara Ann. "A Study of Black
        Identity in 'Passing' Novels of the Nineteenth and
        Early Twentieth Centuries." Ph.D. dissertation,
        American University, 1975.

886.   Reimherr, Beulah. "Countee Cullen: A Biographical
        and Critical Study." M.A. thesis, University of
        Maryland, 1960.

887.   Ritter, S.A.H. "The Propagandistic Craft of Langston
        Hughes." M.A. thesis, University of Kent (Canterbury),
        England, 1973.

888.   Robison, Z. Catherine. "The Color Problem As It
        Finds Expression in Modern American Negro Literature."
        M.A. thesis, University of Utah, 1941.

889. Royster, Beatrice Horn. "The Ironic Vision of Four
      Black Women Novelists: A Study of the Novels of Jessie
      Fauset, Nella Larsen, Zora Neale Hurston, and Ann
      Petry." Ph.D. dissertation, Emory University, 1975.

890. Seydi, Souleymane. "Rudolph Fisher: The Man and His
      Work." Ph.D. dissertation, Rennes (II), 1977.*
      (Robert Rouge.)

891. Skerrett, Joseph Taylor, Jr. "Take My Burden Up:
      Three Studies in Psychobiographical Criticism and
      Afro-American Fiction." Ph.D. dissertation, Yale
      University, 1975.

892. Skinner, Beverly Lanier. "The Poems and Nature Prose
      of Sterling Brown, 'Rugged Individualist.'" M.A.
      thesis, Howard University, 1965.

893. Smith, Cynthia Janis. "Escape and Quest in the
      Literature of Black Americans." Ph.D. dissertation,
      Yale University, 1974.

894. Smith, James Frederick, Jr. "From Symbol to
      Character: The Negro in American Fiction of the
      Twenties." Ph.D. dissertation, Pennsylvania State
      University, 1972.

895. Solard, Alain. "Jean Toomer: Sa vie, son oeuvre, son
      influence." Ph.D. dissertation, Paris (III), 1978.*
      (Michael Fabre.)

896. Souffrant, Marcel. "La Culture française et la culture
      anglaise chez Léopold Senghor, Aimé Césaire, Jacques
      Roumain, Langston Hughes et Richard Wright." Ph.D.
      dissertation, Paris (IV), 1972.* (Mr. Dedeyan.)

897. Starke, Catherine Juanita. "Negro Stock Characters,
      Archetypes, and Individuals in American Literature:
      A Study for College Teachers." Ed.D., Columbia
      University, 1963.

898. Stetson, Earlene. "The Mulatto Motif in Black Fiction."
      Ph.D. dissertation, State University of New York at
      Buffalo, 1976.

899.   Sukho, Emilie. "Les Afro-Americains à la recherche
        de leur identité: James Woldon Johnson's 'The
        Autobiography of an Ex-Coloured Man,' Margaret
        Walker's 'Jubilee' et Alex Haley's 'Roots.'" Ph.D.
        dissertation, Paris (XII), 1980.* (Robert Mane.)

900.   Tate, Ernest C. "The Development of Negro Poetry from
        Its Beginnings to Representative Contemporary Poetry
        in America." M.A. thesis, New York University, 1939.

901.   Tchy, Amon. "La Vie et l'oeuvre de W.E.B. Du Bois."
        Ph.D. dissertation, Pau, France, 1974.* (Robert Mane.)

902.   Thevenin, Joseph. "Le Concept de la négritude chez
        Jean Price-Mars et W.E.B. Du Bois." Ph.D. dissertation,
        Paris (IV), 1972.* (Mr. Dedeyan.)

903.   Thompson, Enola. "Jessie Fauset As Interpreter of
        Negro Life." M.A. thesis, Drake University, 1939.

904.   Tignor, Eleanor Queen. "Images of the Black Male in
        Afro-American Fiction: 1920-1960." Ph.D. dissertation,
        Howard University, 1975.

905.   Tolson, Melvin [B.]. "The Harlem Group of Negro
        Writers." M.A. thesis, Columbia University, 1940.

906.   Walker, Grace Ellena. "Novels by Negro Authors: A
        Study of Subject Matter." M.A. thesis, Fisk
        University, 1933.

907.   Williams, Henry C. "An Analogical Study of W.E.B.
        Du Bois and Marcus Garvey, 1919 to 1925." M.A.
        thesis, Fisk University, 1974.

908.   Wilson, Ronald H. "The Prose of Langston Hughes."
        M.A. thesis, Howard University, 1970.

909.   Wintz, Cary de Cordova. "Black Writers in 'Nigger
        Heaven': The Harlem Renaissance." Ph.D. dissertation,
        Kansas State University, 1974.

910.   Wood, Darlene Iva. "The Fictional Writings of Jessie
        Fauset." M.A. thesis, Atlanta University, 1975.

911.   Wroblewski, John E.   "Claude McKay: Proponent of
        Black Nationalism."   M.A. thesis, Howard University,
        1968.

912.   Youman, Mary Mabel.   "The Other Side of Harlem: The
        Middle-Class Novel and the New Negro Renaissance."
        Ph.D. dissertation, University of Kentucky, 1976.

913.   Zeidman, Nathalie.   "The Image of the Negro Through
        the Eyes of Langston Hughes."   M.A. thesis,
        Roosevelt University at Chicago, 1962.

AUTHOR INDEX

Included in this index are the names of major and minor authors of the Harlem Renaissance, authors of articles and books concerning this period, editors of collections of essays and anthologies, secondary editors, and authors of dissertations. The numbers following each name refer the reader to item numbers in the bibliography.

TITLE INDEX

Titles listed are the majority of the books and articles and stories included in the bibliography. Non-book titles are not listed nor are there entries in the names of the special collections (section VII). Like English items, foreign-language items are indexed according to the first substantive (non-article) word in the title--e.g., *La Voix des Exiles* appears under the V's, not the L's. Numbers following the title refer the reader to item numbers, not page numbers.

"Spirit Bloom in Harlem. The
Search for a Black
Aesthetic During the
Harlem Renaissance: The
Poetry of Claude McKay,
Countee Cullen, and Jean
Toomer," 822
"Sterling Brown," 218
"Sterling Brown: The New
Negro Folk-Poet," 217
"Stone Rebound, The," 540f
"Strong Man Called Sterling
Brown, A," 216
*Studies in American Litera-
ture: Essays in Honor of
William Mulder*, 159
"Study of Black Identity in
'Passing' Novels of the
19th and Early 20th
Centuries, A," 885
"Studies in Black Pastoral:
Five Afro-American Writers,"
876
"Study of James Weldon
Johnson, A," 350
"Study of Literary Criticism
by Some Negro Writers,
1900-1955, A," 814
"Study of Plays by Negro
Playwrights: From
'Appearances' to 'A
Raisin in the Sun' (1925-
1959), A," 799
"Study of Rudolph Fisher's
Prose Fiction, A," 884
"Study of Social Protest in
Contemporary Negro Poets,
A," 803
"Study of the Disunity Theme
in the Afro-American
Experience: An Examination
of Five Representative
Novels, A," 848
"Study of the Language
Structure and Symbolism in
Jean Toomer's *Cane* and N.
Scott Momaday's *House Made
of Dawn*, A," 865

"Study of the Poetry of
James Weldon Johnson,
A," 823
"Study of the Poetry of
Langston Hughes, A," 815
"Subjects and Shadows: Images
of Black Primitives in
Fiction of the 1920's,"
872
"Sur quelques thèmes dans
la poésie de la Harlem
Renaissance," 149
"Survey of the Month," 721-
29
"Survey of the Negro Press,
A," 640
"Swamp Moccasin," 690
"Sweat," 324
"Symbolism and Irony in
McKay's *Home to Harlem*,"
381
"Symbols of the Jazz Age:
The New Negro and Harlem
Discovered," 706
"Symphonesque," 633

"Take My Burden Up: Three
Studies in Psychobiograph-
ical Criticism and Afro-
American Fiction," 891
"Technical Aspects of the
Poetry of Langston
Hughes," 306
"Technical Study of Spirituals
--A Review, The," 681
"Tensions in Jean Toomer's
'Theater,' The," 466
*Their Eyes Were Watching
God*, 320
"Theme and Vision in Jean
Toomer's *Cane*," 434
"Theophilus Lewis and the
Theater of the Harlem
Renaissance," 134
There Is Confusion, 251
"This Year of Grace," 200
"Three Novels of the Jazz
Age," 235